WHERE WE WORKED

WHERE WE WORKED

A Celebration of America's Workers and the Nation They Built

Jack Larkin

LYONS PRESS
Guilford, Connecticut
An imprint of Globe Pequot Press

Lyons Press is an imprint of Globe Pequot Press.

All photos courtesy the Library of Congress unless otherwise noted.

Text design and layout: Nancy Freeborn
Project manager: Kristen Mellitt

Library of Congress Cataloging-in-Publication data is available on file.

ISBN 978-1-59921-960-8

Printed in the United States of America

10 9 8 7 6 5 4 3 2 1

To Timothy D. Larkin and Daniel E. J. Larkin,

with love and admiration.

ACKNOWLEDGMENTS

My thanks go first to Barbara Bauman Larkin, who has been my companion and reliance in everything I do. Steve Culpepper, executive director of the editorial department at Globe Pequot Press, has supported this project from the beginning, and collaborated on its conceptualization. Courtney Jordan provided helpful editorial advice on the first three chapters.

I would also like to thank my unsung heroes—the visual archivists and imaging specialists at the Library of Congress. They have created an extraordinary online collection, making available our nation's greatest single resource for the visual study of the American past. Their work is a superb example of public service, and of tax dollars well spent.

Contents

CHAPTER 1

Working the Land

CHAPTER 2

Workshop and Household

Introduction

"What in the hell does anybody need to know about history?" asked Ed Smith, a tough old fisherman in New Bern, North Carolina, when he was interviewed in 1939. He was sure that history didn't account for the experiences of ordinary people like him, and suspected it was just "a lot of made-up mess about something that never happened." On the other hand, the historical narrative of his own life clearly made perfect sense to him, as he described his hardscrabble days working on the water and as a housepainter.

In its own way, this book tries to answer Ed Smith's question. Despite the conviction of many working people—my own father included—that things "never happened like the history books say," I have sought to do justice to their experiences.

Where We Worked is a book of pictures and stories about the work of ordinary Americans in our past. House and home may be our refuge, but for almost all of us, work is our destiny, and the workplace is our destination. Work—for better or worse—shapes much of who we are, what we know, and how we live.

As the United States becomes a post-industrial society with an economy based on information and services, many kinds of work that once defined our lives are disappearing. Textile factories and steel mills have almost vanished; farms, mines, and timberlands are worked by great machines. Typewriters, once a symbol of efficiency and modern communication, are now relics.

This book explores a world of work that has been rapidly receding from our memory and experience. It is built around the remarkable visual resources of the Library of Congress, which from the 1830s through the 1930s provide a great wealth of photographic and other pictorial documentation of American workers and their workplaces.

The narratives of this book are intertwined with these images. They are based on diaries and travelers' descriptions, reminiscences and autobiographies, eyewitness accounts and oral histories. They try to tell the stories, over time, of wheat growers and sharecroppers, mill girls and housemaids, gold miners and railway porters, farmwives and cowboys, newsboys and stenographers.

Stories of two families in particular—my own and my wife's—are threaded into this narrative in places, not because they were extraordinary, but because they seemed so representative. Readers of this book could provide similar ones from their own family histories, and I hope they will. For me, they provide a sense of personal connection to a vast story.

The overall narrative of this book begins in the 1830s, when, in the midst of a vast tide of westward migration, the Industrial Revolution and sweeping changes in transportation and commerce were just getting under way. It ends in the 1930s, when the great economic engine that had been created over the previous hundred years seemed to have broken down—and just before mobilization for war, war itself, and a host of new technologies would reenergize the economy and create a new and different world of work.

Over the course of that hundred years, the United States became the world's greatest agricultural producer. Americans explored and exploited our country's vast resources of land, timber, and minerals; spanned the continent with railroads, and created an immense industrial base. The United States took in millions of immigrants, and built great cities. In those years Americans were, in the memorable words of one of my own history teachers, "a brutally vigorous people." The nation's stunning economic growth was the result of almost incalculable effort, the work of many millions of hands, and often came at great cost.

Where We Worked focuses on the experience of ordinary workers, in households and craft shops, on farms and railroad lines, in mines and forests, in factories and offices. That is not to say that the stories of elite workers—managers, professionals, officials—are not worth telling. It simply recognizes that their stories have in most cases already been told, often by themselves. Instead, this book tries to represent the unrepresented.

Of course, it's not possible for this book to encompass all the varieties of work in that now-vanished America. The subject is too vast, necessary images and compelling stories were not always available, and space was limited.

Why end in the 1930s? One answer is in the materials, and the fact that the strongest Library of Congress visual collections go up through those years. The other is that World War II provides a clearly defined breaking point, one of history's sudden transitions. A comparable account of Americans at work for the years from 1940 on—those of my own life, since I was born in 1943—would need a very different book based on different resources.

These temporal boundaries have defined this book, with three exceptions. It briefly reaches back to the beginning of European settlement to chronicle the first family farms, and briefly ventures past World War II to complete the stories of my father and father-in-law. And it uses a very few images from the early 1940s where they provided the best documentation for earlier events.

Those years are now in the fairly distant past, the world of three generations ago and more. Does it still matter, to look at how Americans spent those countless days of labor? Only if we want to understand where we came from.

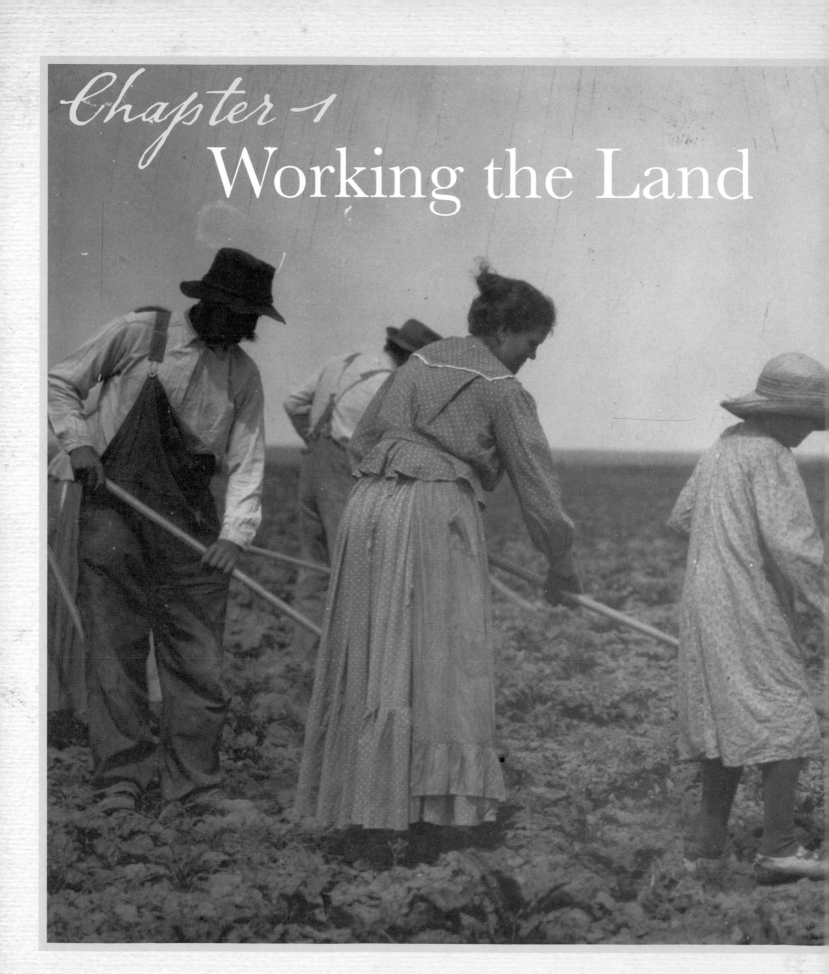

Chapter 1
Working the Land

(*Overleaf*) **Members of the Miller family hoe their field of sugar beets in Colorado, 1915.**

Morris Larkin in his eighties, c. 1940–41, standing between his youngest son, John (Jack, my father), and his oldest son, William (Bill). Bill is holding James (Jimmy), the son of James Sr. (Jim), Morris's middle son. Around 1910, Morris had left his city job for a few years to farm in Indiana so that Bill and Jim had actually done farm work as young boys. My father, the youngest, had been born after their return to the city, and so had never mentioned the farm to me. *Author photo.*

An Unexpected History

Gowing up on Chicago's South Side, with its endless miles of brick bungalows and "three-flat" apartments, I could not have felt more disconnected from the land. The city was full of trees and most houses had lawns, but no one gardened, let alone farmed. The only four-legged animals around were dogs and cats. And the working men I knew were bus drivers and accountants, lawyers and police patrolmen. Right outside the city, though far from view, stretched the fields and silos of Illinois, just about the richest farmland in America. And none of that had anything to do with me, or so I thought.

When I looked back and started to learn about my family's history before Chicago—specifically, about my father's father, Morris Larkin—I found myself just one generation removed from life on a Midwestern farm. I uncovered the shared story of many of our ancestors, of an immense migration from farm to city that swept America not that long ago.

I had always assumed that my great-grandparents found themselves in Chicago after passing through one of the usual ports of arrival from Ireland—New York, Boston, or Philadelphia. I also assumed that they, like the great majority of Irish immigrants, gave up working the land to become city folk, finding jobs as laborers and servants in this country. But when I found Morris as a twelve-year-old boy in the schedules of the 1870 census, I discovered that my grandfather wasn't living in a Chicago tenement. He was on a dairy farm with my great-grandparents in Lyons Township, Illinois, 30 miles from the city.

My great-grandparents, John and Annie, owned some 50 or 60 acres, worth about $900 at that time. They raised corn, kept a few pigs, grew hay and oats,

and had some dairy cows for milk and butter. It was a bit surprising, because most Irish immigrants did not go into farming. The great majority of them had grown up on tiny plots of rented land, growing only potatoes for subsistence. When they arrived in the United States, most had little money and few agricultural skills and often associated farming with poverty and famine. John and Annie Larkin fared a little better. They must have seen farming as a path to independence, as they found the money and skills they needed to work the Illinois prairie.

(Above) **My grandfather Morris Larkin grew up and worked on a Midwestern farm like this one, in Marshall, Michigan, pictured in a panoramic view, c. 1915.**

Farming the Illinois prairie: Two men break up the sod with three-horse riding plows, c. 1903. Morris Larkin worked with similar plows on his father's farm.

Workplaces:

THE FIRST FAMILY FARMS

The first Englishmen to farm in America had not reckoned on how difficult it would be, at first, to work the land. Although most of the Pilgrims had some familiarity with agriculture, they were primarily small craftsmen and traders, who came to the New World to practice their religion in peace. Farming was not at the forefront of their minds, since they expected to develop a successful fishery and trade with the Indians. But at the beginning, fish were hard to find, there was little to trade, and less to eat; as the Plymouth Colony's first governor William Bradford wrote, "[M]arkets, there was none to go to." In addition, they were surprised by New England's bitterly cold winters; it was, after all, at the latitude of southern France.

In their puzzlement, Native peoples taught them about planting corn, and gave them some food. But the Pilgrims found Plymouth a hungry place, and nearly starved. As William Bradford put it, their first harvest "arose to but a little, in comparison to a full year's supplie." They did not yet know enough "of the manner of Indian corne" and were too weak "for want of food, to tende it as they should have done."

Famine—many more deaths, and perhaps the end of the colony—stared them in the face. They took counsel together about what to do—"how they might raise as much corne as they could, and obtaine a beter crope then they had done, that they might not still thus languish in miserie." Up to this point, the Pilgrims had been farming

Captain Thomas Willett House, Kingston, Plymouth County. A mid-eighteenth-century farmstead in Plymouth County, a century and more after the Pilgrims had struggled to create the first family farms. *Historic American Building Survey.*

their scanty fields in common, as members of the Plymouth Company, and failing badly. Some farmed, some shirked, and some stole food. After many arguments, the Pilgrim leaders made a momentous decision—they would farm as family units, giving each household "a parcell of land, according to the proportion of their number." This solution worked, Bradford wrote, "for it made all hands very industrious, so as much more corne was planted then otherwise would have bene by any means . . . The women now wente willingly into feild, and tooke their litle ones with them to set corne." These were the first American family farms.

October in New England *Low's Almanack for 1825* **shows a corn harvest. English people called every sort of grain "corn," so that the unfamiliar maize grown by the Indians became at first "Indian corn." The Pilgrims were imperfectly prepared for practical agriculture to begin with, and the growing of Indian corn nearly defeated them. It would become an indispensable staple crop, and American farmers would eventually simply call it "corn"—the one crop that virtually every one of them grew.** *Author photo.*

By 1880, my grandfather was an experienced farmer in his early twenties, working alongside his father. They raised the same crops but expanded their dairy herd, selling milk to one of the dozens of creameries that had sprung up to supply the fast-growing Chicago market. But between that time and the turn of the century, Morris left the farm for Chicago, one of millions of young Americans, men and women, who gave up farm life for the promise of greater economic opportunity and personal freedom. He found a job as a refrigeration mechanic at a meatpacking plant in the city's vast stockyards, and got married. This might have bitterly disappointed his father, who must have valued his own hard-won hold on the land. But Morris chose otherwise, and became part of a vast tide of movement from the countryside to the city.

FARMING'S ENDLESS CYCLE

What my grandfather and great-grandparents shared with every American farmer since the Pilgrims began to grow corn at Plymouth was the unending cycle of the seasons. On farms large and small, hardscrabble or hugely productive, the calendar shaped the patterns of work and daily life, from plowing and planting through cultivation to harvest.

In the northerly latitudes of America, the farming year begins in the spring—March or April—with a great surge of work to prepare the soil for planting. Horace Clarke of Granby, Connecticut, felt the urgency of the seasons and the endlessness of a farmer's life deep in his bones. On a showery afternoon in May 1836, as he plowed one of his fields for corn, a critical piece of equipment broke. Later that day, he reflected on the farmer's cycle

Haying season was always a time of furious activity. This photograph from 1903 catches the hay flying as five men work together to load a wagon before the crop, which had to be left in the field to dry, is ruined by rain.

This almanac woodcut of 1825 depicts the timeless ritual of haying. Three men are cutting the hay with scythes while the fourth member of the haying gang works behind them to rake it for drying. *Author photo.*

In this early nineteenth-century woodcut, three reapers cut grain with sickles while a fourth binds the sheaves. A fast reaper often cut his left hand, which held the grain against the sickle, while he worked. Scars on that hand were taken as a badge of honor, a sign of hard work. *Author photo.*

(Facing page) Women almost never cut hay on American farms—they were rarely allowed to use "male" implements like scythes—but during the frantic work of haying season, farm women often went out to rake with the men and boys. The heroine of John Greenleaf Whittier's popular poem, "Maud Muller," was a country girl whose wealthy admirer sees her raking in the field and chooses not to speak to her.

of toil and struggle in his journal: "the mold bord or iron to my old first Newgate plow failed today being completely worn out, and that chiefly by myself." The mold board was the critical part of the plow that sliced through the soil, turning over the furrows in which the seed could be planted. After hauling the broken implement back to the barn and finding a replacement, Clarke wrote, "I have followed that plow more miles than any one man did or ever will any plow whatever, in my opinion." He had been farming for over thirty years.

In the summer came the hardest work of all: getting in the hay that fed the cattle and horses. Hay was critical on northern farms because it was vitally necessary for the survival of the livestock through the long, cold winters. Haying season meant backbreaking work during the hottest months of the year. Because hay had to be cut quickly, left to dry in the field, and brought to the barn before it rained, it was exhausting dawn-to-dusk work for the men, and usually drew farm women into the fields as well. One result—in New England, at least—was that children were much less likely to be conceived in July and August than in other months of the year.

The next season of intensive labor—harvesting wheat, oats, rye, and corn—came in the fall, followed by threshing grain and shelling corn so that the crops could go to the mill to be ground into meal and flour. Before refrigeration, the early winter was slaughtering time for beef and pork, so that it could be salted for the coming year's consumption.

Well into the nineteenth century, and in some places, longer, the farming calendar also shaped the patterns of rural social life. Marriages usually took place in the spring, just before plowing and planting, or in the fall, after the harvest had been brought in. The pace of farm work meant that there was little leisure time during the growing season, so that parties, dances, and most neighborly visiting waited for the colder months.

Hagerstown Town and Country Almanac for 1888.

Robert B. Thomas, *The Farmer's Almanac for 1826.* **The pages for the month of March show the astronomical and astrological details, including a chart that maps "the moon's place" onto the various part of the body that it governs each day. On the opposing page, the almanac is advising its many thousands of readers on the proper location of "hog stys" and "necessary houses," or privies. As editor, Thomas waged a fifty-year campaign to improve the work habits and manners of New England's farm families.** *Author photo.*

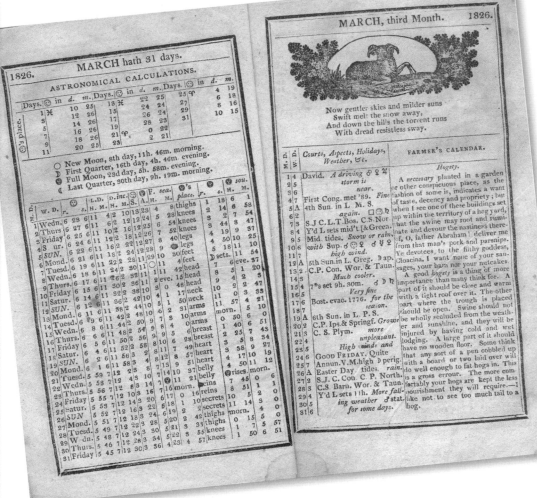

Almanacs

Over the centuries American farmers have read their Bibles, finding a comforting familiarity in its words about sowing and reaping, herding sheep, and yoking oxen. But for hundreds of years, a much smaller book, the almanac, was the indispensable "farmer's bible." Almanacs were the true best-seller in agricultural America, found in the great majority of farm households.

By the 1830s there were hundreds of almanacs, published in editions that matched the latitude and growing seasons of every part of the nation. Just about all farm families used yearly almanacs as calendars and tables of handy information. Some preferred almanacs that provided moral advice or amusing stories; many turned to those that served as guides to improved farming. One of these was the *Farmer's Almanac* published in Boston, which contained a constant barrage of advice about cleaner barns, newer tools, harder work, and more productive work habits. It remains in circulation today as *The Old Farmer's Almanac*, the oldest continuous American publication.

On farms where books were scarce, children valued almanacs as much as adults. "Almanacs figured largely in my reading," Hamlin Garland recalled of his childhood on an Iowa farm in the 1870s. Each one had "a loop of string at the corner so that they might be hung on a nail behind the stove, and a cover of a crude green or yellow or blue." All almanacs predicted the weather, with about the same success that *The Old Farmer's Almanac* enjoys today. Even more important to many readers were the almanac's astronomical and astrological tables. Throughout the nineteenth century these esoteric charts were consulted by traditionally minded farmers, men who governed their plowing and planting by the phases of the moon and the alignment of the planets. This was a mystery to Garland, who was puzzled by the astrology and "signs of the Zodiac" that so interested his elders. "I never knew what all this meant," he wrote, "but it gave me a sense of something esoteric and remote."

Almanacs were testimony as well to the endlessness of the farming cycle, its constant renewal. Every November, as farmers stored away the harvest and turned their thoughts toward the next year, almanac printers all across America brought out their next year's editions. A farmer might travel a long distance to buy one at a country store, or an entire family would eagerly await a visit from a traveling book peddler. An advertisement for a Hagerstown, Maryland, almanac in 1888 reminded readers that it was the same publication "which you, and your ancestors, have been using for nearly one hundred years."

The farmer's almanac long remained a familiar image of American rural life. Edward Penfield's poster of 1915 shows a ruggedly handsome farmer consulting one; behind him is a hay-filled barn and horse-drawn wagon. The poster was an advertisement for the Studebaker Company, which had recently switched from making farm wagons to automobiles.

REVOLUTIONS IN FARMING

As farm families moved West in the nineteenth century, they were mostly hoping to replicate their parents' lives on the land, but with greater scope and prosperity. They wanted independence, a "comfortable sufficiency" of food and household goods, and opportunity for their sons and daughters to farm and marry in their turn. But the process of westward migration and the building of new farms were shaped by two profound revolutions.

Transportation

The first was a revolution in transportation. After 1790 Americans built thousands of miles of improved roads, creating stage lines and freight-wagon routes across the country. In massive construction projects, private and public money went to build canals that connected the interior with seaports; after 1810, the growing mastery of steam power brought hundreds of steamboats carrying passengers and freight to American lakes and rivers. And after 1835, the railroad arrived to link American cities, eventually dominating the nation's transportation system. Taken together, despite failures and fiascos, these achievements vastly shortened travel times for people and goods, meaning that new territories were settled with unprecedented speed.

Tools:

Threshing

Even after the wheat, rye, or oats had been harvested, the hard work of threshing remained. The nutritious inner kernel of the grain had to be removed from the husk and stalk before it could be ground into flour. *Low's Almanack for 1825,* a publication widely read by farmers in the Northeast, shows two men threshing in the backbreaking way that had been traditional for thousands of years. Sheaves of grain are laid out on the barn floor, and each man is using a flail—two sticks of wood attached with a leather hinge—to pound the grain until the heads and the husks are separated. The flail itself is not very heavy, but each man has to strike hundreds of powerful blows to thresh a single bushel of grain. When the grain on the floor is finished, the kernels will be scooped up and winnowed in the open air to remove the chaff, the last pieces of husk. Threshing by hand was a slow process. It took one farmer a full day to thresh eight bushels of grain, less than half an acre's production.

Successful horse-powered threshing machines first appeared in the United States around 1850. Mechanizing the beating and winnowing process, they eliminated the flail and the threshing floor completely. The first machines could thresh wheat sixty times faster than a man with a flail; as they were improved and enlarged, they

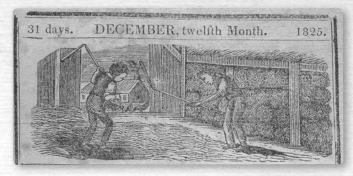

Slowly and laboriously, farmers thresh grain on the barn floor as they had done for centuries. *Author photo.*

became much faster still. By the 1870s mechanical threshers were a commonplace sight on American farms, and there were several competing designs on the market.

Well-informed farmers argued about the relative merits of the "endless apron" mechanism versus the "vibrating tables" of the Aultman-Taylor machine, which adorns the advertising brochure shown below. Aultman-Taylor reached its customers with a promise of durability: "In good hands, and not abused / Sixteen years will see me used." Visible in profile are the machine's power-drive pulleys and its reciprocating arms that pound and winnow the grain. Oddly enough, it resembles a giant grasshopper—an irony that the manufacturer surely did not intend!

The Aultman machine was small enough for an individual farmer to own. In parts of the Midwest, wheat farmers relied on traveling crews who brought their own much-larger threshing machines with them. The crews

(*Left*) **In this advertising poster from 1881, a farmer poses atop the Aultman-Taylor threshing machine.**

(*Facing page*) **A threshing crew is pictured at work with their horse-drawn equipment in Buffalo County, Nebraska, in the 1880s.**

would thresh a single farm's grain in less than a day and move on.

Hamlin Garland remembered the visits of the threshing crew to his family's farm in Green Coulee, Wisconsin. Sometimes they would arrive in the evening, work through the night by the light of kerosene lanterns, and leave at dawn for the next job. For young Garland and his brothers, this was an enthralling spectacle. Staying up late, they stood at an upstairs window to watch as the three-man crew brought in their machine, "which seemed a silent monster" to the children. It was powered by five teams of horses that pulled on long levers, moving in a large circle around the farmyard.

The driver stood atop the power mechanism, "above the huge, savage, cog-wheels 'round which the horses moved." Holding the reins, he governed the motion of the horses and gauged the speed of the machine "by the pitch of its deep bass hum." A long leather belt and pulleys connected the "horsepower" to the thresher itself.

The second member of the crew, the tender, watched the thresher carefully, ready to adjust the mechanism or oil the gears.

The most skilled and dangerous job, "the high place to which all boys aspired," wrote Garland, was serving as the feeder, who brought the grain to the machine. Garland's father threw him great bundles of wheat that "he caught . . . in the crook of his arm, and spread them out into a broad, smooth band upon which the cylinder caught and tore like some insatiate monster." The feeder did this work for twelve hours or so, had a meal and a brief rest, and then was off to another farm to do it again.

Ultimately, Hamlin Garland would leave farm life far behind, becoming an eminent journalist, novelist, and critic with more than forty books to his credit. Yet he would always remember that as a young farm boy, he believed that to have the strength and skill to feed a horse-powered thresher was "the highest honor in the world."

EMIGRATING FROM CONNECTICUT TO EASTERN OHIO IN 1805, DISTANCE 600 MILES, TIME 90 DAYS, NUMBER OF PASSENGERS 10.

Emigrants from Connecticut to Ohio head out on the overland trail in 1805, a journey that could take three months. *Author photo.*

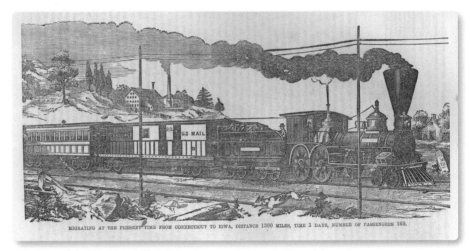

MIGRATING AT THE PRESENT TIME FROM CONNECTICUT TO IOWA, DISTANCE 1300 MILES, TIME 3 DAYS, NUMBER OF PASSENGERS 360.

In 1867, the emigrants' journey from Connecticut to Iowa took three days on the railroad. *Author photo.*

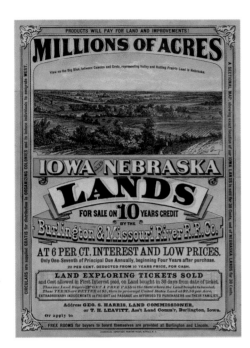

As they expanded westward, American railroads needed to encourage farmers to settle so that they would have profitable customers. They often sold land themselves (the federal government had given them large tracts of land in exchange for extending their tracks) and worked with real estate agents to attract settlers to Iowa, Nebraska, Kansas, and the Dakotas. This colorful advertisement commissioned by the Burlington and Missouri River Railroad in 1872 was one of many that enticed farmers with easy financial terms, attractive images of fertile fields, and free travel to view possible farm sites.

Each succeeding generation of emigrating farm families could move west with greater speed and less difficulty and danger. Even more important in the long run, they could count on swifter, more efficient connections with the markets of the East. The ongoing revolution in transportation connected farm families ever more tightly to the American economy as a whole. They could sell their wheat and corn, pork and beef, in what was becoming a national marketplace for farm commodities—and what would eventually become a global one.

New Tools

The second revolution was the transformation of farm work itself—first with new tools, and then with the application of machinery to its most basic tasks. It would change the working lives of farm families across the nation,

FARMING TOOLS IN USE IN 1790.

The traditional farming tools of early America: a manure fork, a scythe for cutting hay, a hay rake, an iron-shod plow, a farmer-made ox yoke, a sickle for cutting grain, a shovel, a pitchfork, an ax, a hoe, and a crude spike-tooth harrow for turning over plowed soil. *Author photo.*

from the coast of Massachusetts to the far-flung settlements on the moving line of the frontier.

The tools that American farmers used at the beginning of the nineteenth century would have been instantly recognizable to the Pilgrims or the first tobacco planters in Virginia. Over two centuries, they had hardly changed at all. Plows, hoes, shovels, rakes, and axes were made by local craftsmen of wood and wrought iron. They were massive and durable, and if they broke, a neighboring blacksmith or carpenter could fix them.

But by 1840, well before the arrival of agricultural machinery, American farming tools were transformed. Specialized shops appeared to manufacture and sell stronger, lighter tools for virtually every farm task. The old implements, as Francis Underwood of Massachusetts remembered about his father's

FARMING TOOLS OF THE PRESENT TIME,
As exhibited by Robert B. Bradley & Co., 98 State St., New Haven, Conn.

An agricultural implement warehouse in New Haven, Connecticut, in the 1860s. Hundreds of specialized tools were available, including ride-behind plows, four different designs for manure forks, and scythe blades in ten different sizes. *Author photo.*

farm, had been "heavy and awkward"; the new ones were very different—"so light, yet so strong, so polished and so perfectly adapted to use." They were also amazingly diverse. In 1800 a farmer might have eight or ten basic tools; by 1860, he could buy dozens of types from a country store, and find hundreds of specialized ones in a city warehouse just a train ride away.

By that time, the new hand tools were just about universal on farms in the North and West; the South lagged far behind, however, as its labor patterns were shaped by slavery. The improved implements made the simplest tasks—digging holes, raking hay, felling trees—easier. "It would be difficult to exaggerate," Underwood wrote, "the relief that came to working men" wherever these new tools were used.

New Machinery

While new tools lightened farm labor, new machines would change farming far more completely. The 1830s saw an onrush of innovation. Hundreds of enterprising machinists—Cyrus McCormack, who founded International Harvester, was the most famous and successful—began a successful search for ways to make machines that would do the work of six, a dozen, or twenty

In this engraving, *The Reapers* of 1890, the artist has found a way to romanticize the horse-drawn machinery that replaced harvesting by hand. One man rides the lead horse of the powerful, straining team while the other manages the machine. Pictured amid vast fields stretching to the horizon, mechanized farm work has become heroic.

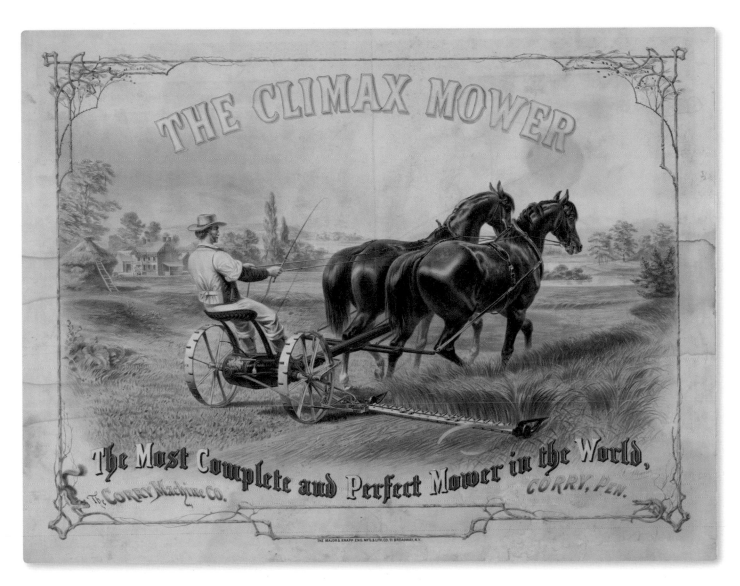

The Climax Mower — The Most Complete and Perfect Mower in the World. The Corry Machine Co. CORRY, PEN.

farmhands. The new machines reproduced, mechanically, the motion of a harvester with his sickle, or a hayer with his scythe.

A careful look at an 1870s advertisement by the Corry Machine Company for its Climax Mower shows us how they solved this problem. Under the driver's seat is the mechanism that takes the rotating motion of the wheels and converts it into the back-and-forth movement of the teeth on the long "cutter bar" that extends to the right. As the teeth move, they cut the hay and lay it on the ground. As the farmer drives his team across the field, the mower cuts a swath of hay wider and smoother than most men could accomplish with a scythe—and far faster. A mowing machine could do the work of a four- or five-man "hay gang." Oxen had been used on American farms along with horses since the early seventeenth century; although they were sturdy and strong, they were too slow to pull mowers and reapers, so they soon began to disappear.

In a business where hundreds of farm machinery companies were competing, in the 1870s the Corry Machine Company was staking its claim in the market with this elegant advertising poster. It shows their mower easily cutting a swath of hay much wider than any scythe could do.

Standing on his freshly plowed field with his family behind him, this farmer in Belpre, Kansas, is posing proudly with a major new investment in farm machinery, c. 1910. It is a steam-powered traction engine pulling a large set of disk plows. Costing several hundred dollars, it out-powered even a five- or six-team horse plow. Farmers had to borrow extensively to buy such machines, putting them at risk if prices fell or a crop was lost. It's not surprising that the photograph emphasizes not the man, but the machine.

By the 1850s, many farmers were using horse-powered reapers for wheat, cutting their hay with mowing machines and gathering it up with "horse rakes." Innovation moved on from these fundamental tasks to mechanize many others, including binding and threshing grain after harvesting, and planting and shelling corn. By the 1890s, many farms were hearing the roar of portable steam engines, far more powerful than any draft animal, that were beginning to replace horse teams. Steam-powered threshing machines traveled from farm to farm in the wheat-growing states, and steam tractors came into use on some larger farms.

The result of all these changes taken together was a great increase in the productivity of farm labor. One farmer growing wheat or cutting hay in 1900 could produce four times as much as his great-grandfather could in 1800. The growing reliance on farm machinery brought another change: In addition to hard work, good judgment, and a feeling for land and livestock, a successful farmer in 1900 needed to have strong mechanical skills as well—enough to run and repair his equipment.

THE COSTS OF TRANSFORMATION

As farmers adopted new technologies and became more and more enmeshed in the world of buying and selling, they lost as well as gained. On the positive side, their work was physically easier, although still extremely hard by today's standards. Overall, their standard of living was improving. Farm families had greater access to cash, and to the consumer goods that the American economy was producing.

"I feed you all," proclaims the farmer in an 1875 lithograph celebrating the centennial of American independence. He himself is a figure of strength and independence, leaning against his plow with its team of handsome horses. He is at the center of the picture, and all the other trades and occupations seem to depend on him. But in reality, farm families at this time were finding the economy more and more perilous and unpredictable. They

In this 1875 lithograph celebrating the approaching centennial of American independence, the figure of the farmer is central, even though farmers were feeling increasingly vulnerable in a changing economy.

Many of the young men in this North Dakota threshing crew, c. 1913, would not spend their lives as farmers. On the farm, they faced diminishing opportunities. The young women standing at the door of the cook wagon were even more likely to leave the country for the city. *Institute for Regional Studies, North Dakota State University.*

were selling their goods in a market where prices were determined by forces —weather, international competition, and transportation costs—that they could not control. Farmers faced a paradox: Bountiful harvests were good for everyone when demand was strong, but hurt everyone when overabundant supply pushed prices down too far. Poor harvests raised prices; they benefited the fortunate farmers whose crops remained whole, but destroyed the livelihoods of everyone else.

Farmers increasingly had to struggle not only with the weather but with some of the nation's most powerful institutions. "I carry for all," the railroad executive says in the centennial print, and no one could deny that the railroads' vast expansion had made possible thousands of new rural communities and millions of new farms. But farmers increasingly felt that "I carry for all" was a lie. They saw the railroads badly abusing their power as the unchallenged transporter of farm goods to market. Without competition, railroads were able to impose high freight rates and shipping practices that threatened to eat up whatever profits farmers could make. Although railroad owners talked about the sacred rights of property and contract, most farmers wanted government regulation of shipping costs.

There is also a banker in the 1876 lithograph, but he is pictured as saying, "I fleece you all." Farmers increasingly found themselves going into debt, driven by the costs of land and machinery, and the seasonal nature of their income and expenses. They wanted lower interest rates and a steady growth in the money supply that would raise farm prices and ease their mortgage payments. Bankers and most Eastern businessmen wanted their loans profitably repaid and demanded a tight lid on prices, inflation, and money in circulation. Railroads, money, and banking—the issues at the heart of the American farmers' struggle to survive in the marketplace—were at the center of bitter political battles after the Civil War.

Increasing productivity led to another paradox for farmers. Over the long run, it meant that their numbers would diminish, as ever fewer workers were needed to feed the nation. A photograph of a North Dakota threshing crew in 1913 (see pages 18–19) shows us twenty-three young men who worked on the machines, and two young women who cooked for them. Fewer than half of them, based on what historians know about the movement of the rural population, would still be on the farm ten years later. Some would have left for a job "in town," 50 miles away. Many would have taken the longer journey to Omaha or Chicago. As farming continued to be an economic struggle, the promise of the city—higher wages, greater opportunity for work and marriage, freedom and anonymity—was pulling young men and women out of the countryside, just as it had my grandfather.

GENDER ROLES

A photograph or a painting can illuminate an entire social universe more
effectively than oceans of ink on the page. Samuel Lancaster Gerry's *New
England Farmyard* is a striking example. Through its detail and flow, the painting shows how farm work was organized between the sexes.

A young woman wearing a bonnet and dressed for work stands in the
foreground, holding a bucket. A cow is already heading to the barn, and she
will soon be milking it. The woman at the back door of the house is dressed
for indoor work, wearing the white cap and collar of a mature woman. She is
holding a broom, caught in the midst of household chores. The two women
have stopped in their work to watch the arrival of a man and a boy in a
wagon loaded with goods. They are probably returning from town. Across
the bottom of the picture, in counterpoint to the broom and milk pail that
signify a woman's duties, are the tools of men's outdoor work—a hay rake, ox
yoke, shovel, and plow.

Men and women worked on the farm in ways that were both distinct and
interdependent. The fields were for men. The house and garden were women's
domain. Men on the farm were far freer to travel than women, who were tied

**Samuel Lancaster Gerry, *New England
Farmyard*, 1849.** *Old Sturbridge Village.*

to the daily routines of cooking, housework, and tending
children. Men and boys took
care of the large livestock
like horses and oxen. Women
and girls tended chickens and
geese, and slopped pigs. Men
worked with plows and edge
tools—scythes, sickles, axes,
and saws   while women rarely
used them.

Men did the rough pro-
cessing—taking grain from
sowing to harvest and threshing—and they also slaughtered
livestock. Women did the fine
processing, turning flour and
meal into bread, salting meat,
preserving vegetables, making
butter and cheese. Very young
children followed their mothers or older sisters while they

On farms that just kept a few cows for family use, women and girls continued to milk, as in this photograph of Alice Butcher milking a cow on the T. J. Butcher place on Middle Loup, West Union, Nebraska, c. 1910.

worked. Then, somewhere between seven and nine, they began to take up the tasks marked out for their gender, the work that they would do as adults.

There were some exceptions to this division of labor. At the peak of summer haying, women across America went into the fields. On Pennsylvania German farms, well past the middle of the nineteenth century, women worked as harvesters in the wheat fields—to the shock and outrage of many

There are two significant things to notice in this photograph, c. 1923. The first is that this farmer is sitting in the barn, preparing to milk, while wearing the headphones of an elaborate radio array. Almost certainly this picture was staged. The second is more fundamental: Dairying has become a male occupation, as we see a milkman rather than a milkmaid.

New England observers who were concerned with female delicacy. Although widows—and, more rarely, single women—could run their own farms, they hired men for the heaviest work. A family with six daughters and no sons, or the reverse, might have to arrange work roles more flexibly. Farm households living near each other sometimes "swapped" children from day to day depending on what kind of work needed to be done.

Dairying became a different kind of exception. Over the second half of the nineteenth century, it ceased to be the sole domain of women. The change started in New England and New York, where farms abandoned grain production in the face of competition from the West. As soon as dairy farming became the farm's central economic activity, men started to take on most of the dairy work. Women's dairying skills were pushed aside by the appearance of "cheese factories" and large factory-like creameries that took milk from many farms and processed it. In 1800, it would have been unusual to see a man milking. By 1900, men well outnumbered women in the dairy barn.

THE FACES OF FARMING

Farmers don't often look out at us from early photographs (or from portrait paintings for that matter) while holding any sign of their occupation. In this they were different from craftsmen, who by 1800 were posing for their portraits with tools in hand, and by 1850 were sitting for similar daguerreotypes. Grant Wood's *American Gothic*, with its hollow-eyed farmer holding a pitchfork, was hardly typical. The tools of agriculture seemed somehow to breach the genteel conventions of portraiture.

But occasionally there is a subtle clue, as in the portrait of Mark White Adams of Cavendish, Vermont, painted in 1837. There is really only one interesting detail in this otherwise-simple portrait of the successful forty-seven-year-old farmer, and that's the leather wallet that he is holding. White was not only a farmer but a drover—a man who gathered beef cattle from neighboring farms and took them on a 150-mile trek to Boston, buying and selling animals along the way. Ultimately he would sell his herd at the great livestock market in Boston. What about the wallet? It signifies the large amounts of cash he needed for his cattle dealing, and was probably made from the hide of one his cattle.

The daguerreotype on page 25 is another rarity, because it shows two farmers who are, in a real sense, posing with the tools of their trade. It shows two young men wearing the long frocks that were favored for outdoor work by farmers in New England and New York. Posing for their portrait as well are two oxen in a yoked team—the draft animals most widely used on northeastern farms until well after the middle of the nineteenth century. Ox driving

Mark White Adams, **1837.** *Old Sturbridge Village.*

Eyewitness:

LEWIS WICKES HINE AND CHILDREN'S WORK

Lewis Wickes Hine (1874–1940) created a career for himself as one of America's first photojournalists, taking remarkably powerful pictures during a time of wrenching historical change. He devoted himself and his camera to documenting the experience of American workers. Born in Wisconsin and educated at the University of Chicago and Columbia, Hine started off as a teacher in New York City. He used photography as a teaching tool, working with his students to document new arrivals at Ellis Island. Gradually, Hine discovered his true vocation—coupling photography with social investigation to teach Americans about themselves, and stir them to action against injustice.

Between 1908 and 1915, Hine was the photographer and researcher for the National Child Labor Committee,

an organization that sought to publicize the harsh working conditions and long hours of hundreds of thousands of American children on farms and in factories. Later, he worked as a photographer for the Red Cross, the Tennessee Valley Authority, and the Works Progress Administration during the New Deal. All his life, Hine remained a tireless advocate for working children, and workers in general. Tellingly, we have almost no photographs of the man who created thousands and thousands of images. Hine's work was about what he could see through the camera lens, not about the man who clicked the shutter. But in a 1908 photograph, we can see him and his camera outlined in shadow, while he takes the picture of a small boy selling newspapers on a sunny day in Indianapolis. It is probably how he wanted to be remembered.

(Above) In agricultural America, virtually all children did farm work, usually beginning quite young. In 1915, Lewis Hine captured five children (ages seven, nine, eleven, thirteen, and fourteen) as they hoed corn on their family's farm near Menomonee Falls, Wisconsin.

(Left) A young boy posed for Lewis Hine on an Indianapolis street in 1908. Hine's shadow can be seen on the pavement.

Two young men in farmer's working "frocks" pose with their ox team in this daguerreotype (1850–60).

was a skill that most farmers needed, and these young men seem proud of it. Oxen were always worked in pairs, and yokefellows usually stayed together as long as both were alive. To teach oxen their repertoire of commands—to start and stop, back up, turn right or left—farmers began to train them early. Calves were selected and paired up before they were a year old. Teams began with quarter-size yokes and worked through several sizes until they reached full growth in three or four years, when they were ready for the serious work of plowing and hauling.

DOWN SOUTH

From the beginning, agriculture in the American South, with its long growing season, was dominated by "staples," or money crops—products that fetched a high price in the marketplaces of Europe. Early in the seventeenth century came tobacco, then rice, indigo, and sugar. Finally came cotton, the king of them all. Slavery—the hereditary servitude of men and women of African descent—emerged as the South's labor system well before 1700. It was a brutal solution to the problem of producing staple crops in large quantities at low cost, and ensuring that there were enough laborers for the exhausting work that these crops required. The South had large numbers of small slave-owning farmers and many farmers who owned none at all, but the great planters, and the money crops on which their fortunes were based, defined its economy and society.

A LANDSCAPE OF FEAR

A cotton field could be beautiful, Solomon Northup thought. "There are few sights more pleasant to the eye," he wrote in 1853, "than a wide cotton field when it is in the bloom. It presents an appearance of purity, like an immaculate expanse of light, new-fallen snow." Yet he also knew that it could be a landscape of fear. Northup was a free black man from New York State who in 1841 was kidnapped while visiting Washington, D.C., and sold into slavery. After twelve years in servitude, he was returned to freedom, and wrote *Twelve Years a Slave*, an account of his experience on cotton plantations in Louisiana.

In Louisiana, cotton was planted "in the months of March or April," he wrote, work that required the use of "two mules, three slaves, a plough

Picking cotton near Clarksdale, Mississippi Delta, November 1940. Cotton had not been picked by slaves in the Mississippi Delta for nearly eighty years when this picture was taken, but the fields looked the same. Not only that, the pickers were the great-grandchildren of slaves, and they were using the same shoulder-hung cotton sacks that Solomon Northup described in 1853.

Four, or perhaps five generations of this slave family in South Carolina pose outside their cabin in 1862. Their master's Sea Island plantation has just been occupied by the Union Army, and they are now free. Slaves constantly struggled to keep their families together against the claims of plantation labor and the constant possibility that older children could be sold and sent away.

and harrow." Within two weeks the cotton plants made their appearance, and hoeing season began. From April to July the slave field hands, men and women, young and old, were turned out every day to hoe or "chop" cotton, to remove weeds and keep the soil turning over. It was a virtually endless process, "a field having no sooner been finished once, than it is commenced again." On the plantations Northup knew, the work was fearful as well as repetitive. "The overseer or driver follows the slaves with a whip . . . The fastest hoer takes the lead row. He is usually about a rod [16.5 feet] in advance. If one of them passes him, he is whipped. If one falls behind, or is for a moment idle, he is whipped. In fact, the lash is flying from morning until night, the whole day long."

Picking started in August, and, as Northup remembered, offered no relief from dread or labor. A new hand, coming to pick cotton for the first time, was "whipped up smartly, and made for that day to pick as fast as he can possibly." Then his or her sack of cotton was weighed at the end of the day, "so that his capability in cotton picking is known." From then on, this brutal measurement determined the cotton picker's quota. Bringing in less would be evidence of shirking, "and a greater or less number of lashes is the penalty." The lowest acceptable figure, Northup recalled, was around 200 pounds a day. The least-productive pickers, after repeated whippings had failed, were usually assigned to other work. The most skillful ones, who might bring in 400 pounds a day, were trapped. If they missed their quotas, they were punished more severely than anyone else.

Hoeing and other plantation work would end without a daily reckoning, but each day of cotton picking concluded with slaves carrying their cotton sacks to the gin house where their day's work would be weighed. "A slave never approaches the gin house with his basket of cotton but with fear," Northup

In defense of slavery, this 1841 lithograph presents an idealized portrayal of plantation conditions. Happy, dancing slaves greet their benevolent owners who feed and clothe them, nurse them when they are sick, and care for them when they are old. An elderly slave says, "God bless you, Massa!"

wrote. "If it falls short in weight—if he has not performed the full task appointed him, he knows that he must suffer." After the weighing came the whippings. Even a slave who had exceeded his quota might not rest easy, for some masters would take note and "measure the next day's task accordingly."

During his sojourn as a slave "on the shores of Bayou Boeuf," Northup remembered that the workday was both long and severely enforced. An hour before daylight an overseer or house slave blew the great plantation horn, waking the slaves, who hurried to "prepare their breakfast, fill a gourd with water, in another deposit their dinner of cold bacon and corn cake" before they walked out to the fields. It was "an offense invariably followed by a flogging, to be found at the quarters after daybreak." Then followed twelve hours in the field—from May through September, in punishing heat and humidity—with a brief break for dinner at noon. If there was still cotton to be

In the 1840s and '50s, Green Hill Plantation in Campbell County, Virginia, grew cotton and wheat. But it was also a training ground for skilled slave field overseers, carpenters, and blacksmiths, most of whom were sold to other plantations once they had learned their trade. Green Hill's owner found this the most profitable part of his business. *Historic American Building Survey.*

The Machine that Made King Cotton

Each boll of cotton, when opened up, has as many seeds as an orange, and the seeds and fibers are tangled together. Cotton couldn't be spun into thread until all the seeds had been removed, and this was a major problem for American cotton growers at the end of the eighteenth century. American "short-staple" cotton, the only kind that grew in most of the South, was full of very sticky green seeds. Removing them by hand was extremely slow work; it took a day to clean a single pound of cotton. This made American cotton much too expensive for sale on the world market.

In 1793, New England inventor Eli Whitney solved this problem. His cotton engine, or "cotton gin," used a rotating toothed barrel to separate the seeds from the usable cotton. His first model, hand-cranked by a single worker, could clean 50 pounds of cotton a day. Over the following decades the cotton gin was steadily improved. Larger versions were horse- or mule-powered, and by 1850, many

THE FIRST COTTON-GIN.—Drawn by William L. Sheppard.—[See Page 814.]

were powered by steam. Whitney's gin made it possible for American cotton to conquer the market and supply the textile mills of England and America. Cotton growing in the South expanded enormously, and so did slavery.

Whitney himself was far more concerned with the patent rights and financial arrangements for his invention than with its social impact. The gin was hailed from the beginning as a triumph of "Yankee ingenuity" that was helping to create national prosperity. Like most Americans of his time, he did not seriously question the institution of slavery. By 1840, there were some voices of criticism; ardent opponents of the slave system, mostly from Whitney's own New England, believed that the United States would have been better off without the cotton gin and the powerful impetus it gave to slavery. Without it, they thought, the Southern labor system might have withered away. Of course, that was an idle wish. The cotton gin was the key to a system of production that stayed in place long after the Civil War.

(Above) Cotton lint is everywhere inside this gin house in Dahomey, Mississippi, c. 1898, with its large steam-powered gins and cotton presses. We can see five African American workers and one white man, perhaps a supervisor. Just as in the cotton factories, the lint in the air put workers at risk for respiratory disease.

(Left) The first cotton gin, drawn by William L. Sheppard *(Harper's Weekly,* 1869*)*.

picked, weighed, and stored, work went on long after nightfall. Then evening chores had to be done: feeding the mules, slopping hogs, cutting firewood. Finally, the slaves returned to their cabins, "sleepy and overcome with the long day's toil."

The work of slaves varied greatly, and was not always as brutal as Northup's experience. Some masters were considerably kinder, and a few gave exceptionally talented slaves great responsibility. Ex-slave Josiah Henson despised his master as ignorant and dissipated, but because he had little hope of change or escape, he confined his ambitions to the narrow world of enslavement in which he lived. As a young man, he was eager "to be first in the field, whether we were hoeing, mowing, or reaping; to surpass those of my own age, or indeed any age . . . and to obtain, if possible, the favorable regard of the petty despot who ruled over us." Eventually, Henson wound up managing his master's plantation for several years. He made it successful, and his master deferred to his judgment about farming and business affairs. Still, Henson was never allowed to forget his status as a slave, someone who could be insulted, ordered about, or beaten at any time. Slavery was always coerced labor; lurking behind the smile of even the most benevolent master was the reality of the whip.

THE LONG HARD DEATH OF SLAVERY

After the end of the Civil War in 1865 and the emancipation of the slaves, everything was different—but nothing had changed. The South was still one of the world's great producers of cotton, sugar, and tobacco, but it was much poorer. The plantation owners who had dominated the South's society and economy had had their wealth and power ripped away. For a while it seemed that the great plantations would be permanently broken up, and the South would become a region of smaller family farms, as many, both in the North and the South, had hoped. But the problems of poverty, race, and the need to produce for the unforgiving global marketplace could not be overcome. The ownership of the South's best agricultural land returned to relatively few hands, all of them white.

African Americans were no longer anyone else's property, but they still had almost no property of their own. They began as landless farmers and laborers, and for the most part, would remain so for many decades. Despite the efforts

In 1939, photographer Russell Lee identified this man in Marshall, Texas, as a former slave. He had probably been born in the 1850s, and had some childhood memories of "slavery days." He holds a surviving artifact of this era—a horn used to call slaves from their cabins to work in the morning, to signal their brief dinner break in the fields at noon, and to call them in from the fields at night.

(Above) "White cotton, black pickers and a gin. Humble and crude, but the crop Uncle Sam depends on to maintain his gold balance." This image from 1915 shows pickers and the gin house and smokestack of a steam-powered cotton gin. Its caption reminds us that the racial hierarchy of the cotton field was still in place and that cotton exports were important to America's international balance of payments.

(Right) This photograph of an African American farm couple in Georgia was taken in 1898. The land ownership and independence that the picture suggests was relatively rare and always fragile in the post–Civil War South.

of teachers, reformers, and some sympathetic Northern politicians, a workable system of land ownership and agricultural opportunity for freed slaves was never created. Ultimately the social and political reconstruction of the South was abandoned by public opinion and political leaders at the North.

With few resources, freed slave families were forced back into the roles they had occupied under the old agricultural system, or something very much like it. More than a few of them, followed by their children, found themselves chopping weeds and picking cotton on a former owner's plantation. Many ended up working plantation land "on shares," receiving seed, tools, groceries, and a rented house, on credit, and paying with a sizable share of the crop they produced. But the terms—steep interest rates, unfair share arrangements, arbitrarily high prices for supplies and low prices for cotton—were so ruinous that each year found them deeper in debt.

Nonetheless, freedom meant something real to them. There was a greater margin for private life. African Americans could marry and manage their own households and could no longer be whipped by a master for missing their quota of cotton. Still, their freedom was partial and had a bitter taste. The slave

PICKERS AND A GIN.

Cotton pickers gather for work at the Alexander Plantation in Mississippi in this 1936 photo. Day labor picking cotton for landowners was the lot of many whose families had no access to land at all, or had failed as sharecroppers.

master's lash was replaced by economic coercion, exclusion from political life, unequal enforcement of the laws, and the constant possibility of violence.

"I Was Dutiful to My Labor"

Ned Cobb of Tallapoosa County, Alabama, was born in 1885 into the black sharecropper's life, one of struggle and oppression. Cobb was a man who deeply understood, even if he could not change, the ways of farming, economic power, and race relations in the early-twentieth-century South. He lived his life as a cotton farmer, struggling to find success and security within a system that frustrated his ambitions at every turn. On his own ground, Ned Cobb was shrewd, tenacious, and enterprising. In an unjust situation that pushed many men into passivity, he was a passionate exponent of the gospel of work. In fact, it's hard to imagine that anyone ever worked harder or more persistently than this son of freed slaves.

Like most African Americans of his time and place, Cobb grew up illiterate with no chance to get an education. "My daddy never did send me to school long enough to learn to read," he said, and as for reckoning, "I can

A sharecropper's house in Hale County, Alabama (Walker Evans, 1935 or 1936). Many sharecroppers lived in houses like this. It was built as two separate one-room cabins joined together with a roofed-over passageway, or "dogtrot."

put down on paper some little old figures but I can't add 'em up." His story would have been lost to history except that an enterprising young historian, Theodore Rosengarten, took down Cobb's reminiscences, in an oral autobiography that was published as *All God's Dangers*.

Cobb learned to work in a very hard school. His father had farming skills enough, but preferred to go hunting in the Alabama piney woods. He charged Ned, his oldest son, to work their rented fields in his stead. "My daddy put me to plowing the first time at nine years old," he recalled. "He wore out a switch on me," Cobb recalled, "[but I] just wasn't big enough for the job, that's the truth."

By the time Ned was thirteen, he was "plowin' a regular shift" to prepare the fields for corn and cotton. Not only did he have to plow "barefoot in that rocky country, anything liable to skin up my feet," he was subject to frequent whippings whenever his father didn't like the way he was handling the mule or the heavy plow. But Ned proved "an apt little kid, and I was willin'. I knowed I had to be willin' under my daddy."

As he grew up, Ned set his mind to learn every kind of work that was available to a black man in his rural community: growing corn and cotton, estimating the productivity of land, valuing cattle, hogs, and horses. He hauled guano fertilizer and seed cotton for a white dealer when he was just sixteen, wrestling 200-pound sacks in and out of freight cars and wagons. At nineteen, he taught himself the job of a logger in a matter of days—how to hitch up an ox team, chain up and move the logs, bring a load down from the woods, and deliver the logs safely to the sawmill. "I knowed nothing 'bout haulin logs,

Young sharecropper and his first child, Hillside Farm, Person County, Alabama.

had never hauled no logs," he remembered, "but put me at anything, I made a success."

When Ned reached twenty-one, his father had nothing to give him. But Ned was sure of his course. He married and began to work land on shares. Despite his energy and intelligence, he had to struggle against his economic bondage to white landowners who dictated the terms on which he could sell his cotton and buy his supplies. He could not read the accounts and papers that landlords and storekeepers waved at him, but he understood their unfairness. "You had to do what the white man said," Ned recalled, "and if you made enough to pay him, that what all he cared for . . . [but] if you don't make enough to have some left, you ain't done nothin', except givin' the other fellow your labor."

In 1932, as times worsened for all farmers, Ned became involved in the Sharecroppers' Union, which attempted to bring black farmers together to oppose the system of "debt slavery." Always courageous, Ned intervened to stop the seizure of his neighbor Virgil Jones's livestock and tools for debt by the deputy sheriff, telling the man "you'll dispossess him of being able to feed

(Above) Hundreds of thousands of white families were tenant farmers and share-croppers as well. In 1913, this family in Corsicana, Texas, was renting a 50-acre cotton farm and working it with their children, "from five years old up." They expected to move every couple of years, the photographer noted, "giving them nomadic habits and [the feeling that] everything is temporary."

(Left) With his feet on the bumper of his shiny new car, a plantation owner has been talking to some of the "boys" who work for him (Mississippi Delta, near Clarksdale, Mississippi, June 1936).

his family." Ned's actions so enraged the white community that he was sent to prison for twelve years. After serving his term, Ned returned to his life on the land, never questioning the rightness of what he had done. His commitment to work remained. Toward the end of his autobiography, he said, "It approaches my mind like this: What is labor? It's a trait of man. God put us all here to work."

(Left) Bud Fields, a white sharecropper in Alabama, rests from picking in his cotton patch, 1935.

(Below) In 1940, this Louisiana cotton sharecropper's small farmstead sits near the edge of the Mississippi River levee, with a two-room house, open-sided shed on the right, and very small barn to the left. This striking early color photograph portrays the lush landscape, which contrasts with the family's humble possessions and precarious economic situation.

Small Hands:

RACE AND POWER

Set side by side, two photographs from the mid-1930s tell a story about power, race, and work. In one picture, a young African American girl, with her cotton sack slung over her right shoulder, pauses briefly to look into the camera. Behind her is an adult figure, perhaps her mother. Both are day laborers picking cotton in the hot sun. At the end of the day, both of them will bring their sacks of cotton in from the field to be weighed.

Weighing the cotton at the end of the day was a work practice that had a long history. During "slavery days" it was often a time of fear, with punishment awaiting pickers who had missed their quotas. Afterwards, weighing became a time of financial reckoning, when pickers, paid by the pound, found out how much they would earn for their day's work.

The second photograph shows another young girl, about the same age, also working out in the fields. But she is a white girl, the plantation owner's daughter. The camera catches her weighing the cotton, not picking it, as she stands in for her father. Although she is young, she is in a position of power, measuring the production and earnings of each of the African American workers who stand around her. Her race and family position have given her authority over them.

(Left) **Picking cotton, Pulaski County, Arkansas, c. 1935.**

(Right) **A plantation owner's daughter checks the weight of cotton brought in by pickers in Kaufman County, Texas, c. 1936.**

RISK: FARMING ON THE GREAT PLAINS

Farming always had its risks. Weather, pests, and the cycles of the economy were generally beyond any farmer's control. But the risks on the Great Plains were magnified to match the scale of its vast and open landscape. The prairies of Illinois, the fields of Ohio, or the rolling hills of Pennsylvania seemed tranquil gardens in comparison. Some found this endlessness, and the abundance that went with it, exhilarating. Others saw it as lonely, even terrifying. "On every hand," wrote E. V. Smalley, a close observer of rural life, in 1896, "the treeless landscape stretches away to the horizon. In summer it is checkered with grain fields or carpeted with grass and flowers . . . but one mile of it is almost exactly like another."

In the 1870s, as the tide of settlement continued into Kansas, Nebraska, and the Dakotas, farm families found themselves moving into an environment more precarious than they could have imagined. They were running up against the permanent realities of the North American continent's climate. The Great Plains are huge and windblown, with hot summers and very cold winters—challenging for farmers, but not impossible. Rainfall was the key. West of Iowa, Missouri, and Minnesota, average annual rainfall starts to decline; responding to this, the trees thin out and then disappear.

Today, geographers mark what they call the "line of semi-aridity"— usually defined as the 98th meridian—out on the Plains. It is an invisible line but an important one. East of the line there is usually enough rain to grow farm crops; west of the line, there usually isn't. But *usually* is a tricky word. Even east of the line, a few years of drought could destroy crops. And west of the line, a few years of high rainfall could deceive farmers into thinking they were safe. None of this was well understood in the nineteenth century. Farmers knew that the climate got drier as they went west, but they were constantly assured by land promoters and railroad officials that whatever rain fell would always be enough.

The earliest time of reckoning came in 1874. Farmers in Kansas and farther north were struggling with a two-month-long drought, as well as a cinch-bug infestation that was destroying crops at an alarming rate. But these were minor nuisances when compared with the hordes of "grasshoppers" (Rocky Mountain locusts) that descended on Kansas, Nebraska, the Dakotas, and northern Texas at the very end of July. It was a plague of Old Testament proportions, as Bible-reading farm families ruefully noted.

This 1898 cyanotype—using a process that fixes the image in gradations of blue, used for many years to make architect's "blueprints"—dramatized the vast horizons on this wheat farm in Brookings, South Dakota.

Plowing in North Dakota in the 1880s. When "the dreaded task of plowing began," Hamlin Garland remembered of his life on a Great Plains farm, "we drove our teams into the field, there to plod 'round and 'round in solitary course." Garland wrote a poem about his experience:

A lonely task it is to plow!
All day the black and shining soil
Rolls like a ribbon from the mold-board's
Glistening curve. All day the horses toil,
Battling with savage flies, and strain
Their creaking single-trees. All day
The crickets peer from wind-blown stacks
of grain.

Institute for Regional Studies, North Dakota State University, Fred Hultstrand History in Pictures Collection.

"The sun was almost darkened," wrote the Topeka correspondent for the *New York Times*, "with the myriads of grasshoppers coming in" from the mountains. "Working rapidly eastward, taking corn, vegetables in their course, they have literally stripped the farms and gardens of almost the entire State." In many counties, he noted, "where the new settlers had staked everything on the chance of a bounteous yield, all is lost." Many of them, "dispirited, ruined," were trying to leave, heading back to their previous communities farther east, with the taste of failure in their mouths. But the plague of locusts did not reappear in succeeding years, and optimism returned. Some who fled returned to rebuild their farms, and many newcomers came west to try for their own "chance of a bounteous yield."

PATTERNS OF BOUNTY AND FRUITLESSNESS

Alternating cycles of hope and despair would prove to be the reality of farming on the Plains. Grasshoppers were bad enough, but the crucial variable was the fluctuating climate. The years from the mid-1870s to mid-1880s were unusually warm and wet. Farmers had enough rainfall for abundant harvests of corn and

"Our Great West of 1874," a satirical poster printed in Kansas, depicts the grasshopper plague that descended on the Great Plains that year. Grasshoppers, along with cycles of drought and bitterly cold winters, presented enormous environmental challenges for farmers seeking to settle on the Great Plains. *Courtesy American Antiquarian Society.*

The William Moore family poses in front of their large sod farmhouse in Custer County, Nebraska, in 1886, just at the end of an optimistic decade of good weather and rapid settlement. Sod houses were the first to be built by settlers on the treeless Great Plains. Building this house with 3-foot-long sod bricks would have required plowing up nearly 2 acres of land to cut the blocks from the earth. This family seems well equipped for Plains farming, with five horses, a flock of sheep, at least one dairy cow, and a working windmill to pump water from a deep aquifer (there was plenty of wind blowing across the Nebraska plains).

wheat, and the winters seemed no worse than those in Iowa and Illinois. These favorable conditions led to a flood of settlers, encouraged by railroad promoters, the advice of agricultural experts, and word of mouth. Some advocates advanced a wonderfully self-serving theory about the climate, now long discredited. They claimed that settlement itself—by breaking the sod and creating cultivated fields—would changed weather patterns for the better: The more farmers there were, the more successful farming would be.

These hopes were dashed during the next fifteen years. From the mid-1880s until the end of the century, the climate of the Plains returned to its more-typical pattern of low rainfall and long, extremely cold winters. In the recurring droughts of those years, hundreds of thousands of farmers abandoned their land and fled to Iowa and Illinois. In 1896, Stephen Crane, journalist and author of *The Red Badge of Courage*, described the devastation: "A prosperous . . . country was brought to a condition of despair: As the drought went on, the hot wind raged like a pestilence . . . farmers helpless, with no weapon against this terrible and inscrutable wrath of nature." They had become "spectators at the strangling of their hopes, their ambitions, all they could look to from their labor."

Crane wrote that "the country died," but it eventually returned to life. The climate cycle continued to turn. At the turn of the twentieth century, and through its first decade, there was another sequence of wet years with warmer winters. Settlers returned, this time better prepared to deal with the inevitable return to semi-arid conditions.

Farmers in North Dakota wait in line to deliver their wheat to the grain elevator. This marked the end of the wheat production cycle. The grain, which came from hundreds of surrounding farms, would eventually find its way from the Midwest to the world market. *Institute for Regional Studies, North Dakota State University.*

Yet it wasn't just uncertain rainfall and unforgiving ecology that made life on the Northwestern prairies hard. There was also the extreme social isolation. American farm families had never lived as close together as their ancestors in Europe, but farms on the Plains were much farther apart from each other than anywhere else. "The average space separating the farmsteads is in fact, always more than half a mile," wrote E. V. Smalley in 1895, "and many settlers must go a mile or two to reach a neighbor's house." Families might go for months without seeing a visitor or a neighborly face, particularly in the long winters.

This created great loneliness, Smalley thought, and bred alcoholism and despair: "An alarming amount of insanity occurs in the new prairie states among farmers and their wives." A farmer might return from the fields, expecting his noon dinner, only to find that his wife had hung herself from the rafters of the barn. Smalley believed that the best remedy for this would be for farm families to live much closer together, and for the men to take longer trips out to their fields to work. But this was unlikely. "There is a crusty individuality about the average American farmer," he concluded, "the inheritance of generations of isolated living."

Sylvester Rawding family in front of a sod house, north of Sargent, Custer County, Nebraska, 1886. Plains families were often miles away from the nearest neighbor or small town. It was lonely for everyone, but women, confined to the house, suffered most from the isolation of their lonely farmsteads.

The Arid Belt, Cowboys, and Cattle

"The great grazing lands of the West," wrote Theodore Roosevelt in 1888, "lie in what is known as the arid belt." They included New Mexico, parts of Arizona, Colorado, Wyoming, Montana, and the western portion of Texas, Kansas, Nebraska, and the Dakotas. For three decades after the Civil War, the western Great Plains were dominated by cattle grazing on the open range. "There are no fences to speak of," Roosevelt continued, "and all the land . . . between the Rockies and the Dakota wheat-field might be spoken of as one gigantic, unbroken pasture, where cowboys and branding irons take the place of fences." Roosevelt knew what he was talking about. Although born to wealth in New York City and educated at Harvard, the future president had transformed himself during what he acknowledged as "a painful apprenticeship" into a competent cowhand and reasonably successful stock rancher.

After 1865, as the great buffalo herds were systematically slaughtered and the power of the Plains Indians was broken by the railroads and the U.S. Army, the immense area from Montana and the Dakotas down to western Texas became "the American West" of both myth and reality—the land of longhorn cattle, ranchers, trail drives, cattle towns, and cowboys. Dry and re-mote, it was, Roosevelt wrote, "one vast stretch of grazing country, with only here and there spots of farm land." Ranchers might cut wild hay or plant a garden patch, but that was all. Individual ranchers owned some of the land on which they established their "spreads," but most of it remained in the public domain, federally owned but open for use.

It may seem that nothing could be farther from city life than cattle graz-ing on the Plains, but the expansion of the cattle business had its origins in the urban, industrial America that was emerging east of the Mississippi. It

An enormous herd of cattle is on the move in San Miguel County, New Mexico. Cow-boys saw this many cattle all at once only during roundups and cattle drives. When grazing, cattle needed a lot of room—about 25 acres of land per animal.

Stock raisers and cowhands on the Northern Plains—as here in Eldridge, Montana, c. 1911—worried less about summer drought killing their herds and more about snowstorms and severe winter cold. Cattle could die by the thousands in a blizzard, and cowboys could freeze to death trying to save them.

was powered by an expanding market for beef; the development of swift railroad transport from towns at the end of the cattle trails, like Dodge City and Abilene; and the growth of an enormous meatpacking industry in places like Chicago, Omaha, and Kansas City.

A Cowboy's Life

Andy Adams of Texas went to work as a cowboy in the early 1870s, when he was eighteen. His father had apprenticed him as a store clerk in the hope of keeping him near home, since both his older brothers had gone off to work on the range. But as Andy wrote in his autobiographical *Log of a Cowboy*, he despised the slow, unexciting pace of life in town, and "took to the range as

BELL RANCH. SAN MIGUEL CO. N.M.

PHOTO & COPYRIGHT 1914 BY
P. CLINTON BARTELL

No. 345 BRANDING CALVES ON ROUND UP. (Photo and copyright by Grabill. 1888

Branding calves during roundup in the Dakota Territory, c. 1888. On the open range, cattle wandered ceaselessly, and herds belonging to different spreads easily became entangled. Calves were branded at the first roundup after they were born, with a mark that uniquely identified them as property of the ranch.

a preacher's son takes to vice . . . the vagabond temperament of the range I easily assimilated." He recalled how his brothers' "wondrous stories . . . about the northern country set my blood on fire."

Since open-range grazing had originated in the Southwest and moved north from Texas to spread across the Western Plains, the largest number of cowboys were Texans, like Adams, or from southwest Louisiana. But the appeal of a cowhand's life drew many young men from all parts of the United States. Roosevelt liked to note that a number of Easterners, himself included, successfully mastered the trade. There were even a few adventurous Englishmen, he said, who were looking for a new start after being exiled to America for bringing their wealthy families into disgrace by drinking, gambling, and debauchery.

A busy day on the Paloduro Ranch, Armstrong County, Texas, c. 1905. Brands were recorded and registered by associations of cattlemen, and cowboys had to memorize hundreds of them to keep track of animals on the range. Male calves were also castrated at branding time, since steers were far easier to handle than bulls.

A substantial number of cowhands—perhaps as many as 30 percent—were African American or Mexican, and a few were from American Indian tribes. Roosevelt, who shared the racial biases of his time, was generally dismissive of "colored and half-caste" hands, but did admit that two of his best cowboys working the trail in 1886 were "a Sioux half-breed . . . and a mulatto."

More than a few white cowboys were actively hostile toward Mexicans, which was strangely ironic. All American cowboys owed their working heritage to the Mexican *vaquero*, who had been chasing cattle since the seventeenth century. The tools of the cowboy's trade, the words he used, and the basic arrangements of his work—from saddles and spurs to the lariat, the branding iron, and the cattle drive—had their origins in Spanish Mexico. Of course, nearly half of America's "great grazing lands" had once actually belonged to Mexico and the *vaquero*. They had been annexed to the United States in 1848 after the Mexican War.

There were never all that many cowboys—no more than a few thousand at any one time—but it did not take long for them to capture the American imagination. In popular magazines and novels, in prints and paintings and

"The Cowboy," J. C. H. Grabill, Sturgis, Dakota, c. 1888. This cowboy poses fully equipped for his work. His pistol and cavalry-style rifle are primarily to protect the herd from predators. His most important tool, besides the horse itself, is his rope, used not only for roping and driving cattle, but also "for every conceivable emergency . . . in helping pull a wagon up a steep pitch, in dragging an animal by the horns out of a bog hole, in hauling up logs for the fire." He has leather chaps to protect himself from thorny brush (although many cowboys did not wear them). Cowboys depended on their horses, but most did not own their own mounts. They used the horses provided by their employers.

touring Wild West shows, they were portrayed as supremely self-reliant individualists. Roosevelt's own writing fostered this image; he called them men who "go armed and ready to guard their lives by their own prowess, whose wants are very simple, and who call no man master." Their lives were starkly contrasted with the humdrum ones of the vast majority of American men, who plodded along on their farms or in shops, offices, and factories. They seemed to embody a freedom that no one else possessed.

Free as they seemed in some ways, cowboys were part of a great economic engine that included railroads and packing houses. They rode the range because American families in Massachusetts, Pennsylvania, and Ohio wanted beef on their tables, and their actual work was far from romantic. They were not warriors or hunters, but mounted herdsmen, responsible for managing enormous herds of free-ranging cattle. Their job was to ensure that the animals they were driving survived winter cold and summer drought. They rounded the cattle up in the spring and fall and drove them thousands of miles east to the railhead towns, where they would be sold.

(Facing page) Bob Lemmons of Carrizo Springs, Texas, was born a slave near San Antonio, Texas, c. 1850. After emancipation, he worked as a cowhand. He is pictured here in 1936, in his mid-eighties.

An African American cowboy poses with his saddled horse, c. 1900. *Denver Public Library, Western History Collection.*

ON THE TRAIL

Cowboys were poorly paid for their difficult and risky work. Trail hands earned more than farm laborers but less than city craftsmen, and often went without work in the winter, when ranchers needed fewer hands. Old cowboys were rare. Most men who started working the range were in their twenties and usually lasted no more than ten years. A few—the luckiest and most able—became ranch foremen or even ranch owners. But most did not. As middle-aged or older men, many ended up picking up odd jobs on ranches or working as stable hands in the cow towns.

But no matter how a cowboy's career ended, the most dramatic and exciting part of the job was the cattle drive. Every year the trail boss—an experienced older cowhand—led ten or fifteen men into the wilderness. Together, they steered a herd of two or three thousand head of cattle across the plains. Some drives were even larger, with twenty-five or thirty men, and twice the number of cattle. Their job was simple: to deliver the animals to market with the fewest possible losses. This was a journey of more than a thousand miles that might take three or four months.

Andy Adams remembered what his brother, an experienced trail boss, told him about the discipline needed on a drive: "Hardship and privation must be met, and the men must throw themselves equally into the collar. A trail outfit has to work as a unit." Along with the men on the drive, and the chuck wagon that carried food and supplies, went another herd, or remuda (from the Spanish word for "change"), of working horses that the cowboys used for replacements when their tired mounts needed to be "swapped out." On Adams's first cattle drive, with fourteen hands, the remuda consisted of 142 horses—"ten horses to the man, with two extra for the foreman." Range work tired horses quickly, and a cowboy could easily wear out two mounts in a single day's work.

Work on the open range was exhausting, dangerous, and exposed to the elements, and it showed. Cowboys' faces were lined and seamed not only by the sun, but by "peril, and hardship, and years of long toil," Roosevelt wrote. A cattle drive involved long stretches of boredom punctuated by sudden emergencies. Cowhands were responsible for keeping the herd together, swimming them across streams, finding them grass and water, and protecting them from predators like wolves and mountain lions.

Because they needed to keep the herd moving as long as possible, and then prevent the cattle from wandering away from camp, cowhands

Five cow punchers are eating on the trail near the Birdwood Ranch in Nebraska, sometime between 1870 and 1890. The trail cook was vitally important, responsible for supplies, repairs, and medical care, as well as food. "Our foreman knew that a well-fed man can stand an incredible amount of hardship," remembered cowboy Andy Adams, "and appreciated the fact that on the trail, a good cook is a valuable asset." *Denver Public Library, Western History Collection.*

At least sixteen cowboys are working this roundup near the Belle Fourche River in the Dakota Territory, heading off straying cattle and "cutting," or separating the herds by their owners brands, 1887.

routinely got little rest. On many stretches of trail, recalled Adams, "they were long, monotonous days; for we were always sixteen to eighteen hours in the saddle." When the herd was agitated by lightning strikes or protracted thirst, all hands worked without rest to keep them calm and prevent a stampede.

"[I]f any of us got more than an hour's sleep," Adams wrote about a night spent trying to calm restless cattle, "he was lucky." A rider could be killed or badly injured if his horse stumbled or if he turned too slowly to avoid a stampeding herd, and chronic exhaustion made such accidents more likely. Thirst and starvation did not afflict the trail hands, who brought substantial food supplies with them, but could threaten the cattle during a

drought or a blizzard. Losing large numbers of cattle on the trail was always a great defeat.

Cowhands' skills were highly specialized, and many tasks that were elementary to farmers and woodsmen were foreign to them. On horseback, the cowboy "shines at the head of his class," wrote Adams, "but in any occupation which must be performed on foot he is never a competitor." He recalled that "there was scarcely a man in our outfit who could not swing a rope and tie down a steer in a given space of time," but when it came to cutting logs to build a makeshift raft for a river crossing, they scarcely knew what to do. "We were the poorest set of axemen that were ever called upon to perform a similar task," he wrote. "When we cut a tree it looked as though a beaver had gnawed it down."

Cowboys lived in an all-male world of work, where almost all of their time was spent on the trail and far away from "civilization." It's no surprise,

Five cowhands sit in front of a group of log houses on a ranch in the Dakota Territory, c. 1887–92. A ranch complex on a Dakota grazing spread was usually a cluster of log buildings and a separate cabin for the ranch foreman. There would also be a mess hall, a long house for the cowboys to sleep, stables, sheds, a blacksmith shed, corrals, and horse pastures.

H. L. Hay's Ranch, Plateau Valley, Colorado, 1911. Ranches on the Western Plains were often many miles apart. In comparison, the far-scattered farm settlements in Nebraska and the Dakotas looked like villages. *Denver Public Library, Western History Collection.*

then, that trail rides just about always ended with a raucous week or more "on the town." Many a cowboy managed to spend most if not all of his accumulated wages on fancy clothes, liquor, and prostitutes. "We sauntered about the straggling village, drinking occasionally," recalled Adams of one such expedition, buying new suits, boots, and hats, and happily listening to a saloon's piano player banging out their favorite tunes. Adams never mentioned visiting a brothel in his autobiography (it would have made his book unpublishable at the time). He only went so far as to say that cowhands spent a good bit of time talking longingly about women.

CHANGES ON THE HORIZON

Free-range grazing flourished for three decades in the American West, from the 1860s through the 1880s, long enough for the cowboy—thanks to wildly popular penny novels and Wild West shows—to become a heroic American myth. Theodore Roosevelt himself did his part to romanticize the life of cowboys and cattlemen, although he also understood the hard, prosaic nature of their work. He saw in them a primitive self-reliance and masculinity that men in industrial America badly needed.

But by 1890 grazing was in decline. Roosevelt predicted correctly that "in its present form, stock-raising on the plains is doomed, and can scarcely outlast the century." Responding to what seemed like endlessly increasing demand, ranchers in the early 1880s recklessly increased the size of their herds. Just as it did in other industries, overproduction drove beef prices down steeply—mostly to the benefit of the packing houses. In some parts of the West, the larger herds overwhelmed the grazing lands. The final blow was the great "die-off" on the Northern plains during the terrible winter of 1885–86. Blizzards and record low temperatures killed half or more of the animals in many herds through exposure and starvation.

This ranch house in Sturges, Dakota Territory, c. 1890, is a considerably more domesticated landscape, the center of a more self-contained ranch. The rancher has a wife, the house is more finished than a log cabin, and the mowing machine at left and the horse-drawn hay rake at right indicate that they are raising hay to feed the stock.

The scope of change on the Plains is evident in this picture showing a young girl, not a weather-beaten cowpuncher, herding cattle. Twelve-year-old Sarah Crutcher "was out of school only 2 weeks this year and that was to herd 100 head of cattle for her father, a prosperous farmer," recorded photographer Lewis Hine in 1917.

This photographic postcard from 1908 captures a more-domesticated ranch life. The hands here are taking at least part of Sunday off to give each other haircuts. On the trail, there was never any downtime for this kind of activity.

As a result, ranchers moved away from the open-range system with its enormous roundups and cattle drives to build more self-contained ranches where they could take better care of their cattle and reduce the risks of blizzard, drought, and heavy losses of cattle. To improve their profits, they began to abandon the hardy Texas longhorns for improved cattle breeds that produced more salable beef per head. These changes were made possible in great part by the invention and widespread use of a new fencing material, barbed wire. Traditional wood or stone fencing had always been impossible on the plains, making it very difficult to control or confine the movement of cattle. Barbed wire was light and strong, and could be strung for miles, demarcating the ranch's boundaries and containing its herds.

Cowboys ceased to ride the open range and became ranch workers, running and repairing fences, cutting hay, and getting the herds safely through the winter. "The great free ranches," Roosevelt noted somewhat mournfully, were like "the great tracts of primeval forests" that generations of American farmers had cut down in order to work the land. True to his convictions about the conquering power of American civilization, he wrote that both were destined to "pass away before the onward march of our people."

"WE WAS STARVED OUT AND WE LIVE ON PERHAPS": THE DUST BOWL

In the early decades of the twentieth century, farming on the Great Plains continued on its careening course of advance and retreat, optimism and crushing disappointment. As international demand for wheat grew during World War I and into the 1920s, Plains farmers expanded their production at an unprecedented speed, gambling once more against the ecological fragility of their region. At first it paid off. As in previous cycles, there were a number of years with adequate rainfall, high productivity, and good prices. But to grow ever more wheat, farmers plowed up millions of acres of drought-resistant prairie grass, putting an enormous stretch of the American land-scape at risk if conditions turned devastatingly dry.

Lawrence Svobida, a Kansas wheat farmer of Czech descent, wrote in 1934 about how much he and the other farmers of the Plains loved their land's abundance. "I believe any man must see beauty," he wrote, "in mile

Father and sons walking in a dust storm, Cimarron County, Oklahoma, April 1936. The farm has long since been buried under blowing sand, and the house itself is partway submerged.

upon mile of level land where the wheat, waist high, sways to the slightest breeze and is turning a golden yellow under a flaming July sun. To me it is breathtaking, the most beautiful scene in all the world." But this picturesque sight of endless cultivated fields would be forever marred in the 1930s, along with the hopes that it embodied, in the greatest environmental disaster in American history.

As it sweeps onward, the landscape is progressively blotted out. Birds fly in terror before the storm, and only those that are strong of wing may escape.

—Lawrence Svobida, Kansas wheat farmer, 1934

It started when the rains stopped coming. Drought came and persisted year after year, worse than anything that nineteenth-century farmers had ever seen, breaking records for lowest yearly rainfall that had been kept since the 1870s. The land dried out, the wheat died, and the topsoil of the Plains, no longer anchored by the native grasses of the prairie, began to turn to dust. The fierce winds of the Plains no longer swept through with relatively little damage, as they had when the soil was firmly anchored. Instead, they picked up tons of loose soil and created enormous choking storms. "With the gales came the dust," Svobida recalled of the years between 1934 and 1940. "Sometimes it was so thick that it completely hid the sun. Visibility ranged from nothing to fifty feet."

The term "Dust Bowl" was coined by an Associated Press reporter describing the great storm of April 14, 1935, or Black Sunday, the day when choking walls of dust seemed to darken half the continent. Dust clouds that overshadowed Kansas could be seen in Washington, D.C. Avis Dungan Carlson, a writer in Kansas, wrote that to stand outdoors in that storm was to feel "a shovelful of fine sand flung against the face." Battered by the relentless storms, "people caught in their own yards grope for the doorstep. Cars come to a standstill, for no light in the world can penetrate that swirling murk . . . We live with the dust, eat it, sleep with it, watch it strip us of possessions and the hope of possessions."

During the Dust Bowl years, agricultural production in the Plains states fell disastrously. Field and garden crops were burned out by drought and, with wells choked and the grass withered and gone, hungry cattle actually died from eating dust. The wheat belt, America's breadbasket, was full of

In June 1938, this farmhouse was one of the few still occupied in the Coldwater district of the Texas panhandle. But the farm itself was already dead, its fields and crops buried by the sand.

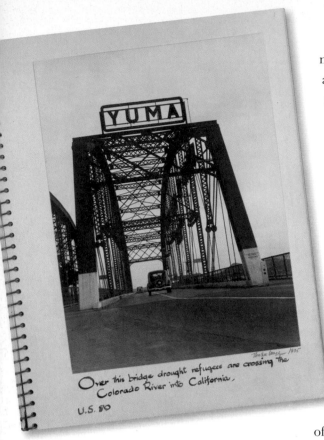

Over this bridge drought refugees are crossing the
Colorado River into California.

U.S. 80

This is a page from the notebook of photographer and journalist Dorothea Lange,
who was recording the Dust Bowl's impact
on the people of the Southern Plains. The
Colorado River bridge in Yuma, Arizona,
took automobile traffic into California—
the promised land of Dust Bowl emigrants.
She writes in her elegant script, "Over this
bridge drought refugees are crossing the
Colorado River into California. U.S. 80 /
Dorothea Lange, 1935."

nothing but sand, and the once-fertile land itself began to disappear. In 1938
alone, the federal government estimated that 850 million tons of topsoil,
from the Dakotas to Texas and Oklahoma, were lost to erosion. The
nation's food supply was not seriously affected, as production moved to
other parts of the country.

But more than the land had been devastated. Men, women, and children in the Dust Bowl states fell victim to dust-related respiratory diseases,
stress, and depression. When Lawrence Svobida realized that his crop had
been utterly destroyed, he "experienced a deathly feeling which, I hope,
can affect a man only once in a lifetime. My dreams and ambitions had
been flouted by nature."

The people of the Dust Bowl joined millions of other Americans as
victims of the Depression years—displaced, unemployed, shell-shocked.
Hundreds of thousands of families made the gut-wrenching decision
to abandon their dust-choked farms and dying communities. Hanging
on to a desperate hope, they became refugees looking for shelter, food,
and jobs. Some headed back east, as their predecessors had done in
earlier crises, but more went west, to the Pacific Coast and the promise
of California. Dust Bowl refugees made their journeys not in wagons but in
old cars and farm trucks, packed with children, clothes, bedding, pots and
pans. In sunny California they found better weather but an economy that
could provide little work other than migrant labor in the orchards and veg-
etable fields. The hordes of Dust Bowl migrants added to the state's already
huge army of job seekers. California growers, who had an oversupply of
workers and faced a Depression-weakened market, deliberately kept wages
low. Many families found no work at all.

Not until 1941, with the American economy starting to recover and gearing up for war production, did the rains return. Farming on the Great Plains
recovered once again; but this time farmers were encouraged, even forced, to
change their practices of plowing and planting and to adopt soil-conserving
techniques. Those who had chosen to stay picked up their lives again, and
some of those who had left returned. More remained in California and the
other places they had fled to; they had created new lives and found work
outside of agriculture.

With all their belongings packed into the car, the members of this farm family from
Abilene, Texas, have become migratory workers in California in 1936. "The finest
people in this world live in Texas, but I just can't seem to accomplish nothin' there,"
said the father. "Two years drought, then a crop, then two years drought and so on. I
got two brothers still trying to make it back there and there they're sitting."

Small Hands:

THE TOBACCO SHEDS

The lower Connecticut River Valley has New England's most productive farmland. Its moderate climate and rich soil make the Valley one of the best places in the world for growing the fine, light-colored tobacco that is used to make the outer wrapping and binding layers of cigars. Early settlers had learned about tobacco from Native Americans, and had grown it in small amounts from the 1600s on. As cigar smoking became increasingly popular among American men after the Civil War, demand for wrapper tobacco grew enormously between 1870 and 1920, and it became one of the region's major cash crops. The long tobacco drying sheds, with their slatted open-work sides designed for the constant circulation of air, once dominated the Connecticut River landscape for many miles. They still can be seen today, although the industry is now small.

Tobacco is a highly labor-intensive crop requiring close attention through its entire growing season. Growing and harvesting the crop employed hundreds of local families. But for the work of stripping the harvested tobacco leaves from their stalks, so that they could be sorted and graded before sale, Connecticut Valley growers often preferred children, who had small, nimble hands and didn't need to be paid very much.

A photograph from 1917, taken inside a tobacco shed on the Hawthorn farm in Hazardville, Connecticut, shows three girls stripping tobacco leaves. "Girls in foreground are 8, 9, and 10 years old," wrote Lewis Hine in his notes. "The 10 yr. old makes 50 cents a day. Twelve workers on this farm are 8 to 14 years old, and about 15 are over 15 yrs." A second picture taken the same week shows seven-year-old Alec, posing with bravado on his way to look for a tobacco-shed job.

The children pictured here came from hard-pressed families whose parents welcomed—or even insisted on—the extra income from their work. In 1870, when large-scale tobacco growing in the Valley was beginning,

few Americans would have thought this strange. After all, children had always worked on their families' farms. But by 1917, in a far less rural America, many would have been ready to condemn both the growers and the parents; attitudes toward the work of very young children had changed significantly. These small workers were ten years old or younger, standing at the stripping tables for long hours, missing school, and possibly absorbing tobacco through their skin. Hine thought that they were too young to be in this workplace, and most public opinion would have agreed with him. Within a few years, children this age would no longer be found in the tobacco sheds.

A former Dust Bowl farmer turned migrant laborer, this man awaits the opening of orange-picking season at Porterville, California, in November 1936.

PICKING AND PACKING

Everything in the United States was done on a large, commercial scale, noted the Frenchman Paul de Constant as he traveled the country in 1914. Accustomed to the small and lovingly cultivated orchards and market gardens of France, he was astonished by how in California and Oregon, "apples . . . apricots, plums, almonds, and peaches" were "hand-gathered in thousands, packed on the spot, and sent off to the nearest [railroad] station without passing through farm or store." De Constant was observing a distinctly American kind of agriculture—growing fruit and vegetables on a large scale, quickly preparing them for market, and selling them nationwide. It was a system that was created after the Civil War.

Before then, most fruits and vegetables couldn't travel very far. Whether eaten fresh, dried, pickled, or turned into preserves, they were consumed close to where they were grown. But starting around 1870, two innovations—the canning process and the refrigerated railroad car, along with the continued

(Above) An advertisement for Sunny South Fruit, c. 1870. Sunny South Farm in Alabama was a pioneer in the large-scale raising of peaches and other fruit for markets in the North, providing work that drew thousands of pickers and packers into the fields. Ultimately, Sunny struggled unsuccessfully with problems of transportation and refrigeration, which were solved by later-arriving growers.

increase in the speed of rail transport—made a major change in America's eating patterns. The tin can—actually, tin-plated steel—was born as a safe way to package food for long-distance transport without spoiling. Reasonably reliable canning methods were developed that used high-temperature sterilization and mass-produced containers that could quickly be soldered shut.

Tinned food became a symbol of the modern way of life, providing American consumers with inexpensive and convenient green beans and peaches year-round. As Andy Adams remembered, even cowboys on the trail relied heavily on canned food.

Tropical fruit—oranges and lemons—had traditionally been exotic items, eaten only rarely. But the coming of refrigerated warehouses and railroad cars made them, and other fresh fruit, far more available as well. Thousands of acres of orange and lemon groves were planted in Southern California and Florida, where the fruit could be packed and rushed in refrigerated cars to stores in Chicago, New York, or Boston. Refrigeration also greatly expanded the market for other fresh fruit, including strawberries, peaches, and raspberries.

(Left) "Irrigating endless avenues of orange trees, Redlands, California, 1919." Irrigation of what had previously been desert land—and providing access to the national market—created vast agricultural wealth in Southern California.

In these views of Riverside, California, c. 1910–20, men are picking in the orange groves using ladders, sacks, and packing boxes that have changed relatively little with time, while packers—primarily women—work inside a large shed. On these "assembly lines" women workers are sorting, grading, and packing the fruit.

Historic American Building Survey.

(Above) On this Colorado peach ranch in 1907, men are the pickers, coming in with canvas bags; women sort and pack in a simple canvas shelter put up in the fields. Stacks of fully packed boxes, marked MOUNTAIN FRUIT, are visible in the foreground. The older boy may be picking; the younger one is probably just staying near his mother while she works. Toward the back of the shelter is a man in a suit and hat—the owner or manager. *Denver Public Library, Western History Collection.*

(Right) Workers sort and pack peas at Ross's Cannery in Seaford, Delaware, 1910.

In 1910, a wagon caravan is ready to set out from Wolfe Street in Baltimore, taking immigrants out to work on the berry farms.

THE WHOLE FAMILY WORKS: A STORY OF THE BERRY FIELDS

As they responded to the increasing demand from city consumers in the early 1900s, the "berry farms" of southern New Jersey, Maryland, and northern Delaware needed more workers than they could find locally. Growers began to recruit seasonal field hands and packers in Philadelphia and Baltimore. Many of the new workers were recent arrivals from Italy, used to agricultural labor at home and willing to bring the entire family into the fields. In late spring and early fall, caravans of horse-drawn wagons would arrive in the cities' Italian neighborhoods to pick up workers. In 1910, Lewis Hine was struck by what he saw in Baltimore: "a street full of . . . immigrants lined up and ready to start for the country to the berry farms."

The Arnaos of Philadelphia were one of those berry-picking families. Orazio Arnao worked as a street-paving laborer; he never learned to read or write, and spoke only Italian all his life. His wife Katherine took care of the reading, the writing, and the English. Like other families in their neighborhood, they must have been glad for some additional income from agricultural labor. A day laborer like Orazio Arnao could not count on full-time employment. In 1910, they spent several weeks away from their tenement in Philadelphia. In May, they planted and weeded on farms in Cannon and Seaford, Delaware. In September, they worked for nearly a month picking strawberries in Brown's Mills, New Jersey. All seven of the Arnaos went into the field.

(Facing page) Ten children stand in front of the living quarters for city families on Hitchen's farm, Seaford, Delaware, in 1910. Lewis Hine noted "17 children and 5 elders live in this made-over chicken coop."

(Below, left) Father and three children of the Arnao family are picking strawberries on Whites Bog, Browns Mills, New Jersey, September 28, 1910. Except during spring and fall berry seasons, they lived at 831 Catherine Street, Rear # 2, Philadelphia.

(Below, right) In 1910, the Arnao family poses in the fields of Truitt's farm in Seaford, Delaware. Two of the young boys hold small berry boxes.

Standing among the palm trees in Canal Point, Florida, the mother and children of this migrant family stand while the father ducks down. They are living in a shanty, 1939.

"Whole family works," noted the photographer Lewis Hine, who recorded their presence—including the youngest, a three-year-old boy.

Like other seasonal farm workers, the Arnaos endured crude and crowded accommodations. When working in Delaware, they shared a former chicken coop, a building about 15 feet by 25 feet, with two other families—a total of five adults and seventeen children. Hine was deeply disturbed by their willingness to employ even the smallest hands to increase the family's income. Working in May and September meant that the children missed several weeks of school. Hine believed that Orazio and Katherine were irresponsibly sacrificing their children's future.

But a look at the family's fortunes after 1910 provides a different picture. Life wasn't easy in an illiterate laborer's household, but Orazio and Katherine kept their family together and continued to work together. In fact, they were able to save quite a bit of money. In 1920, the federal census shows that they had been able to buy a small house in Philadelphia, and were sending the younger children to school. By 1930 the Arnaos owned not only a house but a neighborhood grocery store. Orazio was no longer working; at sixty-four years old, he had been worn down by years of hard labor on the city's streets. But two of his sons ran the store, and one of his daughters was the cashier. His youngest daughters, born after the family photograph was taken in 1910, worked as sewing machine operators, bringing their wages home.

Lewis Hine had not meant it as a compliment when he wrote that the "whole family works." But the Arnao family clearly saw things differently. Working together was their strategy for survival and success.

"NOW WE CAN'T GO NOWHERES ELSE": A STORY OF THE ORANGE GROVES

For thousands of migrant worker families in the 1930s, the orange groves and packing houses of Florida provided episodic employment and meager housing—not much, but better than total unemployment and homelessness. But their lives were precarious in the extreme. Marion Post Walcott spent the late winter of 1939 documenting the lives of families in Florida's migrant worker camps. In February, she spent a couple of days at the Canal Point camp in Belle Glade, near Lake Okeechobee in southeastern Florida.

Walcott was drawn to one family in particular, whose story she found unusually compelling. She didn't record their names, so we will almost certainly never know how they ended up, but Walcott spoke to members of the family and recorded what they told her about their journey to Belle Glade. They had been tenant farmers in Missouri until drought and the Depression pushed them off the land and sent them looking for some other way to live.

(Facing page) A picker sorts low-lying fruit in a Florida orange grove, 1902.

With their last cash, they had put some money down on a car, making installment payments to hang on to it. Traveling and sometimes living in their car, they became migratory fruit-packing workers, moving from job to job. The father of the family was not interested in talking; he ducked down when Walcott took their picture, so his face cannot be seen.

But the mother was willing to tell her story. Aged beyond her years, she was only thirty-two, but had "had eleven children, two sets of twins." Five of them had died in infancy or childhood. This was a terrible death toll, comparable to that of rugged frontier America a hundred years earlier. By the 1930s, life expectancy for most American families had already improved far beyond nineteenth-century standards. This family did not share in that good fortune. Those children had almost certainly died of intestinal and respiratory infections, victims of malnutrition, poor sanitation, and their inability to get medical care.

For a couple of years they had gone from one seasonal labor camp to another. Arriving in Canal Point, Florida, they had completely run out of luck. "She and her husband lost jobs in the packinghouse," Walcott learned, "because they cut down on help." What were things like for them now? Walcott asked. The mother answered that "we have never lived like hogs before, but we sure does now; it's no different from hog livin'."

Walcott also talked to one of the children, a surprisingly eloquent boy of eight. He had become the caretaker of his youngest brother, and was worried about his health. "This little 'un's fell off so since we come here," he said. "It was so fat before. It's had colitis so bad." Then he told her more about what had happened to his family. "My daddy didn't know we was comin' to the wrong place this time," he continued, and "now we can't go nowheres else." They were trapped at Belle Glade, with no way to look for work elsewhere. His father's car had been repossessed. "He'd paid a lot off on it but he didn't git enough work here."

Eight-year-old son of Missouri migrant laborer holds his baby brother up for the camera and tells his family's story, 1939.

Identified as "Wife of packinghouse worker, migrant from Missouri," the mother of the family from Missouri stands in front of the family's clothesline in February 1939.

Struggles:

Trouble on the Farm

Off the farm, the nation's economy was prosperous in the 1920s. Cars, refrigerators, and vacuum cleaners were rolling off the assembly line. Consumers were on a spending spree, and stockbrokers were getting rich. But the American farmer was more vulnerable than ever. While urban America prospered, farmers felt the iron grip of the marketplace. Farm prices were high during the World War I years, and farmers borrowed heavily for land and machinery. But in 1921 prices fell sharply, and farmers' incomes began to fluctuate unpredictably. With uncertain income and the continuing burden of debt, an increasing number of farms were lost to foreclosure each year.

John T. McCutcheon's cartoon of 1926 illustrates the farmer's fundamental grievance, a theme that had resounded in the heyday of the Granger and Populist movements of the 1870s and 1890s: Farmers fed the nation, but the nation as a whole ignored their widespread economic problems. McCutcheon's farmer leans on a fence post, the skyline of a distant city that he provides for in the background, and laments, "Th' East ain't in'trested in my troubles." Politicians were catering instead to businessmen and city consumers. But if all the farmers took a year's vacation, McCutcheon imagined, cities would starve. Urban, industrial America would pay dearly for its neglect of the countryside, offering up "a bushel of diamonds for a square meal," and farmers would finally be heard. At the time of the illustration's publication, this seemed like an impossible fantasy. Farmers were too deeply dependent on the rest of the economy to rebel in such a drastic way. But by the early 1930s, starving seemed like a real possibility.

Farmers were already in trouble, but the collapse of the overall economy during the Great Depression made things much worse. Markets shrank, farm credit became almost impossible to get, and prices fell further. Corn was worth so little that many families burned the ears in their stoves instead of coal. Ruinous prices coupled with an upsurge in farm foreclosures goaded many farmers into resistance. A sizable number of them joined the Farmers' Holiday Association (FHA), founded in 1932 by pioneer farm union organizer Milo Reno. The FHA, whose name echoes the theme of McCutcheon's cartoon, demanded government action to stabilize prices and reduce mortgage debt. Desperate to make the authorities listen, FHA members protested against foreclosures and used a variety of tactics to drive up prices. They withheld their produce from market, forced creameries and cheese factories to close, blockaded roads, and even pulled drivers out of their trucks.

Cartoonist John T. McCutcheon reflected the anguish and alienation felt by many American farmers as prices crashed, c. 1926. "If all the farmers took a year's vacation . . ." (John T. McCutcheon, no. 62, pen and ink drawing).

In 1932 or 1933 an anonymous photographer captured an angry confrontation on an Iowa farm, with FHA members trying to disrupt a foreclosure sale. Captioned WHEN THE BOTTOM FELL OUT OF EVERYTHING, the image shows hundreds of farmers milling around the barnyard, held in check by uniformed state police wielding clubs and batons. The troopers have arrived to protect the court officials, the auctioneer, and potential buyers from the unruly crowd.

The FHA did not succeed in raising farm prices or shutting down the food markets. But responding to pressures from farmers and homeowners alike, twenty-six states passed mortgage "moratorium" laws to postpone foreclosures for up to five years. In 1933 the federal government responded with the New Deal's Agricultural Adjustment Act, which provided direct subsidy payments to farmers for the first time and tried to raise prices by limiting production. These measures provided some relief, but good times would not come again for farmers until the war years of 1941–45.

A large crowd assembles at a foreclosure sale on an Iowa farm in 1932 or 1933, when, as a farmer recalled, "the bottom fell out of everything." Military police are visible at the top and right of the picture to ensure that the auction is not disrupted.

Chapter 2
Workshop and
Household

(Overleaf) **In the finishing room of a Danbury hat factory, c. 1900, a long row of workers ensures that the hats receive their final shape before they are sent to be trimmed.** *Memory Lane Images, Danbury Historical Society.*

A young American mechanic—about the same age that Richard Needham was in 1860—poses for his portrait, dressed in the half-formal, half-casual way that often distinguished craftsmen from storekeepers and clerks.

(Right) In this 1842 illustration of plasterers at work, the younger man is doing the work of an apprentice. Assisting the master craftsman, he mixes plaster while the master applies the first coat over the lath, using his wooden "float" in his right hand. In his left hand is the "hawk," which holds the prepared plaster. *Author photo.*

(Facing page) A plasterer works on a wall in Waco, Texas, 1939.

The United States in the middle of the nineteenth century was for the most part still a handmade world, a universe of wood and iron, of draft animals, of water power and muscle power. In city, village, and countryside, men and women practiced the skills that created the material fabric of American society, working in wood, metal, leather, cloth, clay, paper, and stone. Their work of hand and eye, shaped by early training and years of learning by doing, was no less important than the toil of the farm.

Richard Needham, my wife's great-grandfather, was one of these skilled craftsmen, a plasterer and "stucco worker." Born in County Wexford, in the far southeast of Ireland, Richard came to Boston with his parents and their five other children in 1852. Richard's father, Joseph, could not read or write, but he found work as a laborer for the city, repairing and paving its streets. He had no trade to teach his sons.

But Richard still managed to move a step beyond his father. The census of 1860 tells us that he was working as a plasterer by age twenty-four. He carried ladders and tools; pushed wheelbarrows from job to job through Boston's streets; mixed sand, lime, animal hair, and water to make plaster; nailed lath to walls; and, as he had been taught, skillfully applied both "rough" and "finish" coats of plaster. Richard Needham spent over forty years working at his trade in the city, plastering the walls of hundreds of buildings and making elaborate cornices and medallions to ornament expensive public buildings and the homes of the wealthy.

PLASTERER.

Richard Needham would not have called himself a craftsman or an artisan, terms that are familiar to us today. In Boston's annual city directories he described himself as a "plasterer" and sometimes a "stucco worker." If pressed, he almost certainly would have said that he was also a "mechanic," the term that nineteenth-century Americans used for the millions of men who did skilled work with their hands. Only later was the word given a much narrower definition; with the triumph of the internal combustion engine, the word *mechanic* was used strictly to describe the men who repaired engines, vehicles, and other complex machines.

THE MECHANICS' WORLD

American mechanics had a sense of the history of their individual callings, but in many ways they were the least traditional craftsmen in the world. American settlers had brought with them the skilled work traditions of Europe—blacksmithing, carpentry, printing, pottery, coopering, cabinetmaking—but not the complicated structures, rules, and rituals of the English craft guilds. Under the scattered and decentralized conditions of American life, American mechanics could choose their trades more easily and move between them more freely. No guilds arose with the legal power to limit entry into the trades or regulate how they were practiced. "In this free country," a Philadelphian writing as Charles Quill noted in 1838, "mechanics are not bound down by legal restrictions to the trade which they have learned, but may exchange one line of business for another, at their pleasure."

This meant, Quill claimed, that the United States was a mechanic's paradise. The equality of American manners, and the lack, compared to Europe, of an overbearing aristocracy that despised handwork as low and vulgar, moved craftsmen up on the social scale. "Ours is not the country where one may sneer at the 'mechanic,'" he wrote. With his sturdy independence and access to opportunity, "the American mechanic has no reason to envy any man on earth."

Still, well into the nineteenth century American mechanics expected that their lives would follow a timeworn path. First came several youthful years of learning the trade as an apprentice, living in the master's household and under his authority. The most elaborate apprenticeships lasted seven years and were formalized by a written indenture signed by the master and the boy's father.

This young man, photographed c. 1850, is a cooper, who makes barrels and other staved wooden containers. He leans on a wooden-hooped "slack" barrel that would have held dry goods like apples or grain. He holds an adze that was used to shape barrel staves. The greatest test of a cooper's skill was the building of a "tight barrel" that would hold liquids—like molasses or whiskey—without leaking.

(Above) In a city tailor shop in 1874, a clerk speaks to a customer, while two workmen sew in the back room on their elevated tailor's bench, designed to keep fabric and workmen off the floor, another man presses a garment, and a woman sews on a machine. Identified by his formal clothes, the master tailor is cutting out the garment to be sewn using a customer's measurements recorded on his tailor's tape.

(Left) Tinware production was an expanding trade in mid-nineteenth-century America. Using a variety of hand-operated machines for crimping, creasing, and shaping their sheets of tin-coated iron, tinners produced shiny wares increasingly used in American kitchens and dairies. *Old Sturbridge Village.*

Not yet old enough to learn such a physically demanding trade, a young boy watches as two blacksmiths shape a piece at the anvil in a shop in Ohio around 1897.

Many were shorter, three or four years, and sealed by an oral agreement and a handshake. At twenty-one, the age of legal independence, a young man was acknowledged to have finished his training. He was a journeyman, a free man, no longer subject to his master's will, and could choose where and for whom he wished to work. It was expected that after a number of years of working for other craftsmen, the journeyman would save enough to marry and establish his own shop and household. Having mastered the skills of his trade, he had the resources he needed to be prosperous and independent. He would himself become a master mechanic, ready to begin the cycle again.

In his highly popular poem of 1842, "The Village Blacksmith," Henry Wadsworth Longfellow offered his readers an idealized portrait of such a man, an American master mechanic. Longfellow's blacksmith is a "mighty man," quietly proud of his skills and with the strength and endurance to handle hot iron and strike at the anvil, hour after hour. He works constantly, "week in, week out, from morn till night," except on Sunday, when he goes to church with his family. His hard work has kept him financially secure and out of debt; he "looks the whole world in the face, for he owes not any man." Happy in his work, respected in his community, an exemplary father and citizen, the village blacksmith was everything that an American craftsman should be. Longfellow's poem resonated with a powerful American belief—that a man could create opportunity and comfort for himself and his family with nothing more than determination and the skill of his own hands.

But even as Longfellow was immortalizing an American craftsman, the mechanics' traditional world was changing rapidly. When Richard Needham went to work in the 1850s, formal apprenticeships—with their specified terms of service and assumptions of legal responsibility for the apprentice's instruction and welfare—were becoming rarer. Richard never lived in the household of a master mechanic, as all apprentices once did. He learned his trade informally from a man who was willing to teach him in exchange for free labor; after two or three years, he went off to find work on his own.

By 1860 it was clear that traditional hand skills were losing their centrality in the American workplace, in a process that would accelerate over the next seventy years. It is the familiar story of the creation of the modern economy. Workers in many crafts found that their skills, no matter how precise and painfully acquired, could be replaced by new machines that fashioned shoes, set type, or turned chair parts. In the majority of trades, work became organized on a larger scale. Small shops gave way to large establishments, and master craftsmen were replaced by manufacturers who did not practice the

Carpentry and house building were more resistant to mechanization and mass production than most other trades. Carpenters preserved more of their skills and more of the traditional apprenticeship structure of their trades, although master carpenters lost most of their power to larger-scale contractors. As part of this work crew, a young apprentice can be seen planing boards with a hand-cranked planer, c. 1870.

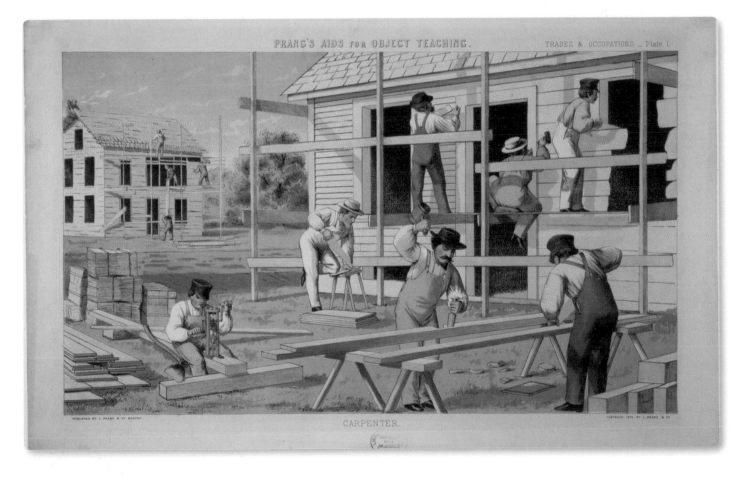

Workplaces:

THE CRAFTSMAN'S WORKSHOP

Views of traditional craftsmen's workplaces at virtually any time seem extraordinarily cluttered, even chaotic. The quantity of tools, materials, and unfinished work is overwhelming to the unfamiliar eye. But a careful look at the shops of a blacksmith, woodworker, and potter reveals that each is organized according to the logic of the craft and the preferences of the craftsman.

(Below) Sawdust litters this woodworking shop with its table saw and profusion of cart and carriage wheels. In the center is the woodworker's "wheel horse," which he uses to clamp the wheel hub securely while he attaches the spokes, constructs the wooden rim, and then bends on the iron "tire." *Historic American Engineering Record.*

(Right) A traditional potter takes recently fired pieces out of his kiln in Stoddard County, Missouri, c. 1930. Working in a tradition brought to the United States from England in the seventeenth century, he is making "redware," a utilitarian pottery known for its reddish color. To the right, wood is stacked for the next firing of the kiln. Just behind the potter is the "waster pile," where broken pots are thrown, with a pile of raw clay in the center. *Historic American Building Survey.*

In this blacksmith's shop in Barnet Center, Vermont, c. 1895, there are plenty of iron scraps and set-aside tools on the floor, along with "clinkers" of burnt coal and pieces of iron slag left over from the forge. At the center is his primary working space, his anvil and the steel "swedge bloc" that he uses for shaping forged pieces. *Historic American Engineering Record.*

trade themselves but managed production and marketing. Often the production process was subdivided so that each worker performed only one or two tasks out of a once much wider range of skills.

A traditional woodworker with his own small shop would construct a chair from beginning to end, starting with selecting the wood to be used. In contrast, one worker in a chair factory might spend the entire workday standing at a lathe turning chair legs while another did nothing but saw out chair seats, and a third assembled them. Although we would not recognize these shops as true factories, they were very different workplaces. Objects that were once the work of single craftsmen were turned out as mass-produced products.

Although Richard Needham's skills were not replaced by a machine, he never became a master craftsman himself. He worked primarily for contractors, who called him in when they needed plasterers and sent him home when work was slow. The traditional ladder of ascent from apprentice to journeyman to master, with its promise of independence, had lost its rungs, coming to an end along with the old system of apprenticeship that had sustained it. Like Richard Needham, the majority of American craftsmen after the Civil War would be employees all their lives.

Again and again, skilled craftsmen in one trade after another confronted mechanization and the reorganization of their work. In the long run, these transformations greatly increased the productivity of the American economy, but for the craftsmen, it was a painful and sometimes brutal process that usually reduced their independence and diminished the value of their skills.

MECHANICS OF COLOR

Before the Civil War, many of America's skilled artisans were not free men. Slaves built and maintained much, perhaps most, of the material world of the South. Prices in the slave market reflected this. "Skilled mechanics . . . fetch from 1,500 to 2,000 dollars," nearly twice as much as "young and sound farm or plantation hands," observed a British visitor to Mississippi in 1862. There were even plantations throughout the region, like Samuel Panill's Green Hill in Virginia, that specialized in training—and selling—expert masons and housewrights. "In slavery days," as the former governor of Mississippi, Robert Lowrey, recalled in 1880, these "Negro mechanics . . . were expert blacksmiths, wheelwrights, wagon-makers, brick-masons, carpenters, plasterers, painters and shoemakers." Unwilling to acknowledge too much skill and independence among African Americans, Lowrey claimed that such workers had always been "under the control and direction of expert white mechanics." But in reality, many enslaved artisans had been working at a highly skilled level for generations and were as self-directed as most white mechanics.

(Right) African American craftsmen are shown undertaking carpentry and painting on a school building in Orangeburg, South Carolina, in 1869. In order to show the skilled work that African Americans were performing, and rebuke segregation in the United States, this image was displayed as part of the "American Negro Exhibit" at the worldwide Paris Exposition of 1900.

(Below) Jacksonville's African American bricklayers pose in 1899 in front of a massive brick wall that many of them may have built. Documenting African Americans who had preserved craft skills and organized for better working conditions, this photograph was also displayed at the "American Negro Exhibit" in Paris.

Before slavery was abolished in the North in the aftermath of the American Revolution, many slaves there had practiced skilled trades as well, often working alongside their masters in the shop. But as servitude disappeared in the North, beginning in Massachusetts in 1783, newly freed African American mechanics met great resistance when they sought skilled work.

Frederick Douglass, the African American abolitionist and orator who began life as a slave in Maryland, had been trained as an expert caulker of ship hulls in the Baltimore shipyards. When he escaped from bondage in 1838 and settled in the free state of Massachusetts, he found that he could no longer work at his trade. White ship caulkers refused to work alongside a black man, and he was forced to take employment as a common laborer. In his *Autobiography*, Douglass argued that the hostility of white mechanics in American towns and cities was the single most important cause of the economic difficulties of free black men. In the North, men of color were increasingly excluded from working in the skilled trades that their enslaved ancestors had practiced. In the South, "Negro mechanics" were able to continue their work, but they were paid less and treated worse than white craftsmen. They found greater scope for their skills, but little wealth, by working within the black community.

PAINTER'S COLIC, THE DANBURY SHAKES, AND OTHER PERILS

"American mechanics work more days of the week than any free men on earth," thought Charles Alexander in 1847. Twelve hours a day in the 1840s, rarely less than ten in 1900, six days a week, their long hours and intense effort often exhausted them. Many, unlike Longfellow's idealized blacksmith, sought solace at the tavern. American men drank considerably more per capita in the nineteenth century than they do today, and mechanics traditionally ended their workdays with a glass or two—or several. Temperance advocates usually marked craftsmen among those especially in need of reformation.

Charles Alexander's anti-alcohol essay of 1847 argued that drink deformed craftsmen's lives; it described a parade of mechanics entering a barroom in an unnamed American city. A "bloated, carbunkled, whiskered young man" tended the bar, assisted by a "pale, sorrowful girl." As the men walked in, the bartender asked, "What will you have . . . brandy? Gin? Punch?" First a young shoemaker entered, "with a pair of newly finished boots," and asked for rum. Next arrived "a ragged man, with livid spots under the eyes," who drank gin and water. This bleary-eyed regular was a "machine maker," a highly skilled and specialized blacksmith who built textile machinery. A bookbinder's hands shook violently as he toasted his drinking companion, a tailor.

A young tailor sits cross-legged on his raised tailor's bench, using his heavy cast-iron "goose" to press the cloth he is holding. His chances of opening his own shop someday declined as the scale of organization in his trade increased.

(Above) **Carpentry was a healthier trade than confined, indoor occupations, although men risked falls and accidents with axes and saws. This portrait of a carpenter, c.1850–60, shows him with the tools of his trade: hammer, saw, plane, and try square for laying out angles and joints.**

(Facing page) **In this engraving, titled** *Facing the Enemy* **(1846), a woodworking craftsman sits in his shop staring at a bottle of liquor and trying to resist temptation.**

The work mechanics often wore down their bodies. Repetitive motion and the constant muscular effort of cutting, scraping, sawing, and pounding not only calloused the hands of cabinetmakers, carpenters, and coopers, but also damaged their shoulders, elbows, and wrists. Blacksmiths, with their heavy hammers and constant striking at the forge, ran even greater risks. Many mechanics battled osteoarthritis and chronic pain. Tailors and printers often wore green spectacles to protect eyes overstrained from fine work or small type.

In Alexander's description of the mechanics' tavern, the rum-drinking shoemaker turns out to have a terrible secret: He has contracted "consumption," the disease that we know as tuberculosis, and had "little prospect of long life." Chronic, incurable well into the twentieth century, and generally fatal, tuberculosis passed from person to person through close contact. It preyed on indoor workers like shoemakers and tailors who labored together in small, crowded, and poorly ventilated shops. The "house carpenter, who works . . . most of all in the open air" was far more fortunate, Alexander wrote, than these men, who were confined "from morning to night in the same spot."

Even more serious were the risks faced by housepainters and hatters, who encountered deadly perils that were seen as inseparable from their trades. Until fairly late in the twentieth century, painters did not buy their paint ready-made but prepared it themselves by grinding up a solid pigment and mixing it with linseed oil and turpentine. One of these pigments, the most commonly used of all, was highly dangerous. "White lead," or lead carbonate, provided the characteristic hue of white-painted villages and pristine interior walls. And, since white was also used as the basis or ground for most other colors, lead carbonate was universally considered indispensable to the painter's trade. "Produced and consumed in vast quantities," it was also poisonous, as painters had known for centuries.

Painters worked and took their midday meals in the midst of white lead dust and open packages of pigment. In the nineteenth century, the dangers were well understood, at least in theory. American magazines aimed at mechanics and manufacturers urged painters to take precautions against accidentally swallowing white lead. They were advised to wash carefully at the end of every workday, and to avoid eating and drinking in close proximity to their paints and paintbrushes. But these safeguards were often ignored by men in a hurry to finish a job, and it was difficult for any painter working indoors to avoid some exposure to the airborne dust.

The results were often tragic. After years of working with white lead, many painters, along with the workers who prepared and packaged it, began to display the symptoms of chronic and irreversible lead poisoning. They were tormented by severe stomach pains or "painter's colic," and crippled by nerve damage. Men were afflicted by uncontrollable tremors and "wrist drop," an

In this image taken from an 1830 painter's manual, three housepainters are shown painting a door, window trim, and one of the wooden pillars of an entranceway. In the foreground are some of their materials, including bowls that they use to mix their pigments. *Author photo.*

inability to raise their hands, so they hung "down uselessly at the wrist," as the *Manufacturer and Builder* magazine noted in 1880. Once these symptoms had manifested, afflicted workmen could no longer work and faced continued decline and death. "In the hope of escaping this evil," noted *Manufacturer and Builder*, "a variety of substances have been proposed as substitutes . . . but none of them have suited the needs of the trade." The editors regretted the cost in lives and health, but saw no alternative. The country, after all, needed both paint and painters. Committed to expansive growth and relentless optimism, the United States was by far the least safety-conscious of the great industrial nations.

By 1913, the *New York Times,* reflecting the nation's slowly rising level of concern, called lead poisoning "the worst of occupational diseases," and advocated strict regulation of exposure. Lead manufacturing was forced to become safer, painters ceased grinding white lead on-site, and safer formulations of lead-based paint were developed. Painter's colic declined and then became a disease of the past.

Until the 1950s, nearly all American men wore hats when they went outdoors. Their shape changed over time, from colonial tricorns to the tall hats of the early and mid-nineteenth century, to the smaller and more-varied bowlers, porkpies, and fedoras of more-recent times, but millions of hats were made and worn every year. Hatters were the specialized artisans who constructed them, making felt—a strong and stiff non-woven fabric—out of beaver and rabbit fur and shaping it into headwear. Originally, men working in the hat trade repeatedly wetted, matted, and pressed the fibers of animal hair into cone-shaped pieces of felt; the most skilled then took the felt and shaped it, by sight and touch, into the distinctive curves of a hat in a particular style. In the second half of the nineteenth century, hatting moved from small shops to factories, as most of these processes were mechanized; however, hat workers remained in close contact with their materials.

This c. 1840 woodcut shows hatters at work making felt for hats, "carroting" the felt to make it more cohesive and pliable, and shaping hats on a wheel of hat molds. The fumes of the carroting process, containing mercury vapor, are visible as well. *Author photo.*

The hatting trade became dangerous in the seventeenth century when the "carroting" process was discovered. Hat makers found that using mercury nitrate to wash the partially shaped felt greatly accelerated the felting process by breaking down the fibers more quickly. The mercury solution temporarily turned the hat fibers orange, which is where the name originated. Over the course of three centuries—carroting with mercury was not forbidden in the United States until 1941—uncounted thousands of hatters breathed in mercury fumes as they worked, and a substantial number had their health destroyed.

Like lead, mercury is a useful metal but a dangerous one. As it accumulates in the body it damages the central nervous system and kidneys, loosens the teeth, and destroys the gums. Victims drooled and slurred their speech, displayed uncontrollable muscle spasms, and eventually suffered irreversible brain damage.

In Britain, the phrase "mad as a hatter" was used to describe the results of occupational mercury poisoning. In America, afflicted workers were said to have "the Danbury shakes." Often called "Hat City," Danbury, Connecticut, was America's largest center of hat production from colonial times to the early twentieth century. In 1887 the community had thirty hat factories

Small Hands:

EARLY TWENTIETH-CENTURY APPRENTICES

Lewis Hine was deeply critical of child labor practices in early twentieth-century America, but from time to time he found traditional mechanic's apprenticeships that still worked. In 1912 he photographed a young man, a "husky tinsmith" of fifteen who was learning his trade in Northampton, Massachusetts. Learning how to make and repair tin-plated vessels and sheet-iron pipes and vents, he worked "eight hours a day, much of it out of doors." Hine contrasted his work life with that of the many young factory workers he had seen: "[C]ompare him to some of our adolescent boys and girls who work in close confinement of the cotton mill 10 hours a day."

A few years earlier, in 1909, Hine documented another apprenticeship, this one in the cigar-making trade. His photograph shows four boys learning the craft at the "School Factory," the well-known De Pedro Casellas cigar factory in Tampa, Florida. The children began in the "stripping department," learning how to separate leaves from stems. As young apprentices the boys would also have carried materials, swept up the shop at night, and been at the beck and call of the master cigar makers. Eventually they would learn the skills of selecting and blending tobacco and move on to rolling and wrapping

the cigars themselves. Their work was not physically taxing, although they spent ten hours a day in the shop, constantly exposed to tobacco. Hine clearly felt that the boys were too young for such work. However, cigar making was a well-paid trade in Tampa, and the boys' parents were willing, as Hine noted, to pay for them "to be permitted to work" in order to learn it.

(Above) **A healthy-looking "husky tinsmith" posed for Lewis Hine outside his Northampton, Massachusetts, workplace in 1912. The usually critical Hine approved of his working conditions.**

(Left) **Young cigar-making apprentices strip leaves as they begin their training at the "School Factory" in Tampa, Florida in 1909.**

and was producing five million hats annually. Workers with the symptoms of mercury poisoning could be seen in most places where hats were made, but Danbury was a city entirely devoted to hat production. Impaired hatters were a common sight in its streets and homes. Like painter's colic, it was simply understood to be a risk of the trade.

Hat making peaked in Danbury before 1900, but the city produced hats well past World War II. They are now no longer made in the city at all, but the unfortunate environmental legacy that created the "Danbury shakes" remains. Although long abandoned, Danbury's hat factory sites, and the nearby Still River, still have strikingly high levels of mercury contamination.

Paths of Change

Printers and shoemakers probably didn't feel that they had much in common, but both trades experienced wrenching change with the advent of mechanization. In a process that began in the 1830s and continued into the 1920s, they found their traditional identities as craftsmen reshaped by the introduction of machinery and the reorganization of their work.

Printers traditionally thought of themselves as the intellectual aristocrats of the skilled trades since their work depended so heavily on literacy. Their work was the conduit through which literature, current events, instruction, political debate—even sacred scripture—reached the reading public. They prided themselves on their mastery of type fonts and paper sizes, on their ability to swiftly translate handwritten copy into lead type viewed in reverse, and to read and correct page proofs.

Printers never worked in "shops" like other tradesmen, but in "printing offices" or "printing houses," a distinction reminding everyone that their product was the printed page. In 1867 Lyman Whiting of Brookfield, Massachusetts, recalled the "the curious awe felt as we walked by the long, low and unpainted 'Printing House.' " He wrote: "Well do I remember how precious a single capital P was esteemed which a lad had brought from the 'house.' The spirit of knowledge seemed to lurk in the dull lead."

Shoemakers, in contrast, were seen as much humbler craftsmen, less well paid and producing a far less dignified product. In colonial America, shoemakers were often itinerant workers, staying a day or two at a farmhouse to make and repair shoes for the family in exchange for room, board, and farm goods, and then moving on. In cities, shoemakers kept shops where they did "custom" work, making shoes to order; the most skilled among them secured wealthy clients. Only they could expect to have the dignity afforded to master craftsmen. As populations grew, other shoemakers gave up traveling to produce ready made shoes that were sold to storekeepers. Customers would simply try on several pairs until they found one that fit.

American printers traditionally had a sense that they were learned and artistic craftsmen, who worked with letters, words, ideas, and information. In this 1840 woodcut from *The Book of Trade,* **one printer is setting type at left. To his right, an apprentice and a journeyman are preparing to print on a hand-operated cast-iron "Acorn" press.** *Author photo.*

Increasingly in the minority after 1850, custom shoemakers like this man shown in an 1870 lithograph, were still able to use the full range of their skills in handcrafting expensive shoes. A female customer has her shoe size taken in the salesroom, while he works at his shoe bench, surrounded by awls, scrapers, shoe knives, shears, and rolls of leather.

SHOEMAKING: FROM SHOP TO FACTORY

In the 1830s, the making of ready-made shoes greatly expanded, making it one of America's most important industries. Centered in Massachusetts and Connecticut, the trade produced millions of ready-made shoes, sold them across the United States, and even exported them to Latin America.

This was not factory production. Shoemakers continued to work with their traditional tools—lasts for shaping the shoe, shoe hammers and lapstones for softening leather, awls for sewing—but their work was aimed at distant consumers, not face-to-face customers. The number of American shoemakers grew tenfold as many thousands of men rushed into the trade. These craftsmen worked not for themselves but for manufacturers, who gave out the materials and the orders, picked up completed shoes, and paid them for each pair produced. Called "sale shoemakers," they worked in small shops, often shared by several men and set in villages or scattered across the countryside. Women working at home were a crucial and complementary part of the workforce. Shoe manufacturers recruited them by the thousands to sew together the pieces of lighter leather that made the "uppers" of the shoe, while men shaped the shoe, built the sole and heel, and attached the uppers.

In 1880, the elderly David Johnson remembered what this work had been like when he was a young man. Four to six workers, and sometimes more, pooled their resources to rent or build a small one-room shop, with two or three small windows and a small stove. There they would spend twelve hours a day, six days a week. Some were cramped "ten-footers," only 10 feet by

These four "sale shoemakers" who produced ready-made shoes are posing in a group, c. 1850–60. Since these workers needed relatively little room, they banded together to rent small shops, where they could converse, keep each other company, and share expenses.

Old-time shoemaker's shop, c. 1880.

Author photo.

10 feet; the average size was "nearer twelve by twelve." Larger ones "were regarded as of almost palatial dimensions." Built as cheaply as possible, they had low ceilings, often no more than 6.5 feet in height. "A tall man with a tall hat on," Johnson recalled, "ran no small risk of damaging his head gear on entering the door."

Because shoemaking was relatively quiet work, shoemakers often carried on conversations or even recited poetry as they sat at their low shoemaker's benches. Homer Merriam of Brookfield, Massachusetts, was a printer's apprentice whose stern master allowed no idle conversation. He enjoyed spending his free time at one of the shoe shops nearby that "was quite a place of resort for myself and several other boys." They listened while the shoemakers engaged in spirited political and religious debate. Eventually Homer's master, finding the shoemakers a bad influence, put their shop off-limits for his apprentices.

(Right) The Henry Wilson Shoe Shop, in Natick, Massachusetts, preserves a workspace like the one that tens of thousands of shoemakers used before their work was centralized in factories. It shows a sitting shoemaker's bench with its leather seat and a standing workbench. *Historic American Building Survey.*

(Below) Shoemakers went in together to rent shops like the Henry Wilson Shoe Shop to serve as a shared workspace. They produced shoes individually, but because their trade was quiet, they were able to socialize, sing, and argue. *Historic American Building Survey.*

When the shoemakers had many orders to fill, Johnson wrote, work went well beyond the twelve-hour day. Men might continue at their benches until ten o'clock at night, and at times "the glimmering light" of the shop windows "would be seen in the dim distance at a much later hour." At first, shoemakers worked at night by the feeble light of a few tallow candles; by 1850, "as whale oil became cheaper," they used lamps, which were a little brighter. But night work strained even the sharpest shoemaker's eyes as they worked with needles and knives, stitching seams and cutting sole leather. As he looked back at his early days from a time of brighter illumination, Johnson wondered "how work, requiring the nicety of the shoemaker's art, could be carried on in those days of candles and dim-burning oil lamps." It was "a mystery."

Just before the Civil War, the machine age began for shoemaking as shoe manufacturers expanded the scale of their operations. Looking for more control over production, they brought workers out of the small shoe shops into larger, factory-style workplaces. In 1939, veteran shoemaker James Hughes of Lynn, Massachusetts, was interviewed by Jane Leary for the Works Progress Administration's "Living Lore" program. In Hughes's view, the beginning of the end for the making of shoes by hand came when, in 1858, "the first McKay machine for stitchin' soles" was introduced.

Properly attaching the sole to the "uppers" of the shoe had always been one of the shoemaker's fundamental skills, one of the things that defined him as a craftsman. "But when the McKay machine come in," Hughes told her, "the shoe was made different." Each new machine could do the work of a dozen or more hand stitchers, making this long-valued skill irrelevant. Some hand workers became machine operators, although they could not always adapt to the new technology. Many more of them were pushed aside. The stitching machine was followed by dozens of others developed between 1860 and 1890 that mechanized other parts of the shoemaking process. They "drove the hand workers out," and most "never come back."

The final blow to the industry's skilled shoemakers came with the introduction of the lasting machine. The laster made the final adjustments between the sole and the uppers that gave the shoe its permanent shape before the shoe was stitched together. It was the most difficult of the shoemaker's skills to master, and as late as 1880, almost no one in the shoe business believed that lasting could be mechanized. A skilled shoe laster could finish no more than fifty pairs of shoes a day.

These assumptions were shattered when Jan Matzeliger, an immigrant of African ancestry from Dutch Guiana, developed a working lasting machine in 1883. His prototype could produce 150 pairs of shoes a day, triple the output of a skilled craftsman. Within a few years the Matzeliger machine, operated by a single worker, was able to last 700 pairs a day.

This sketch of 1885 shows a "laster" building a shoe; he is performing the most highly skilled task of the shoemaker's craft. Within a few years his work would be displaced by the Matzeliger lasting machine.

Women stitch linings and sew shoe uppers in a factory in Lynn, Massachusetts, in 1908. New shoe factories required far fewer skilled shoemakers and employed large numbers of women and children.

With mechanization the costs of shoe production fell drastically, and so did the fortunes of skilled shoemakers. "When the lastin' machine came in," Hughes recalled, "that caused considerable resentment, 'cause them fellas couldn't do nothin' else, and they was out." Hughes himself had been a skilled shoe laster: "Might as well cut the throats of them men as put a lastin' machine in their shop." Consumers benefited from cheaper shoes. Manufacturers increased their profits. And a very old crafts tradition virtually disappeared in less than a generation.

PRINTING: STEAM PRESSES AND LINOTYPES

The printing trade in America became increasingly divided and specialized during the nineteenth century. Thousands of printers worked in small cities and village centers across the nation, mostly producing weekly local newspapers and doing custom work for their communities. Their offices were small, and their work lives were not all that much different in 1900 than they had been in 1830. A journeyman printer in rural America could still aspire to becoming a master, a printer/editor with an establishment of his own.

But small-town printers were in a minority. By 1860 most printers worked in large urban areas, as daily newspapers expanded in size and circulation, and book and magazine publishing became concentrated in Boston, New York, and Philadelphia. Urban printing establishments grew steadily in scale, sometimes employing hundreds of printers. Fast steam-powered rotary presses replaced the old hand-operated, flatbed presses that had linked printers to the tradition of Benjamin Franklin and Johannes Gutenberg. Success on these terms demanded more than crafts skills; printers also required entrepreneurial and managerial talent, and access to capital to purchase expensive equipment. In the cities, the chances that a journeyman might become an independent master printer diminished greatly, although some found small niches as neighborhood job printers.

Traditionally, printers had worked both "at the case," setting type, and "at the press," turning out printed sheets. Urban printers increasingly split these functions, separating the press room and the composing room. Many of them specialized as pressmen, the operators and overseers of ever larger and faster printing presses. Becoming expert handlers of complicated machinery, they separated themselves from the "literary" side of their craft.

Other printers remained in the composing room, becoming specialists in the rapid and accurate setting of type. A skilled "typo"—or "comp," for compositor—would take handwritten copy and stand at the type case with his composing stick. His hands moving in a blur as he took letters from the case one by one, he would turn the text into perfectly formed lines of type

ready for printing, with proper punctuation and spacing included. Typesetters prided themselves on their skill, and in some big-city composing rooms, they held informal races to see who was the fastest.

Unlike press work, typesetting did not require great strength. A number of printing establishments began to hire young women as typesetters. Paid less than half a man's wage, they proved to be no less adept than men, perhaps even more so. Male typesetters resisted fiercely, seeking to keep women out of as many composing rooms as possible.

The year 1886 was one of both dramatic display and remarkable change for American printers. Turning briefly from circus elephants and freak shows, enterprising promoters sought to turn typesetting races into public entertainments. They staged public competitions in New York, Chicago, and Boston, bringing out sizable crowds to watch dueling compositors race the clock. The Boston competition proved embarrassing for male typesetters, however. For the first time, women were allowed to compete after the men had finished, and they proved faster.

By the early 1850s, old hand-operated flatbed presses were being sold off to small-scale printers in the countryside. In city printing offices, they were being replaced by steam-powered rotary presses like these, shown in the Boston office of *Gleason's Pictorial Magazine*, c. 1852. *Author photo.*

Hand typesetting did not disappear altogether with the arrival of the linotype machine. It remained in use in small printing offices, like this New York City office in 1917. A few printing establishments even went against the trend toward mechanization and devoted their services to preserving hand skills and "fine printing."

But feats of speed soon became irrelevant. In the same year that typesetting by hand became a spectator sport, the *New York Tribune* introduced the new linotype machine, radically transforming the work of the newspaper's composing room. Typesetters no longer worked at the type case, picking out letters by hand, but at a ninety-character keyboard. Each keystroke brought down a small metal mold or "matrix" in the shape of a letter, space, punctuation mark, or other character, taken from a reservoir that acted like a traditional type case. As the operator typed, the machine assembled the molds one by one into a line of letters and spaces. When the typesetter finished entering the line, the machine automatically poured hot "type metal" into each mold, creating a complete "line of type" as the metal cooled. The linotype machine then dropped each successive line into a galley tray. When the tray was full, it was automatically sent to the press room to be printed.

The early linotype machines were more than twice as fast as the fastest hand compositors, and they were steadily improved over the years. Because the machines were expensive, setting type by hand remained standard practice in small printing offices for decades. But by 1900 the great bulk of American typesetting was mechanized.

The triumph of the linotype—and its competitor, the monotype—completed the transformation of the printing office into a factory. Once relatively quiet places, smelling of ink and paper, composing rooms became noisy with the constant "clatter and roar" of the linotypes, smelling of oil and the bubbling pots of molten type metal above every machine, and with what newspaper editor's son Douglas Wells remembered in the 1930s as showers of "black, grimy dirt on anything and everything." Not only dirty but massive and physically taxing to operate, the machines served as a good excuse to push women out of the composing room. They also ended the era of typesetters' pride in their speed of hand and eye. "The glory of the composing room is gone forever," said a former champion of hand typesetting in 1895, "and soon will be but a reminiscence."

Sixteen years after the linotype machine was introduced, we can see the composing room of the *New York Herald* in 1902 as an industrial workspace, with ninety-character keyboards at every linotypist's station. The ventilating ducts above each machine are required to keep them from overheating; at the top of each linotype was a "hot pot" of molten type metal.

This is a larger establishment than the country shop that Longfellow describes, where the smith may have worked with one of his sons. Three blacksmiths are pictured in this 1836 woodcut, "striking" alternately at the heavy piece being shaped on the anvil. Striking in sequence maximized the amount of force applied to the iron while it was still hot enough to shape. A fourth blacksmith is filing an already-finished piece. *Author photo.*

Two wheelwrights—blacksmiths who specialize in vehicle wheels and other hardware—work on an iron "tire" for a horse-drawn wagon in this shop in 1903. The tire will be hooped onto the wheel's wooden rim.

Blacksmiths

The Smith a Mighty Man Is He

Henry Wadsworth Longfellow was no mechanic, but a poet and Harvard professor. However, he spent summers as a child on his grandparents' farm outside of Portland, Maine, and knew something about life and work in the nineteenth-century countryside. Out of those memories he created the most famous poem ever written about an American craftsman, "The Village Blacksmith," with its famous opening lines:

> *Under the spreading chestnut tree*
> *The village smithy stands;*
> *The smith, a mighty man is he,*
> *With large and sinewy hands;*
> *And the muscles of his brawny arms*
> *Are strong as iron bands.*

Longfellow's smith is a muscular and "mighty" man, reflecting the highly physical nature of his work. Blacksmiths and related craftsmen in the iron-working trades worked constantly with heavy materials, holding and shaping them with the strength of their arms and backs. Blacksmiths looked for brawny young men as apprentices, who would have both the strength and endurance for long days at the forge. Longfellow's poem also directly responds to the visual and aural drama of blacksmithing. He evokes the shop's clutter of dark iron and soot, fitfully illuminated by the light of the forge, the showers of sparks set flying as hammer strikes anvil, the rhythmic ringing of iron against iron, and the roar of the fire as it is renewed by the bellows.

When Longfellow was writing in 1842, the village blacksmith's trade was becoming more complicated. Smiths had once made most of the iron goods that their communities used. As ready-made hardware, tools, and farm implements came on the market, country blacksmiths became repairmen rather than makers of goods. As smiths adjusted to this new role, some remained in the countryside while many migrated west along with farm families to work in new agricultural settlements. Others became specialized machine builders, or moved to cities and specialized as farriers, shoeing the millions of horses that powered the nation's transportation system until the early twentieth century.

Longfellow exalted the blacksmith's changeless routine of work at a time when work was changing for most Americans. While praising the smith's steady, enduring toil as an example to ambitious men, he was also speaking to himself—a writer with high aspirations sometimes plagued by self-doubt.

Emblems:

"THE VILLAGE BLACKSMITH"

Under the spreading chestnut tree
The village smithy stands;
The smith, a mighty man is he,
With large and sinewy hands;
And the muscles of his brawny arms
Are strong as iron bands.

His hair is crisp, and black, and long,
His face is like the tan;
His brow is wet with honest sweat,
He earns whate'er he can,
And looks the whole world in the face,
For he owes not any man.

Week in, week out, from morn till night,
You can hear his bellows blow;
You can hear him swing his heavy sledge,
With measured beat and slow,
Like a sexton ringing the village bell,
When the evening sun is low.

And children coming home from school
Look in at the open door;
They love to see the flaming forge,
And hear the bellows roar,
And catch the burning sparks that fly
Like chaff from a threshing-floor.

He goes on Sunday to the church,
And sits among his boys;
He hears the parson pray and preach,
He hears his daughter's voice,
Singing in the village choir,
And it makes his heart rejoice.

Longfellow had never done blacksmithing work, but his evocation of strong and virtuous craftsmanship became one of the most widely read—and memorized—poems in American literature in the nineteenth century.

It sounds to him like her mother's voice,
Singing in Paradise!
He needs must think of her once more,
How in the grave she lies;
And with his hard, rough hand he wipes
A tear out of his eyes.

Toiling,—rejoicing,—sorrowing,
Onward through life he goes;
Each morning sees some task begin,
Each evening sees it close;
Something attempted, something done,
Has earned a night's repose.

Thanks, thanks to thee, my worthy friend,
For the lesson thou hast taught!
Thus at the flaming forge of life
Our fortunes must be wrought;
Thus on its sounding anvil shaped
Each burning deed and thought.

—"THE VILLAGE BLACKSMITH,"
HENRY WADSWORTH LONGFELLOW (1842)

A young blacksmith, not long out of his apprenticeship, sits for his portrait c. 1850–60 holding a hammer in his right hand and grasping a horseshoe with a pair of pliers in his left.

Joseph Banyan Hall: "Work—and More Work"

Joseph Banyan Hall was a strong and determined man, a blacksmith born in the Midwest who followed the frontier to Washington State. His story was not the unchanging life of Longfellow's idealized blacksmith, nor was it the struggle with mechanization and the loss of status and opportunity that confronted so many American mechanics in the second half of the nineteenth century. His life was one of movement and successful adaptation to circumstances.

In his autobiography, he set down memories both bitter and sweet. He was born in Potosi, Wisconsin, in 1857. Potosi was a lead-mining town, quickly settled and then "on the decline" as the "mines were soon worked out." Hall despised Potosi. It was "about the most undesirable place in which to have been raised." At fifteen he realized that "there must be a better and broader place somewhere outside" and "planned to get away."

The sum of his experience in Potosi and with his family had been "work—and more work . . . The only idea I ever had of the world was what you could work out of it." Hall went in search of a trade after he turned sixteen, looking for "a place where I could learn blacksmithing."

This self-motivated search reflected the changing nature of crafts training; young Joseph made the arrangements himself and then persuaded his father to agree. He left home in October 1874 to spend three years working in a blacksmith shop 10 miles away in Lancaster, Wisconsin. As it turned out, he hadn't chosen wisely when it came to his instructor. The apprenticeship was a miserable experience, and not one Hall would write nostalgically about in later years. He recalled it as going forth "to battle this cruel world and a more cruel boss." He learned his trade well, but left on the very day his three years were up.

Seeking work and adventure, Hall left Wisconsin for Colorado, where he found abundant work in the mining towns, shoeing horses that hauled ore and supplies, and making and repairing miner's picks and drill bits. "We worked seven days a week on poor food and at a high altitude," he remembered of the town of Leadville, "which made it not too pleasant a place in which to live and work, but I bought into an old shop and soon had some money in my pockets."

After several years in Colorado, Hall continued west to eastern Washington State, where he married and tried farming wheat for a while, while other

The Smith
© C H Gilbert

members of his family came out and settled near him, in "a new country with nothing but open spaces and no trees." When the wheat market bottomed out, he gave up the farm and returned to his trade, building himself a one-man shop in 1895 in the town of Edwall, Washington. He worked there for the next fifteen years as a country blacksmith, shoeing horses and repairing farmers' tools and equipment, and occasionally mending household items.

In 1910, he sold his house and shop for $6,000. "I always thought that this was a fine sale," he wrote, because he had a strong sense that "soon the blacksmith shop was to pass out of the picture." He was right. The automobile, the farm implement manufacturer and dealer, and the hardware store would soon sweep away the need for a blacksmith's skills. Hall moved to Spokane, the principal city in eastern Washington, and became a hardware dealer. He followed what he recognized as the way of the future.

With the fire of the forge in the background, this blacksmith in 1910 is literally striking a glowing piece of metal "while the iron is hot"—a task he surely has done six days a week for forty years or more.

A Woman's Work is Never Done

It has been the fate of most American women to marry, have children, and take on responsibility for running a household—whether in a hardscrabble farmhouse in Tennessee, a middle-class house in Cincinnati, or an apartment in New York City. "A woman's work is never done," wrote Martha Moore Ballard of Hallowell, Maine, in her diary in 1795, "and happy she whose strength holds out to the end of the sun's rays." In that proverb Ballard put words to the experience of millions of American housewives before and since. Ballard was a strong and enormously hardworking woman, but she struck a note of near-universal complaint that would be echoed for two centuries. Cycling endlessly from day to day, much of what women did in the household was what Vermonter Sally Brown in 1838 called the "same dull round of chores"—cooking, clearing away, washing, sewing, mending, cleaning—a repetitive sequence of constantly recurring tasks.

A NEW ENGLAND KITCHEN.
A HUNDRED YEARS AGO.

This 1876 illustration is a nostalgic view of how women's household chores were supposedly done in the past. In reality, all of these activities—cooking, spinning, churning butter, baking, and child care— would most often have been the work of one lone woman, not four.

In 1869, Lyndon Freeman of Parma, Ohio, recalled his mother's life, noting that women's "everyday work of the household" was always liable to be interrupted by "the care of half-a-score more or less of children," along with the needs of husband and neighbors. Women became experts at laying down one task to pick up another. "I am daily dropped in little pieces and passed around and devoured and expected to be whole again next day and all day," wrote Mary Hallock Foote of her household work in California, in a letter to a friend in 1888. Five decades later, Agnes Harrell of Marion, South Carolina, voiced the same sentiment when she described her life to an interviewer for the Works Progress Administration. "There's three meals a day to cook," she said, "and when I do that, the housework, and the washing, there's no time to recreate."

Throughout the nineteenth century, commentators—almost all of them male—marveled at the enormous range of "labor-saving" devices created by ingenious American inventors, from eggbeaters and apple parers to laundry wringers and cookstoves, and then indoor plumbing and electrical appliances. Surely these greatly lightened the American housewife's burdens, they argued. But American women's actual experience of housework was much more complicated than a simple story of mechanical improvement.

This frontispiece from an 1845 cookbook shows a well-appointed traditional kitchen with its open fireplace, iron crane, and heavy iron pots and kettles. *Author photo.*

Housework remained drudgery. Over time, individual tasks became lighter, but others, as if in compensation, became more complicated and time-consuming. Every "labor-saving" invention also seemed to raise the bar of domestic order and cleanliness. The numbingly hard work of wash day—the worst day of the week, as Harriet Beecher Stowe recalled it—was substantially eased in many households in the second half of the nineteenth century by commercially packaged soap and bleach, scrub boards, and hand-cranked clothes wringers. But as household laundry became easier and less laborious to do, standards changed; it was simply done more often.

This pattern repeated itself in the early twentieth century. First commercially available in 1908, the electric vacuum cleaner replaced the old laborious practice of taking rugs outside and beating them—a great net savings of strenuous work. But rugs were usually beaten only once a month, or once a week by the most meticulous. The result was that housewives ignored a good

In an up-to-date kitchen of 1870, this housewife works with a large coal-fired cookstove, has running water, and has a copper boiler for heating water. Her cookstove has lightened the work of preparing meals, but she has additional work to do to keep it clean and free of damaging rust.

Two young women, c. 1880, try out an ice-cream maker, a new appliance that would perk up a housewife's dessert menu, but would also add to her chores. It needed to be packed with ice, salt, and cream, strenuously cranked for half an hour, and then cleaned. *Private collection, used with permission.*

deal of dirt. With the vacuum cleaner it became possible, often mandatory, to clean once a day—and to see every speck of dust or grime disappear. Textile production all but disappeared from the household, as the Industrial Revolution brought an abundance of ever-cheaper fabrics to housewives throughout the country, but this change brought little if any real leisure time to women. With the abundance of fabrics came a superabundance of sewing, and a ratcheting upward of standards for properly clothing a family. Where once two or three dresses sufficed, soon six or eight became the norm.

Cast-iron cookstoves—the first widely sold domestic appliance in American history—grew rapidly in popularity and did make some tasks in the kitchen a bit easier. They were introduced in the 1830s and became commonplace in American kitchens by the 1850s. These appliances promised greater efficiency and ease in cooking, and this was partly true. "Much female strength," the editor of the *New England Farmer* noted in 1837, "has to be exerted over heavy pots and kettles" set at floor level when women were cooking on the fireplace hearth. In contrast, the stove was easier to use since its heating surfaces were waist high, and its "boilers" and kettles of various sizes weighed much less than the larger fireplace implements. Women had to learn new ways of gauging temperature and judging cooking times, but they usually found the cookstove's even heat "more comfortable to cook over than a blazing fire," as Susan Baker Blunt of Merrimac, Massachusetts, remembered in 1901.

The cookstove became a symbol of domestic improvement that women were proud to own, but convenience and pride came at a cost, with additional labor. Unlike fireplaces, cookstoves were vulnerable to rust that would thin and crack their iron plates. The stove's outer surfaces needed to be carefully cleaned and dried at the end of every day, and coated with stove polish

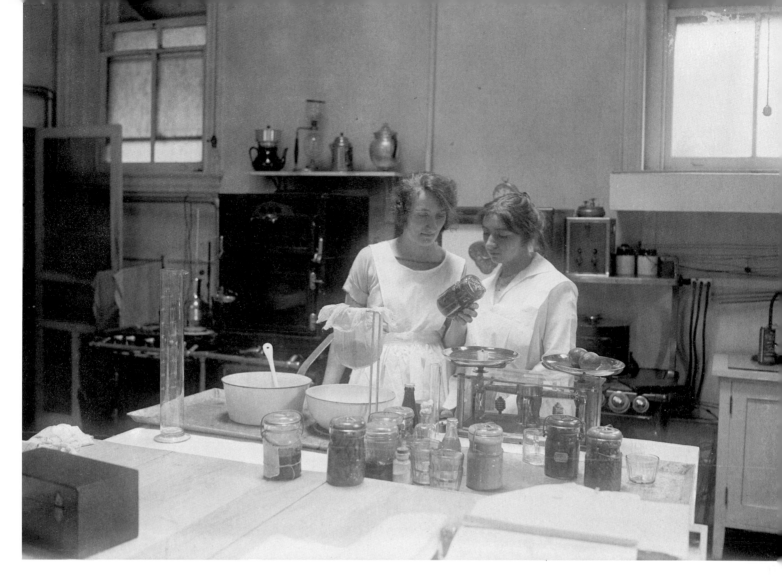

several times a year; these additional tasks added to the time that women needed to spend in the kitchen.

But, in fact, stoves had not been invented or marketed to make women's work easier. The men, who still made the major purchasing decisions for households, had more "practical" ends in view. Stoves were far more fuel-efficient than open fireplaces, and firewood was becoming ever more expensive in Northern cities and villages as woodlands were cleared to make way for cultivation. Stoves reduced the cost of cooking and heating, and made substantially less work for the men and boys who hauled wood and chopped kindling. Farm wives waited decades longer for stoves because their husbands could draw on their own woodlots and saw no reason to make the change.

As gas and electric ranges appeared in the early twentieth century, men and boys were happy to find that their work in the kitchen—bringing in fuel—had completely disappeared. Women were also glad to see the end of scraping rust and polishing cast iron. They still had to cook, however, and the

This 1923 "teaching kitchen" taught the new discipline of home economics. The modern technology of cooking is on display: graduated measures and scales, a gas stove and oven, electric toasters, cooking ranges, and warmers. New appliances eliminated many chores, but transforming cooking into "domestic science" created additional work of its own.

This 1908 photograph of a glamorous young woman heating food in an electric serving dish suggests that new electric appliances make housework effortless, fashionable, and enjoyable.

new appliances had their own way of creating extra work. Freed from the chore of maintaining their old-fashioned stoves, women were urged to use the time they saved to create more elaborate and "scientifically" prepared meals—as well as to keep the glamorous new technology spotless.

COPYRIGHT 1908 BY GENERAL ELECTRIC COMPANY

WOMEN'S WORK: THE WORLD TURNED UPSIDE DOWN

The stirrings of female self-assertion in nineteenth-century America created great anxiety and hostility among American men (and many women as well). As some women advanced their claims of equal rights to property ownership and the ballot and questioned the traditional subjection of wives to their husbands, hundreds of caricatures appeared in the popular press and as widely sold prints, assailing the feminists' demands as unreasonable and unnatural.

Many of these depictions were about housework, showing a domestic world turned upside down. A popular Currier & Ives print of 1869 (shown below) shows a fashionably dressed "liberated" housewife going out to her carriage. The coachman and footman are both female as well. Two men stay meekly behind—sewing, rocking the cradle, and scrubbing clothes. One is clearly the housewife's husband, while the other, doing the menial work of laundry, is probably the displaced footman.

Three decades later, in 1901, a stereograph view shows an updated version of the world turned upside down—again, with the woman free to travel while the man is tied down at home. The young wife wears a bicycling outfit, men's knickers over striped socks. She has on a feminine version of a

"The Age of Iron: Man as He Expects to Be," 1869.

"The new woman-wash day," c. 1901.

man's shirt, cycling gloves, and a straw hat. She puffs on the cigarette in her mouth—in 1901, another major intrusion into the male sphere. Her bicycle, visible behind her, is another symbol of women's emancipation. As bicycles came into wide use in the 1880s, many thousands of women were finding a new physical freedom. "I stand and rejoice every time I see a woman ride by on a wheel," said feminist advocate Susan B. Anthony in 1896, "the picture of free, untrammeled womanhood." As for the young husband, he is busy with his chores. Wearing a long apron over his trousers, he is wringing out clothes in a washtub. The laundry he has already done, including her stockings, is hanging up to dry in the kitchen.

To many Americans on both sides of the centuries-old debate on women's rights, housework was the most telling sign of women's subordination. For conservatives, it was woman's inevitable destiny, both natural and perhaps God-given. For feminists, it was a set of conventional arrangements structured by men's political and economic power. Although women have far more of both in the twenty-first century, the sharing of housework between the sexes remains a complicated issue.

Eyewitness:

Mary Greeley—Worn Out by Hard Work

Mary Woodburn Greeley, Horace Greeley's mother, had her portrait taken near the end of her life, c. 1850–55. Her hard life as a reluctant pioneer wife is etched on her features.

My mother could never be reconciled to this [log cabin] nor to either of the two rather better ones that the family tenanted before it emerged into a poor sort of framed house. In fact, she had plunged into the primitive forest too late in life, and never became reconciled to the pioneer's inevitable discomforts. The chimney of the best log house, she insisted, would smoke, and its roof, in a driving rain, would leak, do what you might.

I never caught the old smile on her face . . . from the day she entered those woods until that of her death, nearly thirty years later, in August 1855. Though not yet sixty-eight, she had for years been worn out by hard work, and broken down in mind and body.

—Horace Greeley, Recollections of a Busy Life, 1857

Beginning in poverty, Horace Greeley apprenticed as a printer and rose to become editor and publisher of the *New York Tribune* between 1841 and 1872, making it one of the most influential newspapers in the nation. His parents, Zaccheus and Mary, left their hardscrabble Vermont home in 1832 for a pioneer settlement in Erie County, Pennsylvania. The labors of a settler's wife destroyed Mary Greeley's health and happiness, as her son remembered in his autobiography.

Greeley had worked hard for his father as a boy, but came to despise farming as hopeless drudgery, seeing Zaccheus as impractical and unskillful. He was unwilling to follow his parents into the Pennsylvania forest, and was glad to escape into a printer's apprenticeship in Vermont. Greeley loved his mother, but even after he became successful in New York City, he did not bring her there to live an easier life; perhaps his father's pride prevented it.

In Service: Domestic Work

Richard Needham, my wife's great-grandfather and the Boston plasterer whose story began this chapter, married Rebecca Hughes in 1865. Born in Nova Scotia, Rebecca came to Boston on a ship from Halifax in 1855 when she was in her mid-teens. Before she married, she spent nearly a decade working as a maid in the households of well-to-do Boston families. The 1860 census simply called her a "servant."

Women from my side of the family also started their lives in America in domestic service. An important part of my grandfather Thomas Murphy's life story revolves around his two older sisters, who left Ireland for America long before him. They came to Chicago and worked as housemaids there and in Milwaukee, Wisconsin, for many years. Pooling their savings, they were able to pay their youngest brother's passage from Ireland and give him an education.

The domestic work that ultimately brought my grandfather to the United States was the occupation of hundreds of thousands of women in nineteenth-century America. In northern cities like Boston, New York, and Chicago, one household in five employed a domestic servant in the years between 1860 and 1900, making it the single most common job for young women. Given the immense drudgery of household labor, families that could afford it employed others to do as much of it as possible.

Before 1840, young American girls from farmers' or mechanics' families often undertook household work for a few years before they married. They were democratically jealous of their rights, refusing to be called servants and usually preferring to eat with the family; but they were willing to work hard. As the pioneering historian of women's work, Lucy Salmon, wrote in 1890, "[T]hey belonged by birth to the same section of the country . . . had the same religious belief, attended the same church . . . and had the same associates as their employers. They were in every sense of the word 'help' as they insisted on being called."

But by the time Rebecca Hughes arrived in Boston, that world was long gone. "The American 'help,' as our grandmothers knew it . . ." had become a distant memory, wrote Grace Ellis in an 1872 issue of the *Galaxy* magazine, a popular family periodical. Very few American-born white women, she

Early occupational portraits of women are far rarer than those of men. This young woman, c. 1850–60, stands drably dressed and holding a broom—the preeminent symbol of housework. But who is she? Few women able to pay for a daguerreotype would have been willing to appear this way.

acknowledged, were willing to work, even briefly, in another woman's household for wages. American-born, Protestant "help" gave way to a "corps of servants . . . composed at the North mainly of the Irish," Mrs. Ellis noted. In Boston, others were British American, like Rebecca. Elsewhere, German and Scandinavian girls served in households along with the Irish. By midcentury the meaning of the word *servant* itself had completely changed; originally it had referred to anyone who worked for another person. Over time the definition narrowed. Americans came to use it only to describe a woman doing the menial labor of the household.

Rebecca may have had an edge in finding work because she was Protestant. Boston newspapers of the 1850s and '60s frequently ran "help wanted" notices from families looking for "a Protestant girl to do general housework." But this was only a slight advantage. Rebecca was still poor, a foreigner, and a servant at the beck and call of others.

The census of 1860 shows nineteen-year-old Rebecca living and working in the household of Harrison Loring, a wealthy shipbuilder. She shared her domestic duties with Margaret Gormley, a forty-year-old Irishwoman. Together they cooked, cleaned, and washed for a household of six. They scrubbed the stove, mended socks, changed beds, emptied chamber pots, answered the door, went on errands, and did whatever else was asked of them.

The periodicals read by prosperous American families in the years after 1870 included frequent discussions of "the servant problem." Writers complained about the inefficiency, slovenliness, and changeability of the Irish "Bridgets" and "Maggies" whom they employed. As the aristocratic Mrs. E. W. Sherwood saw it in 1890, servants had far too much freedom to move from job to job as they chose, leaving their employers with scant notice and greatly inconveniencing them. It was "a perilous state of things," Sherwood wrote in the *North Atlantic Review*, "and not to be endured."

Many young immigrant women, seeking work, dressed up in their best to call on households looking for female servants. This young woman, pictured here, c. 1855, was close to Rebecca Hughes's age at that time.

Her remedy was a system of contracts that would force cooks and housemaids, once hired, to stay in a household for a fixed amount of time—no matter what conditions they endured. Such quasi-slavery never came to pass, of course. But housework remained housework, servants remained servants, and few American employers had either the skills or the inclination to turn their maids and cooks into loyal family retainers.

David Claypoole Johnston drew this cartoon in 1845, just as the flood of Irish immigration was bringing Irish women into American households to work as domestic servants. Johnston caricatured both the maid's inexperience and the mistress's pretensions. *Author photo.*

This 1905 stereographic view follows the tradition of mocking the supposed ignorance and literal-mindedness of Irish servants. The mistress has asked "Maggie" to "scallop" the oysters—that is, to prepare them for cooking in layers with cream, butter, and bread crumbs. Instead, Maggie has given each oyster an ornamental "scalloped" edge with her scissors.

Most employers had little love for their servants, in any case. Rebecca Hughes, along with my Murphy great-aunts, would have been included in Mrs. Sherwood's sneering wonderment at "the confusion of the American experiment" that expected "a creature with no training at all to cook, wash, iron, sweep, dust and take care of children." The imagery of domestic service in the nineteenth and early twentieth centuries testifies to this as well. In cartoons and photographs, female servants were almost never treated respectfully, and were usually figures of fun. Often they were portrayed as slovenly and inept, unable to understand the simplest instructions. On the other hand, young servant girls were sometimes depicted as temptresses who posed a danger to the stability of the family—amorously involved with local tradesmen, or, even worse, with sons or husbands.

After the turn of the twentieth century, the number of domestic servants in the United States began a steady decline. Part of the reason was technology. New household appliances of the electrical era—washing machines, dishwashers, refrigerators, and vacuum cleaners—made living without servants easier for the middle and upper-middle class. But the oral traditions

(Below) In this slightly salacious 1890 stereograph, an Irish maid has misunderstood her mistress. She has been asked to serve the potatoes "undressed," without sauce or topping. She instead comes to the table wearing only her petticoat, undershirt, and stays.

(Left) In this 1905 view, the young servant, Jessie, has just shared an amorous embrace with the "furnace man," whose sooty handprints can be seen on the back of her blouse.

Tools:

WASH DAY

Before 1920, the American wash day was universally reviled as the worst day in a housewife's week, one that began at dawn and left the women of the family exhausted at day's end. In the 1870s photograph below, a mother and daughter are in the midst of doing the family's laundry. The picture seems a bit posed, but the clothes, utensils, and gritty outdoor setting are real enough. Housewives and housemaids did their laundry outdoors whenever it was warm and dry enough, to avoid drenching the kitchen and to spread the clothes out for quicker drying or bleaching in the sun. Back in the kitchen a cauldron of water is on the boil to fill the washtubs.

This 1869 advertisement for an early version of a washing machine was clearly aimed at women who had domestic servants.

The photograph does illustrate one labor-saving device: The zinc or galvanized scrub board visible on the right was first patented in the United States in 1833 and was in fairly wide use by the 1840s.

In a lithograph of 1869, a manufacturer in New York City advertised for a partially mechanized approach to wash day—a hand-cranked "Home Washing Machine and Wringer." One crank turns an "agitator" that scrubs the laundry in the tub, while the other turns the rollers to wring the laundry dry. The scene is not set in an ordinary household, however, but in an upper-class city home's separate laundry room; it even has a tiled floor. The well-dressed mistress of the household looks at the new machine with approval, but neither she nor her daughter (reading a book) will be doing the laundry. That task will fall to the two servants, who may discover that operating the machine is only a little less laborious than doing the laundry by hand.

By 1880, manufacturers of standardized laundry supplies were commissioning advertisements like the color lithograph of 1880 shown on the facing page to market their products to American women. Laundry starch—used to stiffen the collars and cuffs of men's shirts and the ruffles of women's petticoats—was difficult and time-consuming to make at home. When laundry starch became commercially available in the late nineteenth century, it, like many other domestic improvements, proved a mixed blessing.

A mother and daughter do the family laundry outdoors in this stereograph from 1870.

of both the Needham and Murphy families suggest what might have been the most powerful reason. They had strong memories of long hours, limited freedom, capricious mistresses, and, especially, painful condescension. As parents thought about their children's futures, they swore that no child of theirs would ever go out to service again.

"Endless Straight Seams": Sewing

"I got the idea, while I was a small child," wrote Lucy Larcom in 1889 in her autobiography, *A New England Girlhood*, "that the chief end of woman was to make clothing for mankind." Unfortunately, she hated to sew. Larcom's sisters were all remarkable needlewomen capable of "exquisite lace-embroidery" or "expert at fine stitching, so delicately done that it was a pleasure to see or wear." But it was clear that Lucy would never "conquer fate" with her needle. She was tirelessly instructed by her mother and older sisters, but the results "usually ended in defeat and mortification."

In this 1840 engraving "The Hated Task," a young girl is learning to sew under her mother's supervision. She is a reluctant seamstress, and her mother is not pleased. *Author photo.*

Permelia Foster Smith, a physician's wife from Mont Vernon, New Hampshire, chose to be painted with her sewing in 1842—work that was seen as defining womanhood. *Old Sturbridge Village.*

Given the realities of early nineteenth-century domestic life, Lucy's mother and sisters were right to be concerned about her lack of talent with the needle. Needlework was thought to be an essential woman's skill and part of every girl's training at home. In 1840, the majority of American women hand sewed the bulk of their family's clothes, as well as domestic textiles, from towels and sheets to bedspreads and window curtains. Lucy herself ultimately chose a single life, as a teacher and writer—a life that, perhaps incidentally, required far less domestic needlework.

Permelia Foster Smith, a physician's wife from Mont Vernon, New Hampshire, clearly felt that needlework was central to her identity when she posed for her portrait in 1842, shown above. Her husband chose to be depicted with pill bottles and fearsome surgical instruments. She decided to be painted

In 1880, the Gilbert S. Graves Laundry Starch Company of Buffalo, New York, was advertising its product, which would make for smooth, wrinkle-free shirts and blouses, to American housewives. Easily available starch enabled housewives to work harder at ironing the family's clothes.

The number of hours spent ironing probably increased, as standards of respectability moved upward. Women felt obliged to produce pristine and crease-free shirtfronts and collars for their families.

Commercial laundries also became increasingly common in cities after the Civil War, relieving many households, as well as single men and women living "in furnished rooms," of the time-consuming and unpleasant work, but for a price. The 1905 photograph at right shows three women working on whites in a commercial laundry, probably in Boston. Compared to the scene in 1870, this laundry workspace is a technological marvel. Turn-of-the-century advances—running water, large galvanized steel tubs, a hand-cranked wringer, stove, drying rack, and, newest of all, electric lighting—are all here. Most likely, the women pictured working here went back to face their own laundry at home after a day's work.

Three women are working at a commercial laundry, probably in Boston, c. 1905. One is washing, one is wringing, and the third is hanging pieces up to dry on a rack.

In this advertisement from 1908, a cheerful housemaid in a frilly uniform irons a doily with a new GE electric iron. Ironically, the increasing profusion of easy-to-use household technology went along with the twentieth century's long-term decline in the number of domestic servants.

In the South, patterns of domestic service were structured by slavery. Thousands of African American women and men worked in plantation and city households, work that was usually preferable to labor as field hands. After Emancipation, their work became paid labor, but old patterns of subordination and deference persisted. "Wash Day on the Plantation," c. 1887, was probably posed.

with her elaborate sewing table. Its fringed cover conceals a hinged top that opens to store her "work"—all the pieces that she was making or mending. On top of the table is a piece of partially completed embroidery and a pincushion box with her needles and thimbles. Permelia is wearing a decorative lace cap, collar, shawl, and cuffs, all of which she made herself. Lace work was difficult, intricate, and time-consuming, so that it provides powerful testimony both to her skills, and to the importance her society placed on a woman's self-adornment.

About fifteen years after Permelia Smith had her portrait taken in 1842, another young woman, whose name is unknown, sat in front of the then-new daguerreotype camera to have her picture taken, shown at right. Like Permelia, she looks out at us holding her sewing. The camera seems to have captured her in motion, drawing a piece of black fabric through her sewing machine. Her hair is severely parted and drawn back in two buns, in the style of the mid-1850s. Her gaze is direct, even challenging. Her eyes seem a bit shadowed. Hand-coloring has brought the tint of life back to her complexion. Also like Permelia, she is fashionably dressed. She has a lace collar fastened with a brooch, pendant earrings, and lace cuffs that spill out over her wrists. She is no well-off housewife, but a seamstress. Her right hand is highly visible, the third element that balances the picture between her compelling face and the machine. But her hand is not a delicate one. For a slight woman, it is large and muscular—the hand of a women who has been sewing for a living.

By the 1850s sewing was no longer simply a female skill, a household necessity, and a badge of womanly accomplishment. It was becoming a vast industrial occupation. Household sewing remained an important part of women's domestic work, but as the United States became a more urban and industrial nation, an increasing proportion of clothing, household linens, and even decorative pieces like collars and cuffs were being made outside the home. "The manufacture of garments for domestic wear is a never-ending task," wrote a Boston magazine, *Ballou's Pictorial Drawing-Room Companion*, in 1856, about the work of the nation's seamstresses. "The brain is bewildered

In a rare image showing a woman with the tools of her work, "The Seamstress" poses with her sewing machine, c. 1856–58. Early sewing machines like this one (probably an early Singer model) were still quite expensive; a woman working in her own shop would have scrimped and saved to buy one.

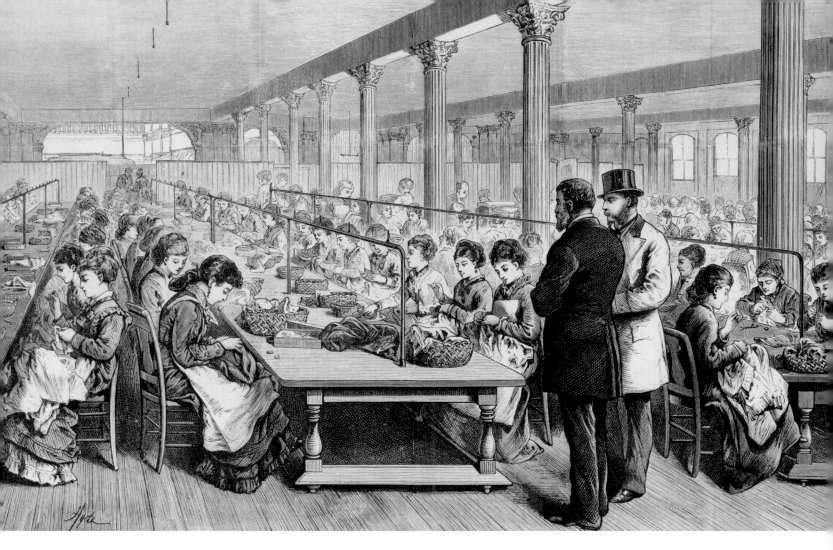

A. T. Stewart's of New York City, one of the nation's first department stores, developed a substantial business in manufacturing, altering, and trimming ready-made clothing. Hundreds of seamstresses are shown at work in the store's upstairs "sewing-room" in this 1875 illustration.

in attempting to estimate the many millions of stitches which must be made daily in these United States alone."

Making those millions of stitches were many thousands of women, an expanding population who found employment in what came to be called the "needle trades," trying to turn their traditionally domestic skills to account in the commercial economy. A rapidly expanding market for ready-made textile goods of all kinds provided them with employment, but often on very harsh terms. "The needle is the natural weapon of every woman who has to battle for herself in the world," wrote William H. Rideing in *Harper's Magazine* in 1880, but "the occupations in which it is available are so overcrowded and underpaid."

The most skillful and fortunate needlewomen, a small minority, were able to set up their own businesses as dressmakers or milliners, and even took on their own apprentices; still, even at this highest level of skill, they made less money than men—about one-third the rate of male tailors, for doing very similar kinds of work. The great majority of seamstresses were women struggling to survive, working long hours for meager earnings. They were single women without families to rely on, widows left without resources, and married women whose husbands' wages could not support their households. They faced a "buyer's market for their labor"; their numbers were large and their skills were commonplace.

Some toiled at home, relying on middlemen who handed out materials and collected the finished product. Others went out every day to their workplaces, which ranged from crowded spaces in tenement buildings to huge factory-scale workrooms, like the hundreds of young women who can be seen in a drawing of the vast fifth-floor hand-sewing room of A. T. Stewart's department store in lower Manhattan in 1875 (shown on the facing page). "This immense establishment," noted the *New York Times* in 1872, was "daily thronged by the wealth, beauty and fashion of New York" who shopped there; in its work rooms labored over seven hundred girls. "They baste, sew by hand and machine, embroider, work buttonholes and make carpets, curtains, all kinds of household linens."

For the prosperous families that shopped at Stewart's, the girls were providing the shirts and dresses, cloaks and lingerie, towels, tablecloths, and curtains that respectable and fashionable family life required. The writer for the *Times* was distressed to discover the meager earnings of the seamstresses in return, the "scanty remuneration paid to hard-working industrious women who earn a miserable living by the needle." He saw as well that the work rules allowed for no discussion of rates of pay, or brief intervals of time away from the sewing tables. Conspicuously posted in the sewing workroom of another New York City store he found a sign reading ALL WHO ARE DISSATISFIED WITH THE PRICES PAID FOR WORK WILL PLEASE LEAVE IMMEDIATELY. ANY PERSONS FOUND LOITERING IN THE ROOMS OR PASSAGES WILL BE INSTANTLY DISMISSED.

Soon after the sewing machine's appearance, an 1856 publication recording the progress of American industry took a highly optimistic view of the social and economic progress that it would create.
Author photo.

SEWING IS MECHANIZED

In the daguerreotype portrait of "The Seamstress" (shown on page 127), the sewing machine is not just a prop, but a crucial part of the picture's meaning; it is also instantly recognizable because its fundamental shape has changed little over the years. But in the 1850s, the sewing machine was something new—a radical innovation. For thousands of years, women had been sewing by hand. Over time metal thimbles and sharper needles came along and made the work more comfortable and a bit faster to do. But the machine, first patented in the United States by Elias Howe in 1846, brought a revolution in speed. It could stitch an uncomplicated straight seam ten times as fast as unaided hands.

As sewing machines became less expensive, and were increasingly available for purchase on the installment plan, they reached more and more families. In this lithograph, c. 1872, the sewing machine is advertised as an enjoyable way to teach girls to sew.

This view of the exhibition and sales room of Hunt & Webster's Sewing Machine Manufactory in Boston, in 1856, shows prosperous families examining the new and still-expensive machines. *Author photo.*

(Facing page) Indicating that sewing machines were becoming more affordable, the Bartlett Company trumpeted their product as "The Sewing Machine for the People." Their 1869 advertisement told its readers that "to one accustomed to a good sewing machine, hand sewing seems drudgery; idling with time."

The sewing machine changed needlework in the household, but also had a pervasive impact on sewing rooms, shirt factories, and sweatshops. The first sewing machines cost about $100, several months' earnings for most American workers in the mid-nineteenth century; for most families, they seemed out of reach. The earliest advertisements show them displayed in elaborate sales rooms intended to interest well-to-do families who might purchase a machine for the women of the house, or for their servants to use.

Trying to offset these high prices, in 1860 the Singer Sewing Machine Company created a new financing scheme—America's first "hire purchase," or installment plan, which allowed customers to pay for a machine in monthly installments over a couple of years. The plan was an instant success, tripling Singer's sales in one year; by 1876, the sewing machine industry was selling over five hundred thousand machines a year. Over the decades sewing

THE
BARTLETT
SEWING MACHINE CO'S NEW PATENT

$25   SEWING   MACHINES. $25

[Trade Mark.]

THE BARTLETT SEWING MACHINE CO.
THE CHEAPEST GOOD SEWING MACHINE
HAND OR TREADLE
669 BROADWAY, NEW-YORK.

We guarantee that any one can use these Machines from our Printed Directions.

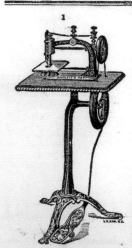

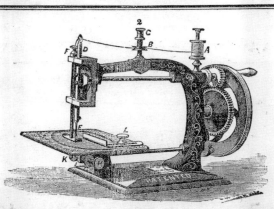

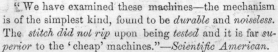

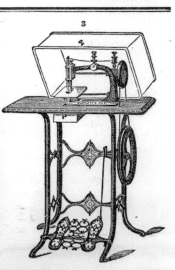

"We have examined these machines—the mechanism is of the simplest kind, found to be *durable* and *noiseless.* The *stitch did not rip* upon being *tested* and it is far *superior* to the 'cheap' machines."—*Scientific American.*

THE VALUE OF THE SEWING MACHINE IS ESTABLISHED.

To one accustomed to a good Sewing Machine, Hand Sewing seems *drudgery ; idling with time—*

STILL THE DEMAND IS

For a Sewing Machine *especially adapted* to the wants of the *masses,* viz: *A THOROUGHLY PRACTICAL* SEWING MACHINE, so SIMPLE that none can fail to *understand* and *successfully use it,* and sold at a price within the *reach of all.*

This machine has been made to meet that want, and is EMPHATICALLY *pronounced by all,*

"The Sewing Machine for the People."

A WARRANTED SEWING MACHINE,

made in as good manner, of as good materials and upon principles which the experience and practice of the past have found to be the best, and necessary to constitute a GOOD FAMILY SEWING MACHINE.

The above Engravings show the Machines made in *a new and beautiful* (patented,) *design of our own* by which we have as much *space inside* the arm for the "work" to pass as in the "Wheeler & Wilson," "Grover & Baker," "Florence," or other Machines, yet combine *perfect PORTABILITY.*

Joseph W. Bartlett
&co

Hundreds of women stitch shirts on their sewing machines in one of the production rooms of the Cluett, Peabody & Co. shirt factory, in Troy, New York, the largest in the world in 1907.

machines became steadily less expensive, down to $30 for a standard Singer model. But installment buying continued to be highly popular, allowing families of increasingly modest means to take a sewing machine home. Most American women, it turned out, were happy to abandon the tedious work of what Harriet Beecher Stowe called "sewing endless straight seams" by hand.

For many American housewives the sewing machine was an attractive and fashionable way to make some of their domestic tasks much easier; some found a renewed interest in creating clothes for themselves or their families. Although its economic importance had greatly diminished by the early twentieth century, domestic sewing remained an important activity in a large number of households.

But for working seamstresses the sewing machine was an increasingly important tool. On a relatively small scale, independent dressmakers and milliners invested in sewing machines to make their shops more efficient. Our young seamstress with the piercing gaze (page 125) might well have been one of them; she was pictured with a sewing machine when they were still expensive. It's easy to picture her scrimping and saving to make the payments.

Clothing manufacturers bought sewing machines by the thousands. The *New York Times* reported in 1877 that the A. T. Stewart Company had installed over one thousand machines in one of its workrooms; their foot treadles had been removed and they were all powered from a central steam engine, so that the seamstresses could no longer control the speed of their work. Like other innovations that mechanized a traditional form of hand work, the sewing machine sped up production and drove down costs, powering a vast expansion of the ready-made garment industry. By 1900 there were sewing machines not only in huge shirt factories and small dressmakers' shops, but also in the crowded, ill-ventilated sweatshops where cheap garments were produced. And they could also be found in the homes of thousands of very poor families who took in sewing work to be done at home. In tenement kitchens in New York and Chicago, mothers and daughters with work to finish often labored together late into the night.

Hand sewing did not disappear, however. On the one hand, the finest detailing and most delicate and intricate stitching could not be duplicated on the machines, so the most elaborate and expensive clothes were in good part still handmade. On the other hand, there were many rural households still without sewing machines, where the needle and thimble were less a tradition than a necessity.

Two Seamstresses

In December 1911, Annie Maier, the sixteen-year-old daughter of a Jewish family in New York City, was photographed working at her sewing machine in the kitchen of her basement apartment. One of hundreds of thousands of American women sewing garments for "home work," she was making doll clothes for the "Campbell's Kids." The Kids were a cherubic pair of children originally created as advertising images for Campbell's Soup in 1903. In 1910 the company began to produce the dolls as promotional items, and they soon became wildly popular. Annie was not working for the Campbell Company, but for a contractor who gave out the materials and a pattern and collected the work, paying her a few cents for each piece.

Annie Maier's pale countenance contrasted sharply with the plump and ruddy good health of the Campbell's Kids dolls, intended as icons of health and good nutrition. Elizabeth Watson, the chief child labor investigator for New York State's Factory Investigation Commission,

Annie Maier, already desperately ill with tuberculosis, was photographed sewing doll clothes in her family's basement apartment in New York in 1911.

worked with photographer Lewis Hine to describe Annie's precarious situation. Annie's desperately ill father had already been sent away to a tuberculosis hospital, leaving the family without a male provider. A private relief society had been assisting them, but Annie had also been infected and had fallen seriously ill herself. The agency refused to give further help unless she would agree to be hospitalized. However, Annie was unwilling to leave her family without the income her work provided. She "refused to do this," wrote Watson, and instead was "working on dolls' clothes with tuberculosis progressing towards its final stages."

The killer of millions of young adults in the nineteenth and early twentieth century, tuberculosis (earlier called consumption) particularly threatened workers who toiled in confined, ill-ventilated, and crowded workplaces. Seamstresses and others engaged in "home work" were as vulnerable as tailors and shoemakers. New York City's eminent lung specialist Dr. Adolf Knopf noted "the frequency of tuberculosis among them," in 1910, and defined it as the city's worst public health problem; it "causes the fearful condition which we are now trying to combat." Given what treatments were

Angelina Guinzali, a young seamstess, hand sews a silk lining in Madame Ball's dress shop in Boston in January, 1917. Her work was more skilled—and far healthier—than the work of home sewers.

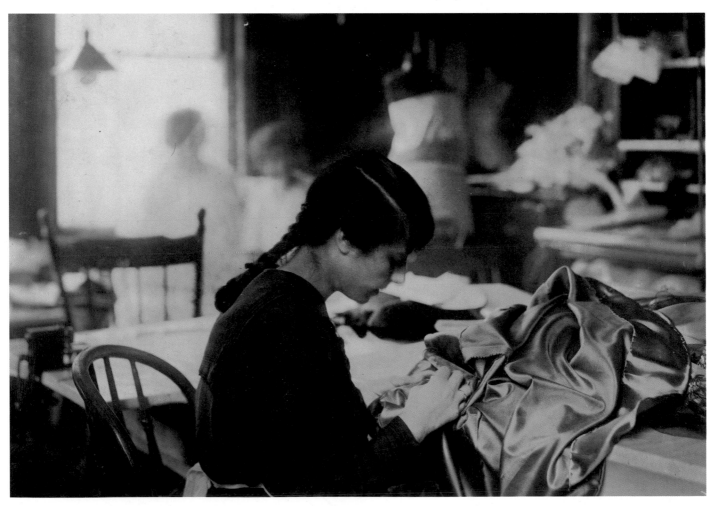

available for tuberculosis at the time, it is unlikely that either Annie or her father were likely to survive very long—whether in or out of the hospital.

Angelina Guinzali was also a needlewoman, but she was more fortunate than Annie Maier. When Lewis Hine took her photograph she was fifteen years old. He caught her hand stitching a silk lining for a gown at Madame Ball's fashionable dressmaking establishment at 603 Boylston Street in downtown Boston. Angelina lived on Salem Street in Boston's North End, a twenty-minute walk from her workplace. Her parents, Alceste and Francesca, came to Boston from Italy in 1885. Angelina was the youngest of their five children. Her older siblings did unskilled work as laborers or in the city's box and leather-belt factories, but Angelina's talent with a needle had found her a good opportunity for a working-class girl her age; she would be able to learn a skilled trade that she could practice until she married, and which would be useful all her life. She would work long hours in the dressmaker's shop and surely be subject to Madame Ball's whims, but earnings and working conditions would be better than those for home workers or shirtmakers.

This dressmaker was not Madame Ball, Angelina's employer, but could well have been her counterpart. She is shrewdly eying the fashions on display and taking notes as women walk by in New York City's annual Easter parade, c. 1905.

Small Hands:

"Home Work"

New York City was the center of the immense American garment industry. Much of its work went on in the crowded tenements of the Upper East Side. There, thousands of poor immigrant families worked in their homes—sewing, knitting, and crocheting clothing that would be sold throughout the United States, in every department store and country merchant's establishment from San Francisco to Boston. Mothers and children took on the work, often laboring late into the night to supplement the wages of husbands and fathers.

The contractors who gave out the work knew little or nothing, they claimed, about the squalid conditions under which most of these goods were produced, or about the fact that very young children helped produce them. "I do not keep track of their homes, or where they do their work," said one manufacturer; another admitted that "I have never gone into any of the places myself."

It was none of their business. As the state of New York focused on child labor and the social problems of "home work" in 1912, Lewis Hine photographed some of these families, and child labor investigator Elizabeth Watson interviewed them. In her report to the state's Factory Commission, Watson recorded what many of these children told her about their lives. Their stories were all very similar. She was struck by the ways in which home work kept them sitting indoors for long periods, took away the hours of sleep they needed for healthy growth, and robbed them of their childhoods.

Angelina: "When I go home from school I help my mother to work. I help her earn the money. I do not play at all. I get up at six o'clock and I go to bed at ten o'clock."

Camilla, nine years old: "I have no time for play; when I go home from school, I help my mother. Half hour

Documenting the abuses of home work, Lewis Hine photographed an Italian immigrant family crocheting caps in their kitchen on the Upper East Side of New York.

I make my lessons. Every morning I get up at six o'clock. I go to bed at eleven o'clock."

Giovanna: "I get up at five o'clock in the morning. Then I work with my mother. At 9 o'clock I go to school. I have no time for play . . . At ten o'clock I go to bed."

Maria: "I have no time to play when I work by my mother, but when I don't work, I mind the baby and clean the house."

Little nine-year-old Antoinette: "I earn money for my mother after school, and on Saturday, and half-day Sundays. No, I do not play, I must work; I get up to work at four o'clock in the morning, I go to bed at 9 o'clock."

HOMEWORK DESTROYS FAMILY LIFE

Keeps the child from school

Encourages father to shirk responsibilities

Prevents proper care of home

Allows unsupervised, greedy manufacturers and parents to make a mockery of childhood

WOULD YOU LIKE YOUR CHILD TO GROW UP
HERE OR HERE

(Above) A mother sews on her machine while two older daughters and a son add hooks and ribbons, in Lewis Hine's depiction of a "Jewish family working on garters in kitchen."

(Right) Using Lewis Hine's photographs, this poster from 1913 was displayed as part of New York State's official campaign against the employment of children in "home work."

Chapter 3
Wrestling with Nature

(Overleaf) Laura Mine, Red Star, West Virginia, c. 1908. The three miners on the right, with their carbide lamps, work underground; the smallest of them was identified as a boy of about fourteen. The man on the far right is called the "bank boss" or foreman. The man on the far left, with tie, cardigan, and straw hat, is most likely the mine superintendent.

Five miners talk after finishing their noon dinner deep underground, in a bituminous coal mine in southern Illinois in 1903. Just behind them, surrounded by bracing timbers, is one of the pillars of coal that holds up the roof of the tunnel.

My first encounter with the American workplace—other than an occasional stop-off at my father's gas station on Stony Island Avenue in Chicago—came in 1948. It was a visit to a coal mine. More precisely, it was the first of several visits I made to the still-remarkable working coal mine exhibit in the city's Museum of Science and Industry. We went 500 feet down in a clanking elevator cage, felt the increasingly thick and musty air, and rode coal cars for twenty minutes through dark tunnels that were illuminated only by the headlights of the small electric locomotive. I met real workmen who had spent years mining bituminous coal in southern Illinois and who were now museum staff. They were friendly enough as they guided us underground, demonstrated how their safety lamps detected deadly "fire damp" (explosive methane gas), and used the latest (c. 1933) mechanical cutters to tear away at a wall of coal. Still, they spoke to us with a certain amusement, letting us know that we were strangers to their dark and difficult world.

I still remember the utter blackness as headlamps were extinguished, and the dramatically staged explosion of a small amount of "fire damp." It was all artifice, of course, as the *Chicago Tribune* noted when the exhibit opened in 1933. Although we were 500 feet below ground on Chicago's lakefront, we were far safer than any miners had ever been.

A line of coal-delivery wagons—mostly horse-drawn, a few motorized—stretches along six blocks as the drivers wait to load up at a coal yard in Chicago in 1909.

Compared to the seemingly prosaic occupations I saw around me, mining coal was a dramatic and dangerous way to make a living. Later I learned that along with logging and the commercial fisheries, it was the riskiest work that Americans could do in peacetime. But at the same time, coal production was not really disconnected from ordinary experience. Among the commonplace sights of my Chicago childhood were the vast piles of coal being delivered to apartment buildings, to feed their big furnaces and heat their steam boilers. What the miners did kept us warm in the winter. Much later, of course, I would come to understand how the work of other Americans who wrestled with nature—loggers, fishermen, oil workers—sustained the fabric of our everyday life.

Their work in particular has been highly dangerous until recent times. The sea, the forest, and the mine are all intrinsically perilous workplaces, and Americans have traditionally chosen speed and productivity over caution when it comes to exploiting natural resources, accepting high levels of risk. Through the nineteenth century and into the twentieth, the people and governments of the United States paid only passing attention to workers' safety in any industry. American ways of work, American technology, and American law were designed to expand production, not to protect workers. American workplaces have become much safer since the middle of the twentieth century, but the occupations that wrestle with nature are still by far the riskiest. Their stories are especially compelling because subduing a continent—extracting the resources that built a great nation and an immensely powerful economy—cost many of them their lives or their health.

IN THE AMERICAN WOODS

Even after two centuries of settlement, the vast scale and abundance of America's forestlands meant that the nation's landscape in 1840 was primarily one of wooden buildings, and virtually all American households cooked and heated with wood. Most farmers did their own logging on a small scale,

Loggers pose with an enormous Douglas fir that they are felling in Reynolds, Washington, c. 1902. The primary tool that loggers used on the great trees is the large crosscut saw visible at the right. Logging on the Pacific Coast had a very different seasonal pattern than in Maine or Michigan. Rainy rather than snowy winters meant that loggers had to encamp in the summer so that they could haul the logs out before the logging roads became impassable with mud.

clearing their lands, opening up fields on longer-settled farms, and maintaining woodlots for fuel. Farmers closest to the cities supplied urban households with firewood and building materials as well.

As cities grew, the railroad emerged, and farms multiplied at the expense of forest, this pattern of highly dispersed lumbering began to change. In New England and other long-settled Northern states in the 1840s, there was concern about "the rapid disappearance of the woodlands." Early railroad locomotives burned wood, and "their great consumption . . . had raised the prices to such an extent" that many observers feared farmers would denude their woodlots, threatening the fuel supply of hundreds of thousands of households and making building materials increasingly expensive.

Portable steam-powered sawmills made it possible to produce lumber right in the logging camp. This sawmill, in a lumber camp in Concord, New Hampshire, c. 1915, burned scrap wood from the ongoing operations.

Of course, this never came to pass. While coal became the primary fuel for railroads and domestic heat, large-scale lumbering emerged as a major sector of the American economy. Lumber production moved from farm woodlots to the great forests of Maine, northern Michigan, and Wisconsin, to the pine woods of the South, and then to the timber stands of the Pacific Coast. After 1850, by lake, river, and rail, the wealth of the American forest would be transported unprecedented distances to construct houses, shops, and factories. Every year logging camps would spring up by the thousands in the American woods, and the rough-hewn men who worked in them would turn loggers into mythic American lumberjacks. Before the middle of the twentieth century, however, sweeping mechanization would industrialize lumbering almost completely.

THE SHANTY BOYS

"In all the more Northern sections of the United States," wrote the experienced timber merchant Charles Flint in 1876, logging was work that had to be done during the heart of winter. And across the nation, from Maine on into the West, "the logging camp is very much the same," he noted. Any account "of the winter operations of one," he wrote, "will apply, with slight modifications, to them all."

"Shanty boys" was the name given to the loggers who spent their winters working in the Michigan woods and living in rudely built camps, or "shanties." After dinner one night in 1892, thirty-one of them posed outside their camp building.

Made out of rough logs, with crude sleeping berths along the walls, and thoroughly dirty and disheveled, this bunkhouse was photographed just after housing a Maine logging crew during the winter of 1889.

But one detail that varied from place to place was the matter of names. The most common American name for a logger was "lumberjack"—simply derived from adding *lumber* to *jack*, meaning "male worker." This is what most of the men who worked in the forests of Maine, Wisconsin, Minnesota, and the Pacific Coast called themselves. But the loggers who worked in the pine woods of Michigan called themselves "shanty boys" or "shantymen," because of the rude accommodations they had for eating and sleeping. Journalist Arthur Hill, writing for *Harper's Monthly*, spent a winter in an isolated Michigan logging camp in 1892 and shared in the loggers' everyday lives, following them as they felled trees and skidded logs in the deep pine woods and writing down their stories.

The men Hill encountered were a varied lot. Some were farm laborers who just wanted work in the winter, a time when farmers had little for them to do. During the warmer months they worked in the fields and tended sawmills; they did not see winter work in the woods as their primary and enduring occupational identity. Hill noted that they were men "who go to the woods late" because they were finishing up the harvest, and "come out early" so that they could be ready for spring plowing. A number of them had families "for whom they faithfully toil and save," or were "steady, thrifty young men" who were scrimping and saving for farms of their own.

But the loggers Hill found most interesting were not steady and thrifty. "The genuine shantyman" was a different article, a man who completely identified himself as a logger and every winter would "go into the woods early and come out late." Shanty boys didn't work much in the summer. They lived off

Emblems:

A Lumberjack Play and a Shanty Boy's Song

The mythical Paul Bunyan was not the only American lumberjack to make his way into song and story. In 1891 Gus Heege wrote a play in American Swedish dialect whose hero was the Swedish immigrant lumberman, *Yon Yonson*. The play proved immensely popular and was staged hundreds of times from the 1890s through the 1920s. Portrayed as strong and competent in the woods, but naive and amusing in his ignorance of American ways, Yon Yonson was a long-familiar figure in American popular entertainment.

Unlike Paul Bunyan and Yon Yonson, Michigan's shanty boys were not fictional, and some of their culture has survived. In their pine woods camps, they sang to entertain themselves in the evenings. Arthur Hill, who spent a winter in a Michigan camp, recorded one "characteristic song, evidently home-made," that he heard

in 1893. In this song, two young women compare their lovers—the stay-at-home farmer and the wandering shanty boy. Not surprisingly, the farmer does not do well in this competition.

The Shanty Boy

As I walked out one evening, just as the sun went down,
I carelessly did ramble till I came to Saginaw Town.
I heard two girls conversing, as slowly I passed them by;
One said she loved a farmer's son, and the other a Shanty Boy.

The one that loved the farmer's son, these words I heard her say,
"The reason why I love him is at home with me he'll stay;
He'll stay home all winter, to the woods he will not go,
And when the springtime comes again, his lands he'll plow and sow."

"I shall always praise my Shanty Boy who goes to the woods in fall,
He is both stout and hearty and fit to stand a squall;
With pleasure I will greet him in the spring when he comes down.
His money on me he'll spend it free when your mossback he has none."

"How can you praise your Shanty Boy who to the woods does go?
He's ordered out before daylight to face the frost and snow,
While happy and contented my farmer's son will lie,
Soft tales of love he'll tell to me while the storms are blowing by."

"I never can stand that soft talk," the other girl did say,
"The most of them they are so green the cows could eat them for hay;
How easy it is to know them when they come into town,
The small boy shouting after them, 'Mossback, how come you down?'"

"What I've said unkind of your Shanty Boy, I do not mean it so,
And if ever I meet with one of them along with him I'll go,
And leave my mossback farmer's son to plough and plant his farm.
While my Shanty Boy so bold and free will save me from all harm."

This production of *Yon Yonson*, advertised in an 1899 theatrical poster, actually tried to re-create a midwinter lumber camp onstage.

their earnings from winter logging, spending much of it on liquor and prostitutes; if they ran out of cash, they did a few odd jobs, but preferred to loaf and drink. But once in the woods, they had greater skill and daring than the steadier men. They were a strong and skillful bunch, reckless risk-takers who could be relied on "for the work which more prudent men will not do."

Hill described how a logging foreman would put his crew together at the beginning of the logging season in early winter. First, he secured a number of steady seasonal workers off the farm; they were easy to hire and not hard to find. Then, to get the necessary skills, he had to recruit at least half of his men from among the true "shanty boys." He would walk the streets, visiting the "boarding houses, small hotels and saloons" where they stayed in the off-season. He paid for drinks and passed the word around that he needed experienced loggers. When he found a likely looking shanty boy, he offered him a job.

If the foreman hired sixty men, Hill wrote, he would usually find only thirty or so at the office on the morning they were setting out for camp. The rest were "still in the saloons," unwilling to leave until their "money is gone, and credit, too." The foreman would return to find them and cajole them into reporting for work, perhaps promising to pay off a bar bill or two. Hill pictured some of these men showing up hungover and penniless, "trembling, broken and bankrupt," but finally ready to spend another season in the woods.

WINTER IN THE WOODS

Logging did not start until a stand of timber was surveyed, or "estimated," as to what it would yield, and then bought by a lumber company or contracted out by its owner. Then the loggers went into the woods, faced with a great

Using teams of oxen and horses, Michigan loggers are hauling—"skidding"—logs after they have been cut to a central collecting point where they will be piled up until the spring, c. 1900.

labor of preparation before they could fell a single tree. First, supply roads had to be cut through the woods to connect the camp with "civilization," along with logging paths so that lumber could be stored and moved to the waterside "banking grounds." Using axes, picks, and shovels, the men had to completely clear the roads of stumps and sink them below ground level so that the logging sleighs—massive sleds pulled by teams of horses or oxen—could run. Then jams and other obstructions had to be cleared out of the stream or lake on which the logs would float to the sawmill in the spring. Just as the weather began to go below freezing, noted Hill, the shanty boys would sprinkle the logging roads with great cans of water, "making a solid bed of ice, over which enormous loads can be hauled."

By the 1870s, loggers were using the large crosscut saw to fell trees and cut them into logs rather than the traditional ax; although it required two men, it made the job much faster. Improvements in steelmaking meant that

In 1870, loggers in Minnesota are sketched in action. One man is felling a tree with an ax. Two loggers are cutting a felled tree into lengths with a crosscut saw.

This 1885 wood engraving captures horse teams hauling logs from the skids to the "banking grounds." Using very long reins, the teamsters perch precariously atop their heavy loads.

the saw was strong and flexible, and its teeth would remain sharp. Logging bosses found that the saw doubled a man's daily output. So wood choppers became sawyers, although they continued to use the ax as an all-purpose tool for trimming branches, cutting scrub growth, and starting cuts. Unlike modern-day loggers, they wore no helmets or other protective equipment—only heavy boots and wool clothing.

"Fallers" took down the trees; judging from long experience, they calculated where to begin the first cut and in which direction the tree would fall. If you were a really skilled woodsman, Hill noted, "you could throw your

This view of a lumbering camp in Michigan, c. 1892, shows the stables, bunkhouses, cookhouse, and shops that made it a "backwoods village."

tree wherever you wished it." Skill was important here, as a mistake could easily kill a man by toppling a 60-foot pine on top of him. Once fallen, trees had to be trimmed of their branches and then "bucked" into manageable and uniform lengths of 15 to 20 feet. Then the "fallers" went on to another tree while the "skidders" chained the logs and dragged them a few hundred yards with oxen or horses to the "skidway," a frame for holding logs. There, the loaders piled the logs up in six to eight tiers, using long, iron-tipped poles called "cant hooks." Finally, large horse-drawn sleds arrived, driven by the camp's teamsters.

When it came to loading the sled, wrote Hill, the loaders needed all their "judgment and strength and skill," as they worked to stack the logs "higher than a load of hay," without tipping them over. The teamsters sledded the logs, sometimes as much as a mile to the banking ground by the frozen waterside, where the "scaler" measured them and the banking crew went to work, carefully placing the logs on the bank so that they would "roll in easily when the ice goes out." Often in subzero temperatures, sometimes battling heavy snow, the logging crews repeated this sequence day after day, as they systematically cleared the timber stand of its usable trees.

Directing all of this work was the camp foreman, whose managerial skills Hill admired. He seemed to be everywhere, "urging, directing," and driving his men toward the highest possible production. Every night he went over the daily counts of the fallers, skidders, loaders, and teamsters; "if anyone's count is short, he wants to know the reason why." Men who fell short were exhorted to do better, became the butt of other workers' jokes, or had their pay docked. The camp cook was also crucial, just as the cowhands' cook was on the cattle drives. Keeping sixty men fed over a day that might last from four in the morning to seven at night, he "sleeps even less than the foreman."

Working together for twelve hours a day or more, these sixty men constituted an isolated community, 20 miles or more over frozen roads from the nearest town. Their camp, like hundreds of others across the American timberlands, was "a backwoods village," with a long bunkhouse for the men; a cookhouse and granary for food supplies; and stables, a blacksmith shop, and a separate office and bunk for the foreman and scaler. The camp's social life, as Hill described it, was far from boisterous. It was usually an hour or so of conversation, jokes, stories, and songs, perhaps some card playing, until an early "lights out." Sundays, he wrote, were "devoted to cleanliness, not godliness": a time when the men took baths, cut each other's hair, wrote letters, organized a camp lottery, or dickered with a peddler who occasionally found his way into the woods to sell watches and trinkets.

RISKS: FALLING TREES AND ROLLING LOGS

Loggers learned quickly that all work in the woods was dangerous—a tree could fall the wrong way, axes and saws could slip, a load of logs could topple. Crew bosses took precautions. Liquor was banned from most logging camps, and foremen tried to keep men reasonably well-rested. But the constant drive for production often trumped safety concerns. Sliced hands, crushed fingers, wrenched knees, and bruised shoulders were regular occurrences. More serious was an infected wound from an ax or saw, the "gashed foot, and . . . burning fever" that could lead to death from septicemia, or a catastrophic injury while loading logs, when "the cant hook fails to catch and stop the rolling log, and there [was] . . . a maimed and lifeless body."

The riskiest work of all came in the early spring after the ice broke up, when the men moved to "attack the great tiers of logs as they lay piled in the landing" and roll them into the now-open stream to begin the log drive. Standing atop a pile of logs, the men would "pitch and pry" with their poles to get the first log in the pile moving, and then "suddenly . . . down thunders the towering mass of logs," into the stream. While most loggers leaped aside, as the foreman cautioned them to do, the most daring shanty boys stayed perched on the logs, riding them as they plunged into the stream. "Nowhere," wrote Hill, "unless it be on the battlefield, is there more reckless daring shown." The foreman found himself constantly cautioning his men and pulling them back.

As the log run began, the logging camp broke up after four months in the woods. Some members of the crew picked up their belongings and their pay and headed home for spring farm work. But many stayed on as members of the "jam crew," who followed the logs downstream to their destination—the sawmills, where they would be turned into lumber. Living in tents and on the move every day, they kept the logs moving, breaking up "logjams" and pulling up logs that had become snagged or caught in low water.

At the end of the run—usually two to three weeks—the "jam crew" reached the town where they had begun their journey to camp and disbanded. They took their wages, stacked their tools and packed up their clothes, and walked back into civilization—the steady men back to their families, and the "shanty boys" back to the saloons and painted women.

The work life of logging camps in the nineteenth century, with its isolation and camaraderie, was shaped by its lack of mechanization. Michigan

A great jam of logs at Chippewa Falls, Wisconsin, is pictured here, c. 1869. Working to free a jam like this was the most dangerous work lumbermen faced.

Logging underwent a mechanical revolution in the twentieth century, as we can see in this 1919 photograph from Clallam County, Washington. An early gasoline-powered chain saw, heavy and unwieldy, rests against the side of a stump at left. Just behind the workers is the smokestack of the large steam-powered "donkey engine," which used a powerful winch to drag massive logs out of the woods.

shanty boys and Maine lumberjacks worked with oxen, horses, and hand tools to supply an industrializing and rapidly growing nation's appetite for wood.

Although loggers worked in seasonal camps well into the twentieth century, their tools and circumstances changed dramatically. Steam winches or "donkeys" replaced horses and oxen; specialized rail lines were pushed into the forests to haul logs; and the first gasoline-powered saws and winches appeared. These changes meant that fewer men were needed on a logging site, and, since it became easier to get in and out of the woods, they were far less isolated.

The traditional world of logging ended for good after 1950, with the appearance of powerful all-terrain trucks and massive log-handling machines. These provided daily access to the woods and made the camps unnecessary. Logging camps became a memory, a kind of work Americans no longer do.

(Overleaf, following page) This 1888 photograph shows the destination of the shanty boys' log drive (probably in Saginaw, Michigan): the "assorting grounds," where the logs were hauled in off the water, and the large steam-powered sawmills.

Workplaces:

THE SAWMILL

Through most of the nineteenth century, wherever there was both flowing water and growing timber, tens of thousands of small water-powered sawmills dotted America's rural landscape. Country millwrights constructed dams on small streams and built waterwheels. Mill owners were usually farmers who had picked up the mechanic's skills needed to work as sawyers, operating and maintaining the mills. Sawyers ran their mills when a sufficient "head" of water was available; hampered by ice in winter and low water in summer, they often sawed day and night during the weeks of high water in the spring. Because logs were heavy and too expensive to move far with oxen or horses, sawmills remained scattered across the countryside.

Until the 1850s, sawyers used the reciprocating sawmill, a technology whose design and operation had changed little since the 1400s. After 1860, reciprocating saws gave way to rotary ones, as it became possible to forge large circular saw blades that cut faster and more efficiently.

The importance of small sawmills declined with the emergence of large-scale lumbering. After 1860, the great bulk of American lumber came from logs moved long distances by water or rail, and sawn by increasingly larger steam-powered mills. Still, many of these mills remained in use for local lumbering operations, although portable steam- and then gasoline-powered sawmills were making them increasingly obsolete by the turn of the twentieth century.

At least two "up-and-down" water-powered sawmills remained in existence in New Hampshire into the 1930s; they were documented by the Historic American Buildings Survey, but did not survive the great Hurricane of 1937.

(Right) **This woodcut from Oliver Evans,** *The Young Mill-Wright and Miller's Guide* **of 1795, displays the schematic design of a water-powered reciprocating sawmill. Versions of this drawing go back to the 1500s, and mills with this basic design were still running in the United States in the 1930s.** *Author photo.*

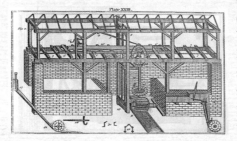

(Below) **Sawyers stand in front of the Weare sawmill in Hampton Falls, New Hampshire, c. 1900. To the left we can see massive logs ready to be rolled into the mill. Behind them is a pile of scrap wood left over from sawing. At the far right and below is sawn lumber.**

(Left) This sawmill in the redwood logging area of Lake Tahoe, California, has a very long, high flume that brings water to a very tall, narrow wheel—a design adapted to a mill site with a relatively small flow of water but a very large vertical drop.

(Below) Two sawyers stand in the Weare sawmill's interior, c. 1900. At the center is the massive log carriage with a log fastened to it. The carriage will advance the log into the saw, which advances it into the serrated vertical saw blade, being adjusted by one of the sawyers. Lever and crank mechanisms driven by the waterwheel below slowly advance the carriage and power the rapid up-and-down movement of the saw and frame.

DOWN IN THE MINES

"King Coal" ruled in late-nineteenth-century and early-twentieth-century America, the indispensable fuel for heating, transportation, steelmaking, and industrial power. By the 1850s, with the development of efficient stoves, coal was in general use for heat in cities and large towns throughout the nation. Railroads redesigned their locomotives to burn coal, which produced far more energy per pound than wood. In 1885, coal produced half of America's energy. (Wood's remaining share was due to its continued use in heating millions of farmhouses.) By 1900, coal provided over 70 percent.

Major coal production started in the anthracite or "hard coal" region of eastern Pennsylvania in the 1830s. Great deposits of bituminous or "soft" coal" were discovered and mined across the nation first in western Pennsylvania, Ohio, West Virginia, and Illinois, then in Kentucky, Tennessee, and Alabama, and ultimately farther west in Colorado and Utah. It drove railroads

A miner checks the tunnel roof around 1910. Wooden support posts and excavated rock are visible at the right, and the coal car is behind him. The debris on the tunnel floor indicates that there has recently been a rockfall.

and steamships, made enormous quantities of coke for steelmaking, and powered mills and factories. Hard or soft, coal powered America's great industrial transformation during the second half of the nineteenth century and on until 1910. It was the energy source that would allow the United States to become the world's fastest-growing and most dynamic economy.

Coal mines began as relatively small, decentralized operations. Miners saw themselves, despite the dark and dirt, not as laborers but as skilled mechanics, wielding picks, shovels, and drills, and blasting powder to free the coal from the mine face. As demand for coal grew, mines were dug ever deeper. Steam power was used to pump water out of the deep mine tunnels and to ventilate shafts. The size and scale of mine operations steadily increased, although coal mining never became as centralized as the railroads or the steel industry.

Coal mining was brutally hard and dangerous work, and relationships between miners and bosses were harsh and often openly hostile. Mine owners worried far more about production than safety, and often treated their miners as expendable units of production, easily replaced. As the industry expanded, intense competition periodically pushed down the price of coal and the rates miners were paid. Not surprisingly, coal mines were frequently theaters of open, often violent, conflict between labor and management.

By 1890, electric-powered machines (steam-driven machines were not safe to operate within mines) could cut coal without the need for blasting it loose. Within ten years, the new machines were mining 25 percent of American coal. Miners saw many of their traditional craft skills become irrelevant. The twentieth century brought continued mechanization to the mines. "Duke" Allison, an Illinois miner who started work in 1936, described the impact of the new technology that not only cut the coal but automatically loaded it as well: "They put machines in that eliminated a lot of handloaders, see, because they used to load the coal by hand. And they had twelve, fifteen hundred guys working at these mines. After they put the machines in, then they was operating with less men . . . As progress goes along they get more production . . . with less men."

"WE COULD TASTE THE GAS": AN AMERICAN COAL MINE IN 1855

The McGuinness coal mine in Pottsville, Pennsylvania, was the deepest one in the United States when Scotsman William Ferguson visited it in 1855. The "Mammoth" coal seam that its miners were working was 22 feet thick and began 438 feet below ground.

J.R.Smith Jun.t Del.

J.R.Smith Sen.r Sculp.t

VIEW OF POTTSVILLE

Taken from Sharp Mountain & respectfully dedicated to the enterprising citizens of the COAL REGION by,

J.R. SMITH . Drawing Academy Philad.a

This 1833 view of Pottsville, Pennsylvania, and its coal mine was made soon after mining began there.

Ferguson began his subterranean adventure with a precipitous descent. He and his companions were lowered 400 feet down in a rickety wooden cage, which rattled their bones with a jolting stop at the bottom. Each of them had been given one of the oil-burning lamps that miners then used, so that after adjusting their eyes, they found themselves "in a pretty large open space, hollowed out of a seam of coal . . . One side was perpendicular, formed of posts, boarded and filled in behind with rubbish. The other side sloped to the floor, and was the roof-bed of the coal seam."

The visitors—all of them genteel and formally dressed—were anxious to be entertained, and prevailed on their miner guide, John, to find them some explosive "fire damp"—one of the great hazards of coal mining. John found a spot where the gas had accumulated, and first let them "see it burn inside the safety-lamp," which the miners used to warn of its presence. But the visitors pressed, and the obliging John went further; he volunteered to "set fire to it, that we might see how it burns." John exploded it for them, and "the effect was beautiful . . . a sheet of pale blue flame." Ferguson's tone grew more serious after he discovered that there had been a number of gas explosions in the mine, with injuries, although there had been "no lives lost"—at least recently.

His sense of danger became even more acute as they entered the east gallery of the mine. It was a new tunnel, still under construction, and Ferguson could tell that the circulation of air was still "very imperfect." To make the site safer, one of the miners had been stationed there to operate a hand-cranked ventilating fan. But he had abandoned his post. As they walked farther into the tunnel gallery it became increasingly obvious that the situation was becoming dangerous: "[W]e could taste the gas, and also hear it fizzing out of the chinks of the coal."

What astonished Ferguson was how casually the miners treated this hazard of their work. Alarming as it was to the visitors, the men who worked underground had become accustomed to it. A few of them were "sitting unconcernedly close by, eating their dinners, with uncovered lights." More than this, they made excuses for their fellow worker, "the delinquent fanner-man," who had left his post—and none of them were willing to replace him

This view from 1891 shows the "coal breaker," where anthracite coal that has been mined and brought up from underground is raised to the top of the building, where it rolls down, broken and sorted into ever smaller pieces by rollers and screens. At the bottom is the breaker house, where the coal is picked free of slate by hand.

at the crank. It was not their job. Ferguson was glad to leave the mine before there was an explosion. Contemplating the lax safety practices characteristic of American coal mining, he contented himself by stating the obvious. It was "by such carelessness," he wrote, "that accidents are caused."

BREAKER BOYS, DOOR BOYS, DRIVERS, AND MINERS

Anthracite coal was hard and shiny, sometimes called "black diamonds." Compared to bituminous or soft coal, it was cleaner to handle and to burn, producing less coal dust, ash, and chimney soot. Anthracite was used in industry, but because it could keep kitchens and parlors relatively clean, it also became the primary fuel for heating American homes. While deposits of bituminous coal could be found in thirty-three American states, anthracite was limited by geography; it existed only in a nine-county region of northeast Pennsylvania called "the anthracite belt."

Because of its hardness, anthracite coal had to be blasted out of the seam. It came out of the mine in chunks of many different sizes, mixed in with slate and other rock. Part of the miners' work was to break up the coal into more-uniform pieces and remove the debris. At the McQuarrie mine, William Ferguson saw a coal breaker for the first time, a 60-foot tower above the mine entrance. After the coal had been hauled up from the depths, it was hoisted to the top of the breaker. The breaker was a system of chutes down which the coal tumbled while it was broken up by huge powered rollers "studded with great iron teeth," and sorted into different sizes by iron screens. At the bottom of the breaker Ferguson saw dozens of boys sitting next to the coal chutes. As the coal poured by, their job was "to pick out any pieces of

Breaker boys are picking slate out of the anthracite coal as it pours down out of the chute in the Kohinoor mine, Shenandoah City, Pennsylvania, c. 1891. Some older men, no longer able to mine, seem to be working the breaker as well.

shale or slate which may have got among the coal"; it was "slow and tedious" work, but required to make the coal "ready for market." These were the "breaker boys," often as young as nine, who would be part of the work life of the anthracite mines from the 1830s to the 1920s.

In 1902, John McDowell was thinking about the breaker boys when he wrote "The Life of a Coal Miner" for the labor magazine, *The World's Work*.

Almost looking like they are sitting at school desks, eighteen boys, c. 1913, are picking slate out of the coal in the breaker house of this Pennsylvania anthracite mine.

The door boy's task was a lonely one, waiting all alone in the dark and cold for carts to come through. The father of the thirteen-year-old boy in this 1911 photograph, "a frugal German miner," swore that his son was sixteen in order to get him a job in the mines. Already ill, this young man died in his mid-teens.

In his experience, he noted, the miner's working life traced a cycle, "a rule of progress that is almost always followed." A man could reasonably expect that he would be "once a miner and twice a breaker boy." A young boy from an anthracite mining community would begin his work at the age of nine or ten, sorting coal from slate. He would take on more difficult jobs as he grew in strength and skill, going deeper into the tunnels, until he became a miner in his twenties. But mining took an enormous physical toll. Experiencing "the descent from manhood to old age," usually in his fifties, a miner would gradually lose his skilled status and return, broken in body, to picking slate out of the coal chute. "That is the rule," asserted McDowell, who has some reason to know what he was talking about. He had worked in the mines himself for twenty-five years before becoming a clergyman and an advocate for miners' welfare.

McDowell recalled how he had lied about his age to begin work sorting slate from coal in the breaker, claiming to be "twelve years old, goin' on thirteen," when he was only nine. "Miners' families were large," he remembered, "and their pay comparatively small." Additional income was more important to hard-pressed mining families than schooling. A breaker boy would work to help feed his brothers and sisters.

For a day of labor, a breaker boy got fifty to seventy cents. He got up at five thirty in the morning and put on his sweat-stained and sooty working clothes. By seven o'clock, wrote McDowell, "he has climbed the dark and dusty stairway to the screen room where he works"—a large space shared with fifteen or twenty others. They sat on hard benches built across the coal chute, and for ten hours bent over the chute to pick the rock out of "a steady stream of broken coal." The work was not strenuous, but it kept the boys seated and unmoving. McDowell recalled that a breaker boy's hands "soon become cut and scarred by the sharp pieces of slate and coal, while his fingernails are soon worn to the quick from contact with the iron chute. The air he breathes is saturated with the coal dust . . ."

All young breaker boys, wrote McDowell, wanted "to enter the mines, and at the first opportunity." At thirteen or fourteen they sought work and slightly higher wages as "door boys." In some mines they were called "nippers" or "trappers." Their work was to open and shut the mine doors, which controlled not only access to the tunnels but also the mine's ventilation. Their work was not physically demanding, but it was lonely and monotonous. Except when they were letting coal cars and miners in and out of the tunnels, door boys worked "alone in the darkness and silence all day," with only a small lamp for illumination. They whittled and whistled to pass the time.

As door boys grew older, they wanted to become drivers, guiding the mule- or horse-drawn cars that hauled coal to the surface. Drivers hitched their animals to a "trip" of empty coal cars and led them down to "the working places" of the mine, sometimes through a mile or more of tunnels. After the cars were loaded, the driver brought his trip train back to the surface, where they were unloaded and taken to the breaker. Drivers ran real physical risks; they were not only vulnerable to cave-ins and exploding gas, but in a narrow tunnel, they could fall and be crushed by their own coal cars.

Around the age of twenty, after ten to twelve years of mine work, most drivers became mine laborers. The practice in the anthracite mines was for each miner to hire a laborer, who worked for him alone; the laborer's task was to load the cars with the coal that the miner cut and blasted from the rock. Laborers were paid by the number of cars they filled each day—McDowell estimated this as "averaging from five to seven, equaling from twelve to fifteen tons of coal." Working side by side, miner and laborer struggled together with unwelcome underground springs and stubborn outcroppings of rock. Both men rose around five, entered the mine together at six, and walked to the coal

In this picture from 1911, Pasquale Salvo was working as a driver for the Pennsylvania Coal Company in Shaft #6 of the Pittston mines. By 1920, he had moved up the occupational ladder to become a miner, working his own part of the coal face and directing a laborer. His father, once a miner, had cycled down to working as a laborer as his strength failed. Pasquale's youngest brother was a breaker boy. (Lewis Wickes Hine.)

face where they were working—sometimes a mile or more. They carried their dinner pails, their lamps, and a heavy load of tools and supplies—from picks and shovels to blasting powder and hand drills. Miners usually hired men they felt they could trust—family members, friends, members of the same ethnic community.

Laborers, in their turn, were anxious to become miners "in the technical sense of the word," meaning men who themselves hired laborers and contracted with mine owners "to do a certain work at so much per car or yard." Since 1889, miners in Pennsylvania actually had to present credentials—at least two years' experience at the coal face as a laborer, and a successfully passed safety examination. The miner's work involved not only physical effort as heavy as the laborer's, but also skill, judgment, and a frightening responsibility. Step by step, he had to determine how to prop up the tunnel roof safely as he bored farther and farther into the coal seam. Anthracite had to be blasted free from the coal face, and he was responsible for locating the blasting holes, drilling them, deciding the amount of explosive to use, and carefully preparing the controlled explosions that would bring down the coal. A wrong decision about bracing the roof or blasting the coal could lead to death or serious injury.

For men working at the coal seams deep underground, the "dangers are many," McDowell told his readers. They might be "crushed to death at any time by the falling roof, burned to death by the exploding of gas, or blown to pieces by a premature blast." Nowhere outside the mining towns, he wrote, "will you find so many crippled boys and broken down men." Life insurance was becoming a popular option for American men in many occupations in the early twentieth century, but no one would insure a coal miner.

Over the course of two or three decades, many miners became what McDowell called "broken-down men." They fell victim to arthritis and crippling knee and shoulder injuries, to poorly healed broken bones, to "black lung" disease from the inhalation of coal dust, to the partial loss of hearing or vision from blasting accidents. Blasting and shoveling coal underground became too difficult. But since miners had no pensions and few had been able to save, they still needed to work. They were forced to move up out of the mine and down the occupational hierarchy. Former miners worked as laborers on the surface, tended the horses and mules that hauled the coal, or returned to the poorly paid work that they had done as boys—sitting astride the coal chutes at the bottom of the breaker and picking slate out of the coal. McDowell had lived the miner's life himself into his late thirties, but he had no love for it. He unsparingly described it as "an endless routine of dull plodding work from nine years until death—a sort of voluntary life imprisonment. Few escape."

(Facing page) **Two miners bandage a third man's injured head and arm at the "emergency hospital" in an anthracite mine in Pennsylvania, c. 1909.**

McDowell was hardly a dispassionate observer, but he didn't exaggerate much. Coal mining was essential to the economy, and employed over a million men in 1900, but it was a trade that shortened the lives of its workers. Unfortunately, the mines were owned by as reactionary and willfully blind a group of men as could be found anywhere in the United States. They could see no need to change the painful cycle of the miner's life.

DIVERS OF THE EARTH

The roads were "made of coal-dust" in Pennsylvania's mining towns, wrote English journalist and traveler Stephen Graham in 1913. The imperatives of coal production had ignored almost every other human need. In the region around Scranton in the northeastern part of the state, he walked through "a devastated countryside" with "bad air . . . vitiated by the fumes of the burning mines." Great deposits of coal had "been on fire ten years, and the smoke rolls from the slag-coloured wastes in volumes, and diffuses itself into the general atmosphere." The houses Graham saw were "wretched frame-dwellings, ruined by the subsidence of the ground on which they were built, and begrimed with the smoke."

At the end of every shift he saw muscular men emerging from the mine shafts "with sooty faces and heavy coal-dusty moustaches," carrying their tin "grub-cans." On their heads they wore "black nine-inch lamps looking like cockades." These were the "divers of the earth." Few, he noticed,

Enormous heaps of refuse rock and coal dust, like these in Nanty Glo, Pennsylvania, c. 1937, scarred the landscape of virtually all mining towns. Trying to keep his house warm during the Depression, the man shown here is searching one of the heaps for pieces of usable coal.

(Above) Six men and one boy have just left their world of underground work in a Scranton coal mine to come up to the surface, c. 1912. Visiting journalist Stephen Graham wrote: "It is strange that a people, most of whom are working all day in darkness," should enjoy life "in the air of the outside world" as much of the miners did.

(Left) Polish coal miner's house near Scranton, Pennsylvania, c. 1912. The landscape of Scranton seemed blasted and desperate to journalist Stephen Graham, but miners' families strove as best they could for the comforts of home and community.

Struggles:

THE ANTHRACITE STRIKE OF 1902

At the turn of the twentieth century, 150,000 men worked in the anthracite mines, producing 60 million tons of coal a year—but there was trouble. Anthracite was a uniquely critical commodity in the American economy. Much cleaner to handle and burn than bituminous coal, it was used by millions of American families to heat their homes. It was the household fuel for cities throughout the heavily populated Northeast and Great Lakes states, as far west as Chicago. But anthracite was found only in the coal fields of eastern Pennsylvania. Any major disruption of production in that one region threatened much of the nation with a very cold winter.

Unrest had always stalked the mines. Mining was a hard business, subject to the cycles of the economy and vulnerable to overproduction. Miners wanted to be paid as much as possible for their brutally difficult and dangerous work. Foremen and managers wanted to control their workers and meet their quotas for production. Mine operators wanted the lowest possible costs and the highest possible profits. As coal production expanded from the 1870s on, mine owners had increasingly recruited immigrant workers from Eastern Europe and Italy. Coal mines became polyglot workplaces, with more than a dozen nationalities represented and as many languages spoken. Labor advocates charged (and most historians have since agreed) that this was done deliberately, to keep the workforce divided, difficult to organize, and willing to accept low wages. Coal mine operators maintained that it was simply good economics.

Despite the barriers of language and culture, the United Mine Workers (UMW) was able to successfully organize thousands of anthracite miners in 1900. Immigrant miners joined the union in large numbers, surprising mine owners and even John Mitchell, the young president of the UMW. The group led a six-week strike that forced mine operators, under fierce political pressure from the McKinley administration, to agree to a pay raise. "Poetic justice has been meted out," Mitchell said.

But owners refused to recognize the union and bitter conflict resurfaced in 1902. Emboldened by their previous success, miners pressed for another pay increase and a shortening of their ten-hour workday. Operators

PENNSYLVANIA – THE MINING TROUBLES IN THE SCHUYLKILL REGION – ATTACK ON THE COAL AND IRON POLICE BY A MOB OF POLISH STRIKERS, AT SHENANDOAH, FEBRUARY 3D.

Labor troubles in the anthracite country long preceded 1902. In 1888, they made front-page news in a popular New York weekly: "Pennsylvania—the mining troubles in the Schuylkill region—attack on the coal and iron police by a mob of Polish strikers, at Shenandoah, February 3d." Mainstream publications almost always took the side of the owners.

(Top) John Mitchell, the president of the United Mine Workers, arrives in the coal town of Shenandoah, Pennsylvania, during the strike of 1902 to address strikers and their supporters. He is riding in an open carriage, escorted by a crowd of boys. Mitchell is sitting to the right, wearing a straw hat.

(Bottom) The Pennsylvania State Militia had been summoned to keep order, and a few hundred troops were sent to Shenandoah in 1902. They were encamped right next to the railroad tracks, with the town and its mining works in the background.

THE MODERN SWORD OF DAMOCLES.

The cover of the humor magazine *Puck* was not amusing in February 1903. Using the well-known image of the hovering Sword of Damocles, it conveyed the widespread fear that the recently ended coal strike had brought to American homes.

argued that union activity was destroying work discipline in the mines and that profits were too low to justify increases. Most owners bitterly resented the way they had been forced to concede in 1900, and resolved to break the union's power this time around. Mitchell asked for discussion and arbitration, but was refused.

The strike began on May 12. With the miners increasingly militant and the owners unwilling to compromise, there was violence on both sides, ranging from fistfights to pitched battles. The companies expanded and armed their private police forces and recruited strikebreakers. Striking miners attacked the "scabs" who took their spots in the mines, and often shunned and humiliated their families. The governor of Pennsylvania, more sympathetic to the owners than the miners, called out the state's National Guard and dispatched them to the coal fields to "protect private property."

(Left) Coal miners, along with their wives and children, gather for an outdoor mass meeting about the coal strike in McKees Rocks, Pennsylvania.

(Right) President Theodore Roosevelt, shown here in 1906 giving a speech, spent months negotiating an end to the coal strike in 1902.

Copyright 1906 J. Horace McFarland Co.

As the strike went on into the fall, fear mounted at the prospect of a nation of American homes without heat. President Theodore Roosevelt foresaw "untold misery . . . with the certainty of riots which might develop into social war." Historically presidents had often intervened in strikes on the side of property rights, to crush "unlawful" union activity in the name of public order. But sensing a disaster in the making, and frustrated himself at the owners' recalcitrance, Roosevelt sought to mediate the strike. Although he lacked the power to force a settlement, he was so determined to prevent a freezing winter and social discontent that he was prepared to seize control of the mines—from both owners and miners—and operate them with the manpower of the United States Army.

After months of frustration, tortuous negotiation, rising public anger, and the intervention of banker J. P. Morgan, Roosevelt arranged an end to the strike and the appointment of a commission of "eminent men" to arbitrate between the miners and the owners. This marked a turning point in American labor relations. Roosevelt, with an expansive view of his responsibilities and angered by "the extraordinary stupidity and bad temper" of the mine owners, was the first president to play a reasonably even-handed role in a major industrial conflict. He had intervened, he said, neither on behalf of the miners or the owners, but in the interests of "the general public." After 163 days, the strike ended on October 22—barely in time for the heating season. Commissioner of Labor Carroll Wright estimated that during the five months of the strike, about thirty thousand men left the region for other work, and nearly ten thousand went back, at least temporarily, to their homes in Europe. But the miners who remained went back to work and kept American cities warm that winter.

In this 1906 photograph, two miners are shown testing their new-model safety lamps, which indicate the presence of dangerous coal gas. Another new safety feature: Electric lighting has been rigged to illuminate some of the mine tunnels.

spoke English. The great tide of immigration after 1880 had drawn millions of Eastern Europeans to America, and many thousands of men—some with mining skills, most with none—including Poles, Russians, Lithuanians, Croats, Czechs, and Hungarians had come to find work in Pennsylvania's mining towns. *How could they tolerate living and working in such an environment?* he wondered. Graham was struck by the vitality of a miner's social life after work—seemingly the one ray of vitality in this bleak world—when he saw the "crowd . . . surging in and out of the cinema houses and the saloons, and heard the American chaff and music-hall catch-words mixed with half a dozen Slavonic dialects."

Still, it didn't seem enough to explain why the miners stayed. He posed the question to a reporter who knew the region well as they looked over "many-roofed Scranton" from a ridge above the city, seeing the smoke from the town's "numberless chimneys and spouts," and its "black chutes and shafts and mountains of slag." Graham suggested that the landscape "would be a beautiful place if there were no Scranton here at all." But his American friend disagreed, saying, "[I]t's good to live in a place like this where we're doing something." He went on, "We have the faith to smash up the beauty of Nature in the hope of getting something better." Scranton, he maintained, was a more accurate expression of human desires than the unspoiled landscape of the Alleghenies. That, wrote Graham, was "perhaps a glimpse of the religion of America."

"A Hazardous Occupation"

Vern "Duke" Allison had a mining heritage. His father had worked all his life in the soft coal mines in Christian County, Illinois, but he wanted his son to take a different path. In the early 1930s, Christian County had been torn apart by a violent labor dispute that fractured the United Mine Workers and led to bloody confrontations between the breakaway "Progressive Miners" and the Peabody Coal Company. Vern's father had not sided with the Progressives, and had gone back to work at the first opportunity. "He still had a family to support and this is the only way that he could do it," Vern remembered. But the decision "caused hard feelings between families and friends," and "there was a lot of conflict." With all this in mind, the older Allison initially discouraged his son from taking a mine job in 1936, when Duke was twenty-one.

Grimy from his day's work, a miner poses for his portrait at Freeze Fork, West Virginia, in 1939.

Small Hands:

MECHANIZING COAL

In the early twentieth century, Lewis Hine caught on camera two machines that were part of the aggressive mechanization of American coal production. He was interested in them not as an engineer, but as an advocate for the elimination of child labor in the mines. In 1913 he praised Arthur Langerfeld's coal-cleaning machine, which he hoped would soon make the work of thousands of "breaker boys" no longer necessary. Earlier he had seen a machine at work in a West Virginia mine that "digs the coal and loads it on the car. With it 3 men can do the work of 50 in the old way." Yet, he noted, they still employed boys in dangerous jobs such as driving mine horses. In the years to come, mechanization would eliminate the breaker boy, and eventually the driver as well. As Hine had so abundantly documented, these jobs were harmful to children's health and normal growth, but hard-pressed families were very reluctant to give up the boys' labor.

(Above) Young boys risked early and irreversible damage to their lungs by working at the coal breakers. Hine noted in South Pittston, Pennsylvania, c. 1911, that "the dust was so dense at times as to obscure the view. This dust penetrates the utmost recess of the boys' lungs."

(Facing page) Langerfeld's coal cleaner was one of many machines developed before 1920 that would automatically separate coal from slate. "Mr. A. Langerfeld and one of his machines for picking coal, which does away completely with the use of breaker boys," wrote Hine in 1913.

(Right) Hine documented this machine in Gary, West Virginia, c. 1908, as an example of the new coal-mining technology that had not yet liberated boys from their work.

In this horrifying photograph from 1910, a coal miner is shown injured or dead—trapped under rubble after a tunnel cave-in. Mining was safer in 1910 than it had been fifty years earlier, but it remained America's most dangerous occupation.

However, in the depths of the Depression, Duke felt that he had no more choice than his father had had. As he told labor historian Kevin Corley fifty years later, if he wanted to stay in Christian County, "the only money that could be made around here was in the coal mines." Finally accepting his son's decision, Duke's father went to speak to the mine superintendent; this was "the way the biggest part of younger guys got started . . . if their dad was working there, and if their dad was a good worker." Duke described the mine's workforce as a network of kinship: "There was families on top of families out there because the dad got them all in, five and six boys."

The mine where he went to work—Peabody #8 in Taylorville, Illinois—was more electrified, more mechanized, and somewhat safer than mines had been at the turn of the century, but the work was still difficult and exhausting.

Duke started out on the "dirt gang," laying track to extend the main line of the mine's electric coal cars, digging "tire holes" for the rails with a pick and shovel. "I wasn't used to it then," he recalled; "it was a rough deal." Later, because he was agile and slender, he worked as a "trip rider." This meant, he said, tending the coal cars that served the mechanical loading machines. As soon as a car filled up, he had to couple it to an outgoing train, and then replace it with an empty car. Squeezing between the cars to reach the couplings risked smashed fingers and broken collarbones. "That is the reason they wanted little guys," laughed Duke, "small guys with small shoulders."

Duke also remembered a major transition in mine safety during his early working years. When he started in 1936, he wore a traditional felt hat, one that offered minimal protection against head injuries. Attached to it he wore a "carbide light," developed in the 1890s; safer than earlier miners' oil lamps, it still burned with a potentially dangerous open flame. Within a couple of years, the steel hard hat, modeled after military headgear from World War 1, became mandatory in the Christian County mines. As Allison remembered, many miners resisted the hard hat because "it was heavy on their heads," and left a mark on their foreheads after a day's work. Along with the hard hat came the much-safer battery-powered electric lamp, which the miners called a "bug light" and disliked as well. Miners "who had used those carbide lamps . . . for years and years," said Duke, found them light and comfortable. The new lamp's batteries were heavy, and the cord that connected them to the bulb assembly got in the way while men were shoveling coal.

Coal company representatives, state officials, and a few miners demonstrate the lifesaving devices available at this coal mine in LaSalle, Illinois, in 1910: underground breathing gear, stretchers, and resuscitation equipment.

He concluded that the miners didn't "like any change that's going to be made, although it was for their safety." The reason wasn't recklessness or a feeling that safety measures weren't manly, Duke thought. Based on long years of conflict and mistrust, the miners' instinct was to resist anything that management sought to impose on them. Ultimately, they came to see hard hats and safety lamps as beneficial, but it took years.

Although safety measures significantly reduced accident rates, the work remained dangerous. Duke remembered no daring down in the mine, only a matter-of-fact acceptance of risk and a sense that "everybody took care of the other guy." A miner who noticed a dangerous situation would let others know; they were all "your buddies when it come to safety." But he also acknowledged that the pressure to produce, coupled with miners' "pride in their work," created other incentives. He described how coal crews working different sections of the mine would compete for the highest daily production. "Well, we loaded two hundred and twenty cars," one crew would boast, and "another guy from another crew" would counter, "we loaded two forty."

Striving for higher tonnage, crews would sometimes push into areas where the tunnel roof was questionable; they wanted the coal, "and they would go in and load it." The results could be disastrous. "Sometimes they would get out and then it would fall in; sometimes it would fall in on the machine, on the men and everything, even before they got it loaded up." When that happened, "a lot of guys [were] killed and crippled up." It was still, he concluded, "a hazardous occupation."

The Gold Rush and Hard-Rock Mining

A burning desire to find gold and silver was one of the most powerful motives for exploring the "New World" of the Americas, and the mines of Mexico and Peru made the Spanish Empire immensely rich. But those who settled the British colonies that became the United States found little of either ore, much to their disappointment. In 1790, Benjamin Franklin noted, "gold and silver are not the produce of North America, which has no mines." For six decades after independence, the United States Mint coined relatively little gold and silver; America used a wide variety of foreign coins—from British guineas to Dutch rixdollars to Mexican silver dollars—for everyday transactions. In the 1830s, there was a flurry of excitement with the discovery of gold deposits in Georgia, although they proved small. But in 1849 gold was discovered in large quantities at Sutter's Mill in central California, just as it became American territory after the Mexican-American War.

The news spread rapidly up and down the Pacific Coast, and—thanks to the new telegraph—across the world with what then seemed astonishing

To St Louis, – 350 Miles.
To California, 1700 Ms.

THE INDEPENDENT GOLD HUNTER ON HIS WAY TO CALIFORNIA.

I NEITHER BORROW NOR LEND.

The Gold Rush of 1849 turned San Francisco into the American West's first city, with a huge influx of prospectors from all over the United States as well as from Mexico, Peru, Chile, and Great Britain. This daguerreotype, c. 1850–51, is one of the earliest views of the boomtown.

velocity. Within a few weeks, a frenzy for sudden riches seemed to seize the nation. The Gold Rush had begun. It was a mass migration of American workers—as well as prospectors from Mexico, Chile, Great Britain, and continental Europe—on a scale that no one had ever seen before. The population of California grew sevenfold in one year, from 14,000 in 1848 to almost 100,000 in 1849. In the next year, California became a state, and by 1852, its population had almost tripled, to over 250,000 people.

The great majority of these new Californians were men who had come to find gold. The rest were men, and some women, who came to make money off the gold hunters. Eastern farmers, clerks, storekeepers, mechanics—mostly single, but some married men as well—gave up jobs and farms and headed for the other side of the continent. They took the long and dangerous ocean voyage "round the Horn" to San Francisco, or sailed to Panama to take the uncertain but (they hoped) quicker jungle railroad route across the Isthmus and then a ship heading north.

No matter how they arrived, these men were seized by a fever—a burning desire to cut short the painful process of economic struggle and accumulation, and literally strike it rich. San Francisco was the port of entry for the hordes of Forty-Niners, and it became the headquarters of the Gold Rush and the American West's first real city. For its first decade it was a "bachelor" city with relatively few families, dominated by young and vigorous men engaged in the reckless pursuit of wealth. Taverns, gambling houses, and brothels flourished, along with a few churches. Because the city grew so rapidly, and the Forty-Niners were literally in a rush to get their "outfits" and head into the gold fields, it became an astonishingly expensive place. Prices for simple food, miners' equipment, housing, meals, and laundry became wildly inflated. Both the city and California's hundreds of mining camps were not only fast-growing, but dirty, crowded, flimsily built, and unhealthy. Their sanitary arrangements were casual in the extreme. Thousands of Forty-Niners died of infectious diseases like typhus and typhoid, as well as from wound infections from mining accidents. A number of them fell to violence as well, either from confrontations over rival mining claims or alcohol-fueled quarrels.

(Above) Two decades after the Gold Rush, Currier & Ives provided an idealized retrospective view in this popular 1871 lithograph.

(Left) Rockerville, Dakota Territory, 1889. Three old-time miners are panning gold from a stream as the water comes to them out of a box sluice, the placer miner's principal tool along with his pan.

One reason for the astonishing scale of the Gold Rush was that the work it required was simple. The gold discovered in the California hills was placer gold, dust, and nuggets found in mountain streams that had long since been eroded from mineral veins locked deep in the rock. Successful placer miners did not need the skills, equipment, or experience required for mining gold or silver underground. They needed luck, and a few simple tools to sift and wash away sand and gravel. A store clerk or a shoemaker could feel that he had as good a chance as anyone else—a belief that was reinforced every time a Forty-Niner struck gold.

Over its four-year run, the Gold Rush became a story of vastly unequal rewards and diminishing returns. Most of the real fortunes created by the Gold Rush were commercial ones, made by far-sighted merchants who decided that transporting, outfitting, and supplying the miners would be far more profitable than searching for gold. Some Forty-Niners did succeed and

These sketches, printed in San Francisco, c. 1852, portrayed the hardships and annoyances of life in the mining camps, for the miners' own amusement. *Courtesy American Antiquarian Society.*

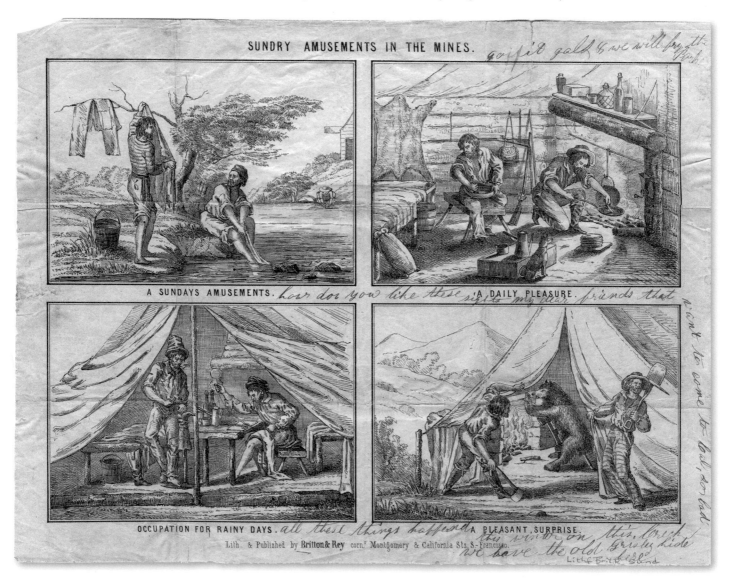

SUNDRY AMUSEMENTS IN THE MINES.

A SUNDAYS AMUSEMENTS.

A DAILY PLEASURE.

OCCUPATION FOR RAINY DAYS.

A PLEASANT SURPRISE.

Lith. & Published by Britton & Rey cornᵣ Montgomery & California Sts. S.-Francisco.

James Marshall, pictured here, was the carpenter and sawmill builder who began the Gold Rush, discovering the precious metal while building a sawmill in Coloma, California, in 1848. He won fame but never profited from his discovery.

became wealthy beyond their dreams, but they were a well-publicized few. A number of miners made at least a bit of money, enough to repay their expenses for the journey and a bit more to start a new life in the West. Others became "hooked" by prospecting and mining, and set out to stake new claims in Nevada and Colorado. Most men failed more completely and returned home with empty pockets, sometimes broken in health as well. As the years went by, though, more than a few disappointed Forty-Niners remembered that time fondly, as the great adventure of their youth.

GOLD AND SILVER

One of the enduring legacies of the Gold Rush was the culture of extraordinary restlessness it created among the men who worked as miners in the American West, as they chased the promise of riches from one boomtown to another. Census records from 1850 to 1920 show that Western miners moved more often than any other group in America. The most mobile, rootless men in the nation, they had never really been cured of the "gold fever" that had brought them, or their predecessors, into the West.

In California, as the easy productivity of Gold Rush placer mining dwindled, miners found ways to get at harder-to-reach gold-bearing sands and gravels—deposits that were buried under several feet of rocky debris. Starting in 1852, they developed the technique of hydraulic mining, which used streams of water at high pressure to wash off the "overburden," as it was called, and get at the gold. In contrast to the individualism and simple tools of placer mining, hydraulic mining meant cooperative work and investment

2358. "A Golden work." Hydraulic mining at Rockdrville, Dak.
Photo and copyright by Grabill, 1889.

Hydraulic mining at Rockerville, Dakota Territory, 1889. These miners are using water at high pressure to wash the debris off what they hope will be gold-bearing sands in the Black Hills of what is now South Dakota.

in more-expensive equipment. To work a claim, a group of men labored together to build a high mountain reservoir, the higher the better, to create enough water pressure and a system of flumes and ditches to carry the water to the site. Hydraulic mining continued in the state until 1884, when it was prohibited because of the damage it did to downstream farmland.

From the late 1850s on, most Western miners turned to the far more time-consuming work of freeing gold and silver ore from solid rock. Some would work in small mines, with no more than a few dozen workers, well into the twentieth century. But an increasing majority of them would become like

coal miners—industrial workers laboring underground for large corporations. The West's first great silver strike, the Comstock Lode discovery of 1859, attracted thousands of miners, as the Gold Rush had. But this time, they were men seeking employment, not individualists hoping to strike it rich.

Nevada journalist William Wright (under the pen name of Dan DeQuille) wrote about the enormous veins of silver discovered in the Nevada Territory around Virginia City in his 1889 *History of the Comstock Lode*: "[T]heir immense richness attracted hundreds and thousands of persons from California, and all parts of the Atlantic States and Canada." Between 1860 and 1880, a great number came to Nevada in pursuit of prosperity, but in a pattern very different from that of 1849.

Exploiting the Comstock Lode required the organization of labor and capital on a large scale. "The mills and hoisting works are a striking and characteristic feature of the place," noted Wright. "The immense waste dumps, high trestle-work car tracks, trains of ore cars on the railroad, clouds of black smoke belched from many tall stacks, trains loaded with wood and timber, all tell that mining is the great industry of the city; then much of the street talk heard is of mines and mining stocks."

The silver mines of Nevada's Comstock Lode were developed very quickly after they were discovered. By 1861, small but smoke-belching industrial villages had been built to process the silver ore, like the Gould and Curry Silver Mining Company's Reduction Works in Virginia City, Nevada, c. 1861. *Courtesy American Antiquarian Society.*

(Above) The deeper that mine tunnels went, the hotter they became. Miners coped with the tropical conditions in the Comstock mines by working bare-chested. These are groups of miners from four different mines, c. 1890: the Ophir mine, the Gould and Curry, the Savage, and the Chollar. The centerpiece honors the three Bickell brothers who lost their lives in a fire in the Gold Hill mine in 1869.

(Right) This 1876 lithograph shows a cutaway view of the extensive square timbering that supported the deep shafts of the Comstock mines, and depicts the miners at work with picks, carts, and wheelbarrows, excavating and hauling silver ore.

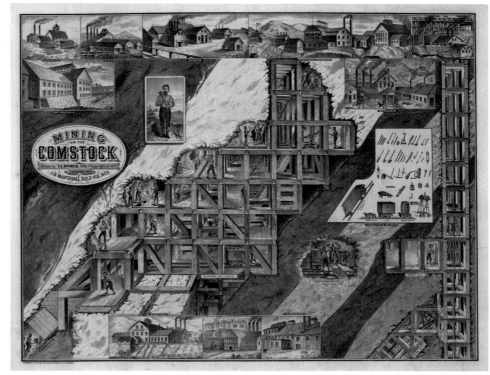

The great majority of miners at Comstock went to work not for themselves, but for mining corporations. As a Danish journalist explained to his readers, the notion of a miner as "a man who simply has to thrust his spade into the ground to find a nugget" was untrue; "a miner is a common mine worker who labors for a company." Reaching that "immense richness" of silver ore meant building miles of tunnels, managing the work of thousands of miners wielding picks, drills, and blasting powder, and investing in machinery for crushing the ore and "reducing" it—separating the metallic silver from its less-valuable surrounds. Entrepreneurs and investors became very wealthy, managers did well, and most miners made a living.

"I'm a Hard-Rock Man"

Hank Simms had mining in his blood, as well as a fair helping of trouble. He was born in Oregon in 1859, the son of a gold-seeking Forty-Niner from Illinois who stayed in the West to become a farmer. Simms shared his story with a Works Progress Administration (WPA) interviewer in 1938, beginning with the year 1880, when at twenty-one, he "lit out from the homestead" to try his hand at mining.

The eight-man crew of the Montana gold mine (its name is on a sign over the entrance) pose with their picks and shovels, c. 1889. Behind them is a loaded ore cart. It runs on a set of narrow tracks that begins right at the miners' feet.

2349. Montana Mine.
Photo and copyright by Grabill, 1889.

In the early 1880s Simms worked at the gold mines in California's Feather River country with "the best of the old hands." They taught him mining, he said, "from the ground *down*. You don't learn from the ground up in my business." After all, the logic of the miner's trade led not upward, but downward, into the earth. He learned to make his own rock drills from bar steel and became a first-rate rough carpenter who could fell trees and safely timber a mine shaft on his own. Drawing on the expertise of the men around him, and studying every aspect of the business, he went on to learn blasting, mine construction and excavation, and assaying ore.

Simms had worked in too many mines to count, he said, up and down the Pacific Coast, mining every metal except tungsten. "By god, I knew every creek and cow between here and Mexico, and right back up to Alaska." He claimed that he and his brethren prided themselves on being footloose, true "journeymen" of the mines. "Every once in a while we just drug down our pay on principle, and went down the road to a new job. They'd call us hoboes now, I guess. But in them days we was known as Overland Johns." The "Overland Johns" saw themselves as the elite troops of the mining industry, men who could walk into any mining town, display their skills, and get any job they wanted. "If a man kept moving he had to keep on his toes," Simms told his interviewer, "and that made good mechanics of us old-timers."

Simms would talk about little except mining, and it turns out that he held back much of his life story. He spoke as if he had always been a footloose bachelor miner. However, the records of the federal census tell us that he had tried for a while to lead a settled life. He actually had married in 1884, and although he traveled a great deal for his work, he returned often enough to have five children with his wife, Mary. In 1900 he was still with her, working as a miner but living on a small farm in McMinnville, Oregon. Soon afterward he abandoned his family, disappearing entirely from view in the public records—a sign that he had begun to lead the life of an itinerant miner. Mary remained in McMinnville with the children, eventually calling herself a widow, although Simms was still alive. This was how he became a true "Overland John."

Hank Simms followed the path of the "Overland John" until he was almost seventy. He spent what he earned, saved little, and wound up living in a small room in the Odd Fellows Home in Portland, Oregon. He acknowledged that he had followed mining "for fifty or sixty years and dug a shaft straight into this poorhouse . . . Miners is fools, and I'll bet that for every dollar lifted off the bedrock on this coast, two has been sunk back in the game." Simms spoke as if he didn't regret too much the life he had led, although he was utterly silent about his family. For a man like him, he told himself, there was no other way. "I guess that if a man has miner's blood in him," he said, "he can't never make it on top the ground. He's like a mole; he can tell his way around by the kind of rock he's in, but the wind don't make sense."

(Facing page) Three "hard-rock" miners are at work with picks in the stope, or working area, of the California gold mine, in Eagle River Canyon, Colorado, in 1905. Note the timbering that supports the stope at the left and right of the opening. Safe design and placement of the timber supports were critical skills for miners.

Workplaces:

THE STAMP MILL

Visiting a Western gold-mining operation in 1876, Charles Bartlett was awed by "the enormous stamps, sixty in number, crushing and breaking the quartz and hard rock." The noise was so great that no one could speak, but he thought the rhythmic pounding of the stamps "had a musical cadence to which the ear soon becomes accustomed." Mechanizing a technique that miners had used for a thousand years or more, steam-powered stamp mills used heavy steel cylinders or "stamps" to crush gold-bearing quartz and rock so that it could be further processed. Stamps were set in frames of six or eight apiece. As the rotating camshaft turned, each stamp was lifted up and then dropped, using its weight to crush the material.

Once the ore was "crushed and pulverized," Bartlett reported, it was taken to "the separators and amalgamators," where "the vestiges of earth, quartz and rock disappear." He was watching what he called "the quicksilver process" for extracting gold. The ore was spread over sheets of copper coated with mercury. Gold was chemically nonreactive, but it would combine with the liquid metal to form a temporary "amalgam." Then the gold-mercury amalgam was scraped off, leaving the rest of the ore behind. Finally, the gold-mercury amalgam was heated to evaporate the mercury and release the gold. The mercury vapor was recovered and returned to liquid form to be used again.

(Right) This photograph shows an interior view of the Deadwood Terra Gold Stamp Mill in Terraville, Dakota Territory, 1888. The stamp mill crew is cleaning out and tending to the machines.

(Below) An exterior view of the De Smet Gold Stamp Mill in Central City, Dakota, in 1888, shows the smokestacks of the steam engines at the far left, the long covered causeway connecting it with the mines, and the long flume for the mill's water supply.

"The Richest Mining District in the World"

The search for gold and silver never ceased, but as new technologies in the late nineteenth century transformed the economy, the great fortunes to be made and the hard-rock mining work to be had came from copper mines—extracting a metal that was not precious or valuable as currency, but was becoming vital to the American economy. The first surge of demand for copper came with the telegraph, invented in 1848. Creating an American telegraph network that spanned the nation required hundreds of thousands of miles of copper wire. In response, production expanded greatly in the mines of Michigan's "copper country," then the country's largest. In the 1880s, demand for copper expanded again due to a second, and far greater, wave of technological change—the development of electrical generating stations, and transmission lines that distributed power to homes, factories, and offices. Over the next decades, electric lights, electric motors, electric appliances, the radio, and the telephone would transform American life; in order to manufacture them, an increasingly electrified nation would consume enormous quantities of copper.

As demand accelerated, mining entrepreneurs scoured the mineral-rich West to find deposits of copper ore. The greatest find was in the town of

In the copper mines of Calumet, Michigan, miners in 1916 descend on a tram that will carry them almost a mile down the mine's sloped shaft.

The heavy timbering is a sign that these copper miners in Michigan, c. 1916, are working deep underground. Copper had far less value per weight than gold, so these miners were digging enormous amounts of copper ore, as we can see in the long line of heavily loaded carts that these miners are pushing to the unloading site.

Butte, in southwestern Montana. Copper miners came to work "under the hill" in Butte in 1895, and soon the immense diggings, wholly owned by the Anaconda Copper Company, were being called "the richest mining district in the world." Digging for copper in Butte, where mineshafts went more than 2,000 feet deep, was no less dangerous than working in the coal fields. In the deepest shaft of the Butte mines the temperature could rise as high as 107 degrees Fahrenheit, and the relative humidity was close to 100 percent. Most miners stayed because it was the only work they knew. These conditions, along with cave-ins, other mine accidents, and lung-damaging dust, exhausted all who worked there, injured most, and killed many outright. It is now estimated that between 1895 and 1950, over 2,200 miners died in Butte's honeycombed tunnels. Many of these deaths were not reported by Butte's daily newspaper, which also minimized its reporting of mine accidents; not coincidentally, it was owned by Anaconda Copper.

Not all copper was found thousands of feet under the earth as it was in Butte. Many huge deposits of low grade ore lay close to the surface. At the turn of the twentieth century, American mining engineers were developing "open-pit" techniques that could strip off the overlaying soil and rock so that copper ore could be efficiently excavated and hauled away. This new technology allowed miners to work aboveground—they dug, loaded, and hauled ore, but did not have to contend with tunnel collapses and explosions.

In 1906, open-pit copper-mining operations began in Bingham Canyon, Utah. As open-pit technology overtook deep mining in productivity, Bingham Canyon by the 1920s overtook Butte as the "richest hole on earth." Mining ended in Butte nearly sixty years ago but continues in Bingham Canyon to this day. Now that enormous trucks and excavators have replaced picks, shovels, and wagons, the mine produces the same quantity of copper now as it did a century ago, with a vastly smaller workforce. At ½ mile deep and 2½ miles across, it is one of the largest man-made excavations on the planet, visible from space with the naked eye. Since most of Butte's workings are underground, it is less dramatic from the air. Still, with its bleak expanse of mine heads, ore bins, and waste piles, it too is a striking industrial landscape. In a way that is both ironic and appropriate, both Bingham Canyon and Butte have become National Historic Landmarks. They are monuments to the immense and sometimes deadly labor of extracting copper from the earth, part of creating modern-day America.

A copper miner emptying a "tip car" of rock waste onto an ever-growing pile looks out at the smelters and processing plants of Butte, Montana, in 1905. The city was enriched by the copper industry, but it also became a landscape of industrial desolation.

(Above) Abandoned in the 1930s, the original head frame of the Butte Copper Mine dominates a desolate landscape.

(Left) In 1942, the stepped and terraced mountainside displays the working of the Utah Copper Company's huge open-pit mine in Bingham Canyon, Utah. Open-pit mining required enormous machines and relatively few workers. Looking tiny in the vast pit, a train of loaded ore cars passes by the mine's main shops.

On The Water

American fishermen—whalers on the faraway Arctic Ocean and Pacific grounds, trawlers for cod and haddock off the New England coast, oystermen on the Chesapeake shore—also wrestled with nature. From the beginning of European settlement, theirs was a commercial trade. They fished far less for subsistence, to feed their families, than to bring the sea's abundance to market. Like loggers, fishermen were comparatively small in numbers, always less than 1 percent of the workforce. Yet their work on the water, always physically taxing and sometimes extraordinarily risky, exerts a similar pull on our imaginations.

"A Boat Under Me"

Born in Portugal around 1890, Captain Joseph Captiva of Provincetown, Massachusetts, was a fisherman who made his living in the coastal waters off Cape Cod. Provincetown had a three-hundred-year-old fishing tradition, where men went out to catch cod, haddock, and flounder and took their hauls to the fish markets of Boston and sometimes New York. "Captain Joe is around fifty and looks a good deal younger," wrote Alice Kelly, who interviewed him for the WPA in 1938. "A little over medium height, he is exceedingly solid and powerful and is considered by everyone who knows him, 'one fine-lookin' feller.' " Kelly said, "I have given his story in his own words," but regretted that she couldn't convey "the singularly musical lilt" of his speech.

Arriving at nineteen, Captain Joe brought his family's Portuguese fishing traditions to America. In "the old country, we was all fishermen," he said, "me and my brothers. My father fish too. And his father." Alerted by relatives already in Massachusetts, he and his family had come for the prospect of "good money" and good fishing. "Anybody'll tell you," Captiva told Kelly, "they ain't no men can fish better than the Portuguese." Proud of his skills and his heritage, he could imagine no other way to live: "I wouldn't never be happy without I had a boat under me." By the 1920s, it was estimated that Portuguese and Portuguese Americans had 90 percent of the Cape Cod fisheries.

Captiva no longer worked for anyone else; he had his own boat. He was a trawler fisherman, using his sizable diesel-powered boat to "drag with big nets along the bottom" for bottom-feeding fish like cod, haddock, and flounder. He had recently invested in improvements to his boat, and fished with a crew of four: himself, two fishermen who also served respectively as engineer and cook, and his son Francis, who was in his early twenties. The crew divided the profits of the catch. "I get most because the boat, she's mine," he told Kelly, and "all the men takes their share."

(Facing page) **All trawler fishermen agreed that keeping the trawler's dragnets in repair was a constant battle. "While one net is down," noted the photographer in 1942, "a second is being mended by all hands aboard the Portuguese drag trawler,** *Francis and Marion.***"**

(Left) Portuguese fishermen are hauling in their catch off Cape Cod aboard the *Frances and Marion*.

(Below) In search of cod and flounder, the dragnet trawler *Frances and Marion* is heading out to sea from Provincetown harbor in the spring of 1942. Along with Captain Joe Captiva's similar vessel, she was part of the Provincetown trawler fleet, individually owned boats with small crews.

(Facing page) After bringing their catch to the Fulton Fish Market in New York, these Massachusetts fishermen take a brief moment of relaxation on their boat before heading back to the fishing grounds, c. 1943.

Indifference to weather and constant hard labor were accepted parts of the fisherman's life. This shines through in this early morning portrait of a fisherman rowing out to his anchored trawler at four thirty on a cold March morning in Provincetown Harbor, 1942.

He exulted in the physical challenge of his work, in struggling with storms, dealing with the heavy dragnets, and hauling the catch aboard on a wind-whipped, rocking boat. "I don't never get tired," he said. "I like to fight. Fight wind and cold and weather. I don't feel the cold no more." With lost boats and drowning accidents, commercial ocean fishing was more dangerous than mining. But he dismissed the hazards of his trade, saying, "I don't never get scared . . . I never think about drowning any more'n you think about danger in the streets." Still, to keep closer to his family, he had grown less adventurous. He no longer went out to fish the Grand Banks off Newfoundland, where the men would "stay away six months, work night and day." Instead, he fished closer to home, usually staying out for no more than a couple of days. "They's just as good fish near home," he explained, "and not so hard work.

"The boy's good fisherman," Captiva said of his son. Portuguese boys, he thought, were more likely to stay with fishing—"they do more like the old man." Captain Joe clearly looked forward to teaching him how to handle the vessel and the crew, since "the boat, she'll be his."

Joseph Captiva retained his self-confidence because his trade had not been destroyed by the Depression. He continued to be able to sell his catch, although prices fluctuated and credit was sometimes harder to find; "we make a big lot money some seasons, and then for a long time we're broke." Even so, he had been able to buy a new engine for his boat. Families still ate fish, and the destructive consequences of overfishing were still some decades in the future. Captain Joe acknowledged that his wife worried about him and their son when they went out to sea. But he knew that "she wouldn't really want me to come ashore. Her people was fishing folks too. She knows I wouldn't be no good on land."

HUNTERS OF THE SEA

Whalers were not true fishermen, with hooks and nets, but hunters. They tracked their warm-blooded prey, the largest creatures on Earth, across thousands of miles of ocean, caught them with harpoons, and killed them with lances thrown like javelins.

From the 1830s through the 1870s, whaling was both highly visible in American life and an important part of the nation's economy. At its peak in the 1850s the whaling fleet accounted for over seven hundred ships and eighteen thousand men. Whale ships sailed around the globe, but the business itself was highly concentrated. The great majority of whaling vessels embarked on their long voyages from the two ports of Nantucket and New Bedford in Massachusetts.

Whaling—with its bloody chases, years-long absences from home, and risk of violent death on the immense loneliness of the ocean—was a dramatic and deadly serious trade. But it owed its existence to the most prosaic demands of nineteenth-century domestic life. Whale oil—boiled, or "tried," from the animal's thick coat of blubber—was the clean-burning fuel that illuminated American houses, as oil lamps replaced flickering candles after 1820. Whale-

In this 1850 lithograph view of a sperm whale fishing ground in the Pacific, several ships have stopped to hunt a "pod" of whales, about a dozen of whom can be seen in the water. At the far left, the boat steerer or harpooner is preparing to strike at a whale. At the far right, a whale has been harpooned, and the line that holds it is visible, along with a flurry of blood. In the center, other whaleboats are pursuing whales. Two boats in the foreground are "stove"—crushed and broken up by a powerful blow from the flukes.

SPERM WHALING WITH ITS VARIETIES.

(Above) Whale ships are pictured in port, c. 1880, returning after a cruise that might last four years. Casks of oil—the products of a successful voyage—are on the dock.

(Right) In this American domestic scene from around 1840, the parlor is illuminated by an Argand lamp that burns sperm whale oil.

bone—actually the tooth-like lattice of baleen found in the mouth of the right whale—was indispensable to women's fashion, since it was used to stiffen corsets. Whalers pursued and killed these great animals so that American parlors could be well lit and American women could be fashionably slender.

New Englanders had been hunting and killing whales in small numbers near shore since the late seventeenth century, but the search for ever more oil and whalebone made whaling in the nineteenth century a business of great distances. Whale ships cruised into the Arctic or far into the Pacific Ocean, seeking the grounds where whales could be found in larger numbers. Every voyage was driven by the imperative to produce—to fill the ship with casks of oil and bundles of whalebone, and then to return successfully to port. Whalers were constantly on the watch. The first duty of every sailor was to "sing out" when a whale or its telltale spout was sighted; captains often forbade loud conversation, singing, and whistling on deck to avoid scaring off the whales, whose hearing was acute.

A young woman is pictured in 1899 wearing an expensive corset that has given her the whalebone-reinforced "hourglass figure" required by the high-fashion standards of the time.

A whaleboat with its six-man crew is shown, c. 1860, attacking a "right," or baleen whale. As the boat closes in, the harpooner is preparing to strike, attaching a line—actually a heavy rope—to the whale. Next the harpooner and boat header at the back will exchange places and the mate will kill the whale with his lance.

Whaling was like war, with long periods of boring shipboard routine punctuated with bursts of deadly excitement. Its dramatic and bloody centerpiece was the chase. When a whale was sighted, the ship lowered its boats in pursuit. Whaleboats were strongly built craft, usually with a crew of six. The boat header—usually one of the ship's mates, or officers—was in command. Second to him was the boat steerer or harpooner, who, as the boat approached the whale, stood in the bow with his harpoon—a steel-tipped spear with barbs designed to hold the animal fast, and attached to 1,500 feet of line.

"I leap in the lowered boat, we row toward our prey where he lies," Walt Whitman wrote of the whaleboat's attack in *Leaves of Grass* (1867), imagining himself as one of the boat's oarsmen. "We approach stealthy and silent." He described "the mountainous mass" of the whale; still unaware, "lethargic, basking." Then came the harpooner's strike: "I see the weapon dart from his vigorous arm," he wrote, and the wounded whale swam to escape, running out the harpoon line, towing the boat on a long and veering chase—what whalemen called a "Nantucket sleigh ride."

Finally, the exhausted whale ceased to run, and the boat moved in for the kill. The harpooner moved from bow to stern, switching places with the boat header, a difficult feat on a pitching boat. The boat header proceeded to finish the whale with a long, steel-barbed lance, "driven through his side," as Whitman wrote, "press'd deep, turn'd in the wound." Then the great creature died spouting blood, with "one convulsive leap . . . then flat and still in the bloody foam."

Once the whale was killed, the frantic excitement of the chase gave way to the tedious work of butchering. The whale had to be towed back and lashed to the ship, so that the grisly process of severing the head and peeling the thick blanket of blubber could begin. The most skilled crewmen—usually the captain and mates—attacked the carcass with 16-foot-long cutting spades. After the initial cuts had been made, one of the harpooners took a perilous leap from the pitching deck onto the whale's back. Keeping his footing on the slippery carcass, he attached the "blubber hook," linked to a massive chain that would "unwrap" the blubber from the body in a 6-foot-wide strip.

These whalemen, c. 1930, are shown stripping the blubber from a whale carcass.

Then the blubber would be cut into sections, sliced into ever smaller pieces, and then "minced" into narrow strips. The strips, called "Bible leaves" for their thinness, were finally readied for boiling in the great "try pots" that were set up on deck in seagoing brick hearths. For two or three days, almost the whole ship's company worked long shifts to keep the fires burning and the try pots filled, as every scrap of blubber was rendered into oil, poured into casks, and taken below for storage. William Abbe, who sailed on a whaler in the late 1850s, remembered the miseries of the work. Wearing "clothes soaked with oil," crewmen wrestled with firewood, blubber, and barrels, "slipping and stumbling on the sloppy decks" made slick with oil and blood.

The American popular press of the 1840s and '50s often portrayed whaling as a thrilling adventure undertaken by daring young men. But the romance of whaling was mostly illusory. Life on a whale ship, wrote former crew member Ben-Ezra Stiles Ely in 1849, was "one of many hardships, and of few bright prospects. It demoralizes most persons who devote themselves to it." The adrenaline rush of the chase aside, whaling was miserable work, and poorly paid. The whale ship's hierarchy was almost military, and the captain's power virtually absolute. Some observers likened service on a whale ship to temporary slavery. Discipline was rigid and could be harsh; until 1850, recalcitrant crew members might be flogged. In a ship on an active whaling ground, the hours of work were long and sleep was limited. "We have to work like horses and live like hogs," complained young Robert Weir, who shipped out on the *Clara Bell* in 1855. All but the captain and mates slept in cramped, unpleasant, and often foul quarters. Food was salt meat and hard biscuits, bad more often than not, and sometimes scanty. Scurvy, a disease of severe vitamin C deficiency due to the limited shipboard diet, could make sailors' lives miserable, or even kill them. Accidents were numerous.

Although whalemen felt little romance, they needed and admired bravery. "In this business of whaling," former whaleman Herman Melville wrote in his great novel, *Moby-Dick: or, the Whale*, "courage was one of the great staple outfits of the ship, like her beef and her bread." Chasing whales was exciting but very dangerous. Tangled up in rapidly uncoiling harpoon lines, men could lose fingers, hands, even feet, or be pulled overboard. Some whales fought back before they were killed; a blow from their powerful tail flukes could kill a man instantly or destroy a boat. Sperm whales, which had teeth rather than whalebone, were doubly dangerous; their scythe-like jaws were as deadly as their tails. Seasoned whale hunters were not without fear, but they were accustomed to the hazards of their trade. Melville described one of the *Pequod's* mates, Stubb, "taking perils as they came with an indifferent air . . . calm and collected, as if a journeyman joiner engaged for the year."

Whalers were a rough and various lot. Captains and mates, with few exceptions, were white Yankees, but crewmen could be found in all shades of white, black, red, and brown: whites from across the United States, Portuguese, African Americans, Native Americans, South Sea Islanders, West Indians. Captains justified their harsh discipline by claiming that many in the crew were ignorant and brutal men who needed to be controlled. Crew members often responded by deserting their ships, and captains found themselves recruiting fresh hands in their ports of call. Once in port, whalemen were notorious, even among sailors, for drinking, carousing, and pursuing women.

Whaling began its long decline in America with the development of cheaper and more-efficient sources of nighttime lighting. Plants that manufactured and distributed "coal gas" for illumination were built in a number of American cities in the 1850s. Kerosene, at first extracted from coal and naturally occurring asphalt, was a superior lighting fuel, but could be produced only in limited amounts. When petroleum was discovered in the United States in 1859, it provided a virtually unlimited supply for kerosene production. Manufactured gas in large cities, and kerosene everywhere else, soon replaced whale oil in American parlors, kitchens, and offices. The whaling fleet diminished from seven hundred ships to fewer than two hundred by the late 1870s, and its decline marked the fall of the economic fortunes of New Bedford and Nantucket.

What kept American whaling alive at all into the early twentieth century was the continued demand for whalebone in women's fashion; although cheaper stiffening materials became available for corsets, well-to-do women insisted on more expensive baleen under their clothes. Late-nineteenth-century whalers, intent on harvesting baleen, often abandoned the blubber entirely, and bowhead whales, which had the most baleen, were hunted nearly to extinction. Finally, between 1900 and 1910, the corseted hourglass figure, dominant since the 1850s, went permanently out of fashion. The market for whalebone collapsed, and American whaling lost its last reason for existence.

In its April 1861 issue, *Vanity Fair* imagines the whales celebrating the discovery of oil in Pennsylvania; kerosene would soon displace whale oil for lighting, pushing American whaling into irreversible decline.

TONGING FOR OYSTERS

Oysters can be found in many places along America's Atlantic coast, but their richest source has always been the great Chesapeake Bay estuary where they grow in the muddy bottoms of its tidal rivers and creeks, and along the deeply indented shores of the bay itself. In the early years of European settlement they were harvested by hand, by men and women wading into the water and picking them out of their shallow beds. But as population and demand for oysters grew, fishermen were impelled to gather them from deeper "oyster bars" farther offshore. Probably no later than the late seventeenth century, Chesapeake watermen began using oyster tongs, which became the tool and symbol of their trade.

Most of the oyster tongers who lived around Chesapeake Bay, wrote R. H. Edmonds in his 1881 history of the industry, were skilled enough at their work, but in his condescending view they were also "illiterate, indolent and improvident." About two-thirds of them were white, the rest "Negro." Living amid the great bounty of the Bay, they did not have enough need to work hard to make them satisfactory citizens. "A tongman can, at any time, take his canoe or skiff and catch . . . a few bushels of oysters," Edmonds told

Standing near the bow of his boat, c. 1905, a Maryland tonger feels for oysters at the bottom of the bay. His catch is on the culling board beside him.

In this "Song of the Tongs," from the humor magazine *Puck* in 1905, the words are a racist caricature while the image provides a vibrant depiction of an African American oyster tonger at work. It was estimated in 1881 that about one-third of all Chesapeake tongers were black.

his readers, "for which there is always a market." He could sell his oysters when he needed money for his family, catch fish in the summer, shoot ducks and eat oysters in the winter, "live in comparative comfort," and have a little cash left over "to be spent for strong drink." In circumstances like this, he complained, "it is almost impossible to get them to do any steady farm work." Tongers supplied the demand for oysters from respectable families in the cities, but outsiders saw them as far from respectable themselves.

Tools:

OYSTER TONGS

Nobody is sure precisely when and by whom oyster tongs were invented. Certainly they were traditional tools by the early eighteenth century, and by the beginning of the nineteenth they were being used by thousands of oystermen. Oyster tongs were designed to reach the bay or river bottom from a boat and gather up the harvest. Usually over 20 feet long, they were a pair of wooden shafts hinged like an enormous pair of scissors. Below the hinge were two long-tined metal rakes facing each other. Standing up in his boat, the waterman held up his tongs, spread them open, and carefully lowered them to the bottom. The tongs were heavy, and hard to manage because of their length, but an experienced waterman could use them to feel for the oysters. "An old oysterman," said James Hicks, describing a family work tradition that went back to the 1880s, "he can take the tongs, and he can feel on the bottom whether it's oysters or shells with . . . the feel of the iron heads." Once the oysterman had located the oysters, he closed the tongs, gathered them up between the rake heads, and lifted them to the deck of his small boat. Then they could be sorted, bad ones and empty shells tossed back, and the rest readied for sale.

Oystering with tongs was slow and patient work; unless a bed was particularly rich, each pass with the tongs, called a "lick," might bring up only a few oysters. It also required a great deal of strength; unusually muscular arms and shoulders distinguished tongers from men whose work was less physically demanding. Tonging also "necessitated very great exposure to the cold," as Edmonds noted. Oysters were harvested in the colder months, from September through April, and tongmen spent their days standing upright on small boats without shelters.

Standing on opposite sides of the boat, oyster tongers in Rock Point, Maryland, 1941, drop their catch on the "culling board" at the stern.

Quicker, more-efficient ways to harvest oysters arrived in the nineteenth century. By 1830, the oyster dredge appeared in the Chesapeake, brought in by New England oystermen who had nearly exhausted their own region's catch. The dredge was a cage of iron mesh, dragged by a boat along the bottom; its iron teeth scraped up the oysters and guided them into its mouth. Dredging was much faster than tonging, and "dredge boats" multiplied; their crews worked more like trawler fishermen, throwing out the dredges behind the boat, hauling them up when they were full, and storing the catch. Mechanically operated tongs appeared in 1890, operated first by hand cranks and then by powered winches.

But hand tonging survived, albeit with a declining fraction of the total catch. Tongers cherished their independence, and clung to their traditional lifeways on the shore. Their costs were small, so their prices could remain

"Market boats" sailed the Chesapeake Bay, waiting to buy oysters from tongers. Here, a tonger—his small boat pulled up against the larger one—delivers his catch, c. 1905.

(Above left) **A long line of iron oyster dredges, ready for use in the Bay fisheries, sit on a Baltimore street in 1905. Dragged behind an oyster boat, their frames scraped the oysters off the bottom and caught them in the iron mesh.**

(Above right) **Two African American women and a man stand in the yard of a small oyster tonger's house on Chesapeake Bay, 1905. "Having secured a house," R. H. Edmonds complained of oystermen's families, "but little time or money is spent on improving it."**

competitive in the marketplace. Some worked steadily to accumulate savings, and a few were respectable farmers who oystered in their spare time. But most were more casual. "Owning a small house and an acre or so of land," Edmonds wrote, along with a boat or a share in one with a father or brother, they were content. The men who worked on dredge boats labored for others.

The boat owners and dredgers who used the new techniques were driven to produce, to harvest enough to meet an ever-increasing demand, particularly as faster transportation and refrigeration expanded the distance that fresh oysters could be shipped. Concerns that the continued expansion of dredging would lead to overharvesting and destruction of the oyster beds were already being voiced in 1881; "the hitherto seemingly exhaustless beds of the Chesapeake may be exhausted, if the present rate of dredging is continued," warned Edmonds. Regulation and limitation would eventually be needed to prevent an "oyster-famine."

Edmonds thought that the tongmen's casual, unambitious, and disorderly ways marked them not only as shiftless but as relics of the past. But in an important sense, their way of work would be part of the future. After much destruction, confusion, and conflict, dredging and mechanized oyster harvesting have now come to be strictly limited to protect the oyster beds and the ecology of the Bay. Hand tonging is again the most common way of oystering. Harvesting oysters patiently with tongs, "lick" by "lick," is now an act of ecological responsibility.

BOOMTOWNS AND ROUSTABOUTS:
WORK IN THE OIL FIELDS

The very earth seems greasy, and the streams are coated with the steel-blue scum of petroleum. —ROBERT FERGUSON, 1865

In August 1865, Scottish traveler Robert Ferguson was on a journey deep into America's recently discovered oil fields, in the northwestern counties of Pennsylvania. He passed through Titusville, where the first oil well had been sunk in 1859, bringing up the "rock oil" that had at times bubbled up to the surface and had long been ignored as a nuisance. In the next six years, petroleum had become an immensely valuable commodity as techniques were developed to refine crude oil into kerosene, and to adapt lamps and lanterns to burn the new fuel. Cheaper and cleaner-burning than whale oil, kerosene quickly became the most widely used illuminant in the world and pushed American whaling into irreversible decline. As this became clear, *Vanity Fair* ran a cartoon showing a group of formally dressed whales "celebrating" the discovery of the oil wells of Pennsylvania, shown on page 209.

Celebrating the success of the early oil industry, a group of men and women pose atop one of the large wooden storage tanks of the Leroy Well in the Pennsylvania oil fields, in the mid-1860s, while two workers stand at the top of the derrick.

In this view, the oil-drilling and -pumping equipment of 1891 is contrasted with the "primitive" technology of 1859 at the first oil well in Titusville, Pennsylvania.

(Facing page) This stereographic view of the Pithole, Pennsylvania, oil field in 1866 shows oil-drilling derricks, large wooden storage tubs, and workers busy filling smaller barrels with oil and loading them on horse-drawn wagons.

AN OIL BOOMTOWN: PITHOLE, PENNSYLVANIA

As Robert Ferguson disembarked from the train of the Oil Creek railway at its depot in Venango County, he found enormous piles of oil barrels waiting for transport and a powerful stench of petroleum in the air. There were also signs warning newcomers to TAKE CARE OF YOUR POCKETS, an indication of the oil region's notorious lawlessness. Ferguson boarded a lightly built open carriage headed for the boomtown of Pithole, and bounced for 6 miles over roads that were rutted, muddy, and blackly slick with oil.

Pithole was an astonishing place. Before January 1865 the town had not existed. On January 8 a great gusher was struck in an open field, quickly named the United States Well. Other highly productive wells were soon discovered nearby, and thousands of oil seekers streamed into the area. By the time Ferguson arrived, Pithole had become "a city eight months old—with ten thousand inhabitants, twelve hotels, a daily paper, a 'Temple of Fashion,' billiard-rooms innumerable, a theatre, and an 'Academy of Music' "—not to mention taverns, brothels, and many flimsy boardinghouses. Oil was "the be-all and end-all of existence" in the town, Ferguson noted; "if you hear two men talking together, it is certain to be about flowing wells, and pumping wells, and so many barrels a day."

This early oil refinery, c. 1870, in Erie, Pennsylvania, is transforming crude oil into kerosene, which will be barreled and shipped all over the world.

Most of the primarily male inhabitants of Pithole were oil field workers, along with a few dozen "oil princes" who owned the wells and had their own boxes at the theater. But just as in the California Gold Rush, there were thousands more who had come to profit from supplying the workers' needs, from food and lodging to entertainment and illicit pleasures. And then there were hundreds whose work was more shadowy, men who accosted unwary newcomers on the town's muddy streets. They were speculators, Ferguson discovered, looking to raise money for a new drilling venture, or outright confidence men, "lying in wait to let you in for some newly-formed oil-stock."

Out in the oil fields, Ferguson saw men clambering over the wooden derricks that supported the steel drills that bored new wells, raised and lowered by hundreds of stationary steam engines. Other workers tended steam-powered pumps or tapped the large storage tanks, incessantly filling barrels with oil that would be taken by wagon to the railhead. A heavy film of oil covered everything, including clothing, hands, and faces.

The oddest oil workers whom Ferguson encountered were the "oil smellers." They were the heirs to an ancient European and later, American, folk tradition of dowsing for water with a hazel wand—a practice that many American farmers believed was the best way to locate new well sites or hidden springs.

But these men dowsed for oil. An oil smeller walked over the ground holding a forked hazel bough upright in front of him, Ferguson reported, "till on coming to the spot where oil is to be found, it is claimed that the rod suddenly turns round in his hand till the stem points to the ground." Ferguson was told that the possessors of this rare talent could make "a professional living by it," but he made no estimate of how many wells oil smellers had discovered.

Oil, unlike coal, could be extracted quickly from the earth; Pennsylvania's coal-mining communities remained for generations, while its oil towns usually had much shorter life spans.

Although the Pennsylvania oil fields as a whole would remain productive into the twentieth century, Pithole was destined to collapse almost as quickly as it came into being. Ferguson had arrived at the town's peak of population and prosperity. By early 1866, its wells were drying up, taking with them the sole reason for the community's existence. Seeking new opportunities, oil men—from "oil princes" to "oil smellers"—poured out of Pithole as fast as they had poured in, and two destructive fires swept through its hastily constructed buildings. Within a year its population declined from fifteen thousand to two thousand, and by 1870, Pithole was an empty ghost town—an early and extreme example of the boom-and-bust cycle that would define work in the oil fields.

"DISCOVER OIL, COAX IT OUT OF THE GROUND, STORE IT, AND SHIP IT"

As demand continued to increase, exploration for oil went far beyond the borders of Pennsylvania, and oil fields were discovered in California and in the Midwest. But in 1901 the industry was transformed almost overnight when the Spindletop gusher, by far the largest oil strike up to that time, came in near Beaumont, Texas. Hundreds of oil companies were incorporated within a year, and over the next decade, tens of thousands of workers poured into the oil fields of Texas and Oklahoma. The industry's center of gravity moved from Pennsylvania to the Southwest.

Without a change in the market for petroleum, the enormous discoveries in the Southwest would only have produced a huge oversupply and drastically falling prices. Instead, they coincided with the development of the internal combustion engine, which ran on gasoline—previously considered an almost useless by-product of the oil-refining process. The number of gasoline-powered vehicles in the United States grew with astonishing speed, from eight thousand in 1900 to four hundred thousand in 1910, and nearly ten million in 1920. The American motorcar created a huge and ever-expanding demand for oil. This was just in time, as it turned out, because the market for

Oil wells in the field called the Merchants' Gusher, part of the great Spindletop strike in Beaumont, Texas, in 1901. The drill rig has been removed from the derrick in the center of the picture, replaced by an oil pump connected by pipes to a storage tank.

kerosene was waning. In the first decade of the twentieth century, the kerosene lamp would lose its dominance to another innovation, Edison's electric lightbulb.

Oil added a third dynamic of boom and bust to the region's economy, already shaped by cattle ranching and semi-arid farming. The industry brought new jobs for many, and long-term opportunities for some. Gerald Forbes, an early chronicler of the oil boom, recounted how farmers in the oil-rich regions of Oklahoma "were attracted from their fields and crops by the high wages" that the oil companies would pay for unskilled labor. "I never did go back to the range anymore," said Rowdy Buell of Katy, Texas, who left his work as a cowboy for the oil fields around 1910. "I made a lot more money wet nursing oil wells," he recalled, "than I ever did punching dogies along and riding hoss."

Work in the industry was determined by the cycle of exploration, drilling, production, and decline, as well as by changes in price and demand. Exhausted wells and fields were abandoned, and workers moved on to the next strike. When gushers arrived in remote locations, as they usually did, they generated thousands of jobs in hastily built camps, with men, and even entire families, living in tents and flimsy shacks. Some oil towns, like McCamey, Texas, outlasted the oil boom and became permanent communities. Most disappeared when the oil ran out. Oil field men—from "roughneck" laborers and foremen (called "gang pushers") to engineers and managers—were among the most transient of American workers, moving constantly from one oil lease to another as oil was struck in one place and ran out in another.

Forbes described how the first drilling crews would descend on a thinly settled county of farms and ranches, creating a separate community of oil derricks and hell-raising in their midst—an oil boomtown. The drillers were young, well-paid by the standards of the region, mostly single, and, as Forbes lamented, "without the stabilizing influences of family and property." Like

(Above) **This panoramic view of the Burke-Burnett oil field in Texas in 1919, with over one hundred wells visible, shows the vast extent of the southwestern oil strikes.**

(Facing page) **A customer pumps gas at a Dome Gas service station in Takoma Park, Maryland, in 1921. Also in the picture are two other elements of the gasoline distribution system—a railroad tank car and a gasoline tank truck.**

At a well in Kilgore, Texas, c. 1939, three workers are on the derrick floor. Two are loosening a section of drill pipe using heavy wrenches, while the third, most likely a "gang pusher" or foreman, looks on.

their predecessors in American mining towns, lumber camps, and whaling ports, they worked long and difficult hours and wanted "recreation and entertainment when not on duty." And just as before, their wants were supplied by "bootleggers, gamblers and prostitutes, ever willing to separate the oil field worker from his pay," who put up their own tents and shacks near those of their customers.

Oil field work was not as risky as mining, but it had real dangers nonetheless. The steam boilers that powered pumps and drills could explode. Constant exposure to petroleum was not good for the lungs, eyes, or skin, and oil in storage could generate lethal vapors. In the 1920s, simply gauging (measuring) the depth of the oil storage tanks was a hazardous enterprise. The gauger would climb a long run of wooden steps to the top of the tank and open the hatch, but before dropping in his measuring line, he would, as the daughter of one oil field worker remembered, "run a little way up the catwalk to wait for the first rush of poison gas to be carried away by the air." If a man didn't wait for the toxic cloud to disperse, or returned to the hatch too soon, he could be poisoned, sometimes fatally.

Perhaps the greatest danger came from working close to the well itself. Tons of steel drilling tools hung high in the derrick, suspended on thick cables and powered by steam-driven winches. A frayed cable or a cracked

pulley could kill. "J. E. Ray, aged about 25 years, was killed instantly Monday night," read an obituary in the Wilson, Oklahoma, *Gazette* for July 20, 1920, "while working on an oil well on the Carter lease." As he worked on the well platform, a heavy piece of machinery had fallen off the cable and crushed his head. "This is one hell of a way to make a living," a Mexia, Texas, oil worker said in 1923 after a friend had died in a boiler explosion, "and if I didn't have to do it, I'd never work another day in a damned oil field."

Eyewitness:

Estha Briscoe Stowe, "An Itinerant Oil Field Family"

Born in 1916, Estha Briscoe Stowe had spent her first few years of life on the small cotton farm in Waldrip, Texas, that her parents, John and Vina, were working on shares. In 1920 her father, eager for better opportunities, heard that there was work available in the oil fields, "paying five dollars a day for unskilled labor." As she wrote in her account of her early years, *Oil Field Child*, "he felt compelled to give it a try." With that decision, she recalled, "we became an itinerant oil field family." For the next nine years the Briscoes followed John's work, moving just about every year to a new oil field. At every move they found rough housing in just-built encampments, living at various times in tents, cabins with low walls and canvas roofs, a curtained-off corner of a bunkhouse, even an unused tool shed—and, once or twice, a company house. John followed the oil and the call of higher wages. He rose from the ranks of unskilled roustabouts to become a foreman, or "gang pusher," supervising crews that installed the pipes that connected wells to storage tanks.

Most oil field workers were not married men with children, so the Briscoes were in the minority. They formed neighborly bonds with the other families that shared their itinerant life. Estha's mother struggled with leaky roofs and sandstorms, rudimentary stoves and sanitation, and cramped quarters. Her husband was determined to save enough money from his wages to set himself up as a country storekeeper, and she shared his ambition.

Estha herself grew up as "an oil field kid," picking up the schooling that the camps and boomtowns offered, and finding friends among the few other children. The oil fields were their playground, and they "learned early to stay away from all company equipment the way city kids learn to stay out of the streets. Each lease was dotted with tanks, racks of pipe, cable tool drilling rigs, old boilers, and other paraphernalia used to discover oil, coax it out of the ground, store it, and ship it. There were no fences to keep us out of danger, and our tent homes were always located near some of these things."

Oil field children knew about above-ground steam lines, dangerous, perpetually operating oil pumps, and "slush pits" that caught what was brought up out of the hole during drilling, "filled with greasy water and slimy drilling mud." They watched as heavy equipment was hauled around the site. In 1921, oil companies still used multiple teams of mules; by 1925, there were "trucks and

An oil field laborer, or roustabout, soaked with sweat, rests briefly on an August day in the Texas Seminole field, 1939. His crew has been digging ditches for oil pipes that will connect wells and storage tanks.

tractors, just coming into use . . . much faster, but not so much fun to watch."

After every explosion and accident, Estha wrote, "my parents talked of leaving the hazardous oil fields," but they felt forced to wait until they had saved enough. Finally, in August 1928, John Briscoe bought a grocery store in Graford, Texas, and the family left their itinerant life for good. John Briscoe had been both careful and reasonably fortunate. He had emerged from a decade in the oil fields with enough money to start a business, and with his health more or less intact.

An oil field worker in Kilgore, Texas, takes a break near the derrick, next to the tools his crew will soon be using. Estha Briscoe Stowe recalled: "Roustabouts had their own terms for many tools and operations used on the rig floor, and a new man, called a greenhorn, had to learn in a hurry if he wanted to survive."

Chapter 4

Power and Production

(Overleaf) **Leopold Daigneau, a mule spinner at the Chace Cotton Mill in Burlington, Vermont, poses with his young assistant in 1909. Operating the more complex spinning mule, which made the finest thread, was the most physically demanding job for a textile operative. Better paid than work at the spinning frame, it demanded considerable strength and was usually done by men. Mule spinners frequently harassed women who tried the work.**

AMERICA'S MACHINE AGE

In 1864, the Anglo-American writer Thomas Nichols observed that America had become the preeminent land of the machine, and he celebrated the achievement. Nichols visited hundreds of different factories, "full of machinery in rapid motion," powered by water and steam. He watched thousands of intricately moving machines make cloth, wire, pins, clocks, watches, buttons, nails, rivets, boot lasts, shingles, house doors, and mirror frames. The English had invented the railway and the locomotive, he noted, but it was Americans who had already built 30,000 miles of track and were using the railroad to conquer the continent.

All of this stemmed, he was sure, from an ingrained American preference for "every kind of labour-saving machinery," a two-hundred-year-old tradition of mechanical ingenuity. "Would any one but an American have ever invented a milking machine?" he asked. "Or a machine to beat eggs? Or machines to black boots, scour knives, pare apples, and do a hundred things that all other peoples have done with their ten fingers from time immemorial?" Americans did believe in the millennium, he concluded; for them it was a vision of a future "time when machines will do everything."

In his exuberant celebration of American power and production, Nichols was thinking only about abundant output and impressive technology. The workers were somehow secondary, required only "to watch the machines and supply them with material." Eventually, Americans might make work disappear completely.

Fifty years after Nichols's visit, the English writer Stephen Graham took a much darker view of American machinery and American work. While Nichols had celebrated the power of America's machines, Graham found it frightening. He was struck by the expanding practice of time and motion study in American industries like steel manufacturing, which used photography and film to break down every task into its component parts, and then retrained workers for maximum efficiency. "Each man," he lamented, "is drilled to act like a machine, and the drilling enters into the fibre of his being." In factories, Graham claimed that human beings had simply become the living links between "immense complicated engines," so that "flesh and blood is grafted into steel and oil." American companies took "the last ounce of energy out of their employees," and as for those who could no longer produce, "they are the old iron, and their place is the scrap-heap."

Both observers were right, in part. The achievements of American technology and industrial organization that Nichols wrote about were very real. They led to vastly increased productivity and a sustained, long-term rise in the overall standard of living. But, as Graham saw, the human costs of

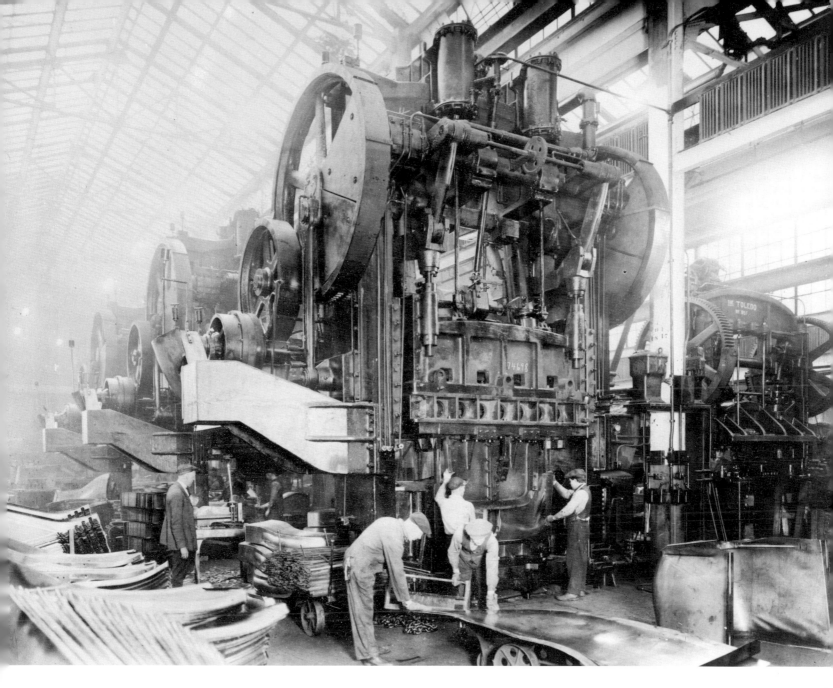

Workers operate the stamping presses that are turning out steel panels for auto bodies at the Dodge Main plant in Hamtramck, Michigan, 1915. *Historic American Building Survey.*

industrialization were high. Risks and rewards were distributed very un-equally, and workers' health and safety were rarely considered. Managers and workers struggled for control in the workplace, and the managers usually won. Workers had little protection against mass unemployment during eco-nomic downturns, and many of the new mechanized workplaces were brutal environments. At the same time, industrial workers built lives for themselves and their families. Most achieved only intermittent, precarious security. Yet, many found opportunity for improvement, and still more were able to pass it on to their children.

As the nation moved from an economy based on agriculture and crafts to one of large-scale mechanized production, tens of millions of Americans learned the ways of machinery. They built railroads, tended looms in textile factories, labored on the meat-packing lines, handled red-hot ingots in steel mills, assembled automobiles, stood at lathes creating intricate metal shapes, or drove electric-powered streetcars along their routes. The American quest for power and production is made up of their stories.

THE LATHE HAND AND THE MOTORMAN

Both my father, Jack Larkin Sr., and my wife's father, Edward Walter Bauman, were very good with machines. Jack and Ed were both handsome city boys—one from Chicago and one from Elizabeth, New Jersey—who had taken a two-year technical course in high school. They shared something else: They both entered the workforce at perhaps the worst possible time in American history, the Depression years of the mid-1930s. In one way or another, they continued to work with machinery all their lives, but followed diverging paths. Both men were true children of America's machine age.

About sixty strong, the workers in the machine room of the Thomas and Betts Company pose on the factory floor in 1938. Edward Walter Bauman, my father-in-law, is the handsome young man with black hair, in the fourth row back, third from the right. *Author photo.*

A machinist turns an aircraft part on a lathe in a production shop, 1942.

Ed was the orphaned child of Polish immigrants who had been informally adopted at a very young age by Gustav Bauman, a German machinist. He remembered scavenging in the Elizabeth railroad yards for scraps of coal, eating only potatoes for supper, and picking up pitchers of beer for his father at the local tavern. With his older brother Joe and "Pop" Bauman, he grew up in the city's industrial center. For several years they lived across the street from the sprawling plant of the Thomas and Betts Company, a manufacturer of electrical equipment and fittings. After he turned eighteen, Ed went there to work as a "lathe hand," taking on his adoptive father's occupation. He learned the machinist's trade, setting up and running the precision machines that made connectors and switch components—the little-seen but indispensable conduits of electric power.

Ed was fortunate to find work in 1936, and he repaid his employer with loyalty; he worked at Thomas and Betts for forty-seven years. Edward Walter Bauman followed a classic American path of upward mobility. Coming up out of near-poverty, he was cheerful and full of energy but usually self-contained, committed to hard work and success. At night he took courses to learn more mathematics and improve his writing skills; on the shop floor he studied ways to make the manufacturing process more efficient. During the war, he was not allowed to enlist because his work was ruled essential to the war effort. He rose from lathe hand to machinist, from assistant foreman to foreman, and then into management. This was sometimes a bumpy ride, with a few reversals along the way. He was not, he was quick to say, very good at

In 1942, Jack Larkin Sr. had just completed his U.S. Navy training as a diesel mechanic.
Author photo.

(Facing page) Gasoline pump at a Shell station, c. 1940.

office "politics." My father-in-law was not at all a boastful man, but he was proud of his achievements and the complexity of his work. He was at home among the workers and machines on the factory floor.

Jack Larkin Sr. took after his father, Morris, who ran refrigeration machinery at the stockyards; like Ed, he was also handy with tools and engines. Jack was fascinated with automobiles and worked on them when he had a chance; as the youngest in the family, he enjoyed driving his oldest brother Bill's car. His brothers and sisters said that he had "gasoline legs"—would always find an excuse to take the car even for a short errand, rather than walk. Steady work was hard to find in Chicago in the 1930s, and for some years he found odd jobs, including a brief stint in the "steel mills"—the vast South Side Works of Carnegie Steel.

By the late 1930s Jack had found employment as a sheet-metal worker, building and installing ductwork for heating and ventilation—an industrialized descendant of the tinsmith. His life, like millions of others, was changed by the war. He joined the navy after Pearl Harbor, was chosen for training as a diesel engine mechanic for a new class of diesel-powered ships, and spent the war on anti-submarine duty in the North Atlantic.

After the war, he briefly tried white-collar work in an insurance agency, discovered that he couldn't stand office routines, and then found a way to do what he had always wanted to do: Partnering with an old friend, he opened a Shell Oil filling station and garage on Stony Island Avenue in Chicago. Both men would pump gas and change tires; Jack would work on cars, and his friend would keep the books. Sadly, the partner was an embezzler. Over the course of a couple of years, he falsified the books, drained the cash, and then disappeared, leaving only the partnership's debts behind. My father's dream of the gas station and garage disappeared as well.

In 1948, he badly needed a job, and found one as a "motorman" for the Chicago Consolidated Surface Lines, driving not an automobile but a trolley car. Later, as the street railway tracks and overhead lines disappeared from the city's streets, he drove a bus for what had become the Chicago Transit Authority. This was the work that he would do for the rest of his life. My childhood memories are of his uniform with its shiny buttons, his coin changer, and the pads of unused transfers he brought home. It was perfectly honorable work, but I later came to understand that for him, it signified a kind of defeat. For years he worked on "split shifts"—four hours on, three hours idle and unpaid, and then another four hours of work. He endured the physical pounding of guiding heavy vehicles on city streets and the stress of dealing with difficult passengers.

He was a kind and often humorous man, an exceptionally good driver who knew every street in Chicago, but he did not like his work. He had no

A streetcar motorman in Washington, D.C., in 1936 stares intently at the track ahead.

use for the Transit Authority's management and little more regard for the transit employees' union, which he saw as run for the benefit of its leaders. As far as he was concerned, neither organization responded to the real needs and grievances of the workers. He wanted something else, but was never able to find it.

TEXTILE WORKERS

BEGINNINGS

When Charles Dickens visited Lowell, Massachusetts, in 1841, the factory city was one of America's great tourist attractions, ranking with Niagara Falls. It was so new, he marveled, less than two decades old, with its "fresh buildings of bright red brick and painted wood." Even the powerful Merrimac, "the very river that moves the machinery in the mills (for they are all worked by water power)," seemed to him a youthful and tumbling stream. Lowell was a city of cotton and woolen factories, at that time the fastest-growing place in the United States.

A view of the textile factories of Lowell, Massachusetts, from across the Merrimac River, c. 1850.

But it wasn't just the scale of Lowell and the speed of its growth that interested Dickens; it was also what the city seemed to promise for the future. He acclaimed Lowell as a community with factories but without a permanent class of factory workers. "There is no manufacturing population in Lowell, so to speak," he wrote, "for these girls (often the daughters of small farmers) come from other States, remain a few years in the mills, and then go home for good." This offered hope, he thought, that the Industrial Revolution could come to the United States without the great social evils that it had brought to Britain, where a large population of surplus workers, low wages, illiteracy, alcoholism, and bad housing had created industrial cities that Dickens called "great haunts of desperate misery."

Although they certainly wished to avoid creating factory towns like Manchester, England, the merchants, manufacturers, and bankers who built Lowell were not primarily interested in social reform. What they really wanted was relatively cheap, reliable, and tractable labor. What better source, they reasoned, than the moral and industrious daughters of the New England countryside? They recruited their factory operatives from young unmarried

(Above) **Kirk Boott was one of the principal builders of Lowell. The Boott Mills were the city's largest and stayed in operation from 1825 until 1956.**

(Right) **An owner and an overseer converse while mill girls walk into the Middlesex Woolen Company, Lowell, Massachusetts, c. 1848.** *Old Sturbridge Village.*

women born in the country towns of New Hampshire and Vermont, women whose labor was not needed at home on their fathers' small farms.

Dickens had an eye for attractive women, and he admired Lowell's "mill girls" because they were so different from the impoverished women he had seen in the English mills. They were well-dressed, uniformly neat and clean, remarkably healthy in appearance, and "had the manners and deportment of young women: not of degraded brutes of burden." He noted too that the masters of Lowell wished to keep them under scrutiny and away from temptation. They did not live on their own, but "in various boarding-houses near at hand" to the factories, run by women carefully chosen for their moral character. Boardinghouse keepers, ministers, and local church congregations would keep watch over their lives outside of working hours. They worked long hours, Dickens thought, but were treated fairly.

Educated in New England's rural district schools, the mill girls were not only literate, but many of them were great readers; hundreds of them could be found on the subscription lists of Lowell's circulating libraries. Observing that it would astonish his English readers, Dickens noted that the parlors of their boardinghouses often contained a jointly owned piano, and that several of them had banded together to found a literary magazine, the *Lowell Offering,* "written exclusively by females actively employed in the mills."

Many thousands of these young women came to Lowell in the 1830s and 1840s. The substantial majority of them, as Dickens said, worked there for a few years and then left factory labor for good. The great majority of

them married—many to men whom they had met in Lowell. Some had gone into the mills to send money back to their families—a few helped put their brothers through college—but most mill girls worked for themselves, buying clothes and books, and saving for the future. At the time of his visit, Dickens reported, nearly one thousand of them had accounts at the Lowell Savings Bank, averaging about $100 each—about half a year's wages.

Lowell in 1841 was America's industrial showplace. Most of New England's textile factories were much smaller and less visible, situated on smaller streams in villages of a few hundred people. But when taken together, the factories of what was called the "Rhode Island system" added up to just as much output and employment as Lowell and the other large mills on the same model in cities like Lawrence, Massachusetts, and Manchester, New Hampshire.

The factories in the Rhode Island system recruited a very different population of workers. "In collecting our help," wrote mill owner Smith Wilkinson of Pomfret, Connecticut, "we are obliged to employ poor families, and generally those having the greatest number of children, those who have lived in retired situations on small poor farms, or in hired houses," without any land at all. While young single women made up part of the workforce, it was far more common for an entire family to go into the mill together, moving into a tenement house owned by the company. Fathers usually did the outdoor labor, while their children toiled in the mill and their wives kept the house.

Unlike the Lowell factories, which paid cash, the Rhode Island system mills used the traditional system of rural credit, paying workers in store goods and rented housing. Children's wages went directly to their fathers. Unlike the mill girls, these working families were truly poor, and sometimes illiterate. They were usually far more transient as well. They rarely stayed much more than a year with a single employer, often only for a few months. Frequently they moved restlessly from one factory village to another, looking for "better situations."

"Bands, Wheels, and Springs in Constant Motion"

For workers newly arrived from the countryside, used to time measured by the sun and the seasonal rhythms of the farm, the factory was a strange place. Its bells called them into a world of precisely structured hours and close confinement. "You cannot think how odd everything seems," wrote a mill girl in the *Lowell Offering*, about her first week of work. Even experience in hand spinning and weaving did not help much with the new machinery, and as a new hand, Susan Miller felt that "the sight of so many bands, and wheels, and springs in constant motion, was very frightful." The noise of hundreds of machines working in unison was deafening at first, and over time it undoubtedly injured the hearing of many mill workers. Miller recalled leaving the factory with "the noise of the mill in my ears, as of crickets, frogs and jew's-harps, all mingled together in strange discord."

In every textile mill, a small minority of men performed the most-skilled mechanical and supervisory jobs; women, girls, and boys tended the machines. They watched over the working of spinning frames and power looms, scanning them constantly for broken threads, defects in the cloth, empty bobbins, full spindles—tasks that required concentrated attention. It took several weeks for most mill workers to become reasonably comfortable with the machinery. Success depended on vigilance, quickness, and deft manipulation. Some never acquired the skills and had to leave. Unlike mining or steelmaking, most textile factory labor was not physically strenuous. Instead, operatives faced prolonged standing and what they all remembered as "long hours of confinement."

In this woodcut, c. 1836, a male operative at the right runs the spinning mule; to the left, the mule is stopped while a woman repairs broken threads and a boy crouches under the threads to clean out debris. *Author photo.*

In the smaller mills, many workers just off the farm were slow to adapt to the clock time and work discipline of the factories. N. B. Gordon was a "mill agent" who ran a small cotton factory in Mansfield, Massachusetts. In his work diary for 1830, he worried about having enough water in the millpond to run his factory, about repairing broken machines, and about finding reliable help as workers came and went. Much to his frustration, he was rarely able to report "all hands at work." Usually, one or two went missing through the day, and a few others would "come in after breakfast," or even "after dinner," at one o'clock. More than once Gordon reflected sourly that there were "but few good hands in the mill." In January, there were "a poor lot of weavers at this time & bid fair to be worse." On "Election Day" in May, a traditional holiday in the Massachusetts countryside, he was forced to have the "Factory stopped"; angrily he noted that he "could not peaceably work the mill as all hands seemed determined to have the whole day."

Gordon's worst moment that year came when he discovered that one young boy in the mill was actually sabotaging the machinery, hoping to slow down the pace of work. Lewis Kingman was a "piecer" whose job was to repair broken threads on the spinning mules, the machines that spun the factory's strongest yarn. He had secretly been slipping the leather belts that powered the machines off their pulleys, each time bringing production to a sudden stop. Finally, Gordon caught him trying to cut the belts. "For Boldness and Cunning the above tricks surpass all description," the enraged mill agent wrote.

Young Lewis did not keep a diary that told his side of the story. But Hiram Munger, who had also worked as a child in a small Massachusetts factory, would have understood Lewis's rebellion. "The treatment of the help in those days was cruel," he remembered years later, in 1857, "especially to poor children, of whom I was one. Although I was young, I recollect of thinking that life must be a burden if I was obliged to work in a factory under such tyrants." His experience of factory life had been "American slavery in the *second* degree."

"AN ARMY OF OPERATIVES"

At the time Dickens wrote, America's Industrial Revolution was homegrown. As a later student of the textile industry recalled, its workers—whether farmers' daughters or poor families—were "almost exclusively Americans, both by birth and descent." But this would soon change. During the 1840s, conditions in the industry became increasingly more difficult. Factories of all sizes faced increasing competition that drove prices and profits down. Desperate to cut costs, they lowered wages and introduced the "speed-up"—running the machines faster—and the "stretch-out"—giving each worker more machines to tend.

Tools:

THE SPINNING FRAME

The transition of textile production from hand work to machinery was a wrenching and enormously productive transformation. It began in England in the middle of the eighteenth century, as mechanic-entrepreneurs like Hargreaves and Arkwright searched for ways to mechanize—and indefinitely multiply—the movement of the spinner at her wheel, and later, the weaver at the loom. Over decades of inventive insight and trial and error, they solved innumerable problems of design, marketing, and finance, and created the first textile factories. They were the early heralds of a process of technological innovation in manufacturing that would transform the world and transform the nature of work.

The Industrial Revolution came to the United States in 1791 with Englishman Samuel Slater. When he arrived in Rhode Island, he was carrying in his head laboriously memorized specifications for the textile machinery that was driving Britain's industrial prosperity. The written plans would have been contraband; as one of the foundations of national prosperity, information about textile

SPINNING BY HAND WITH A SINGLE SPINDLE.

(Left) Hand spinning on the wool wheel or walking wheel is illustrated in this c. 1860 engraving. *Author Photo.*

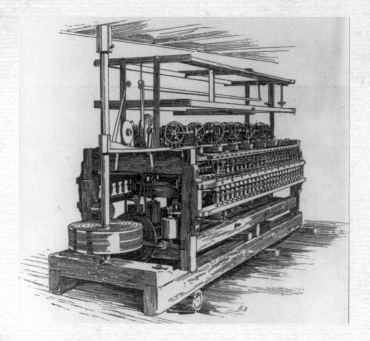

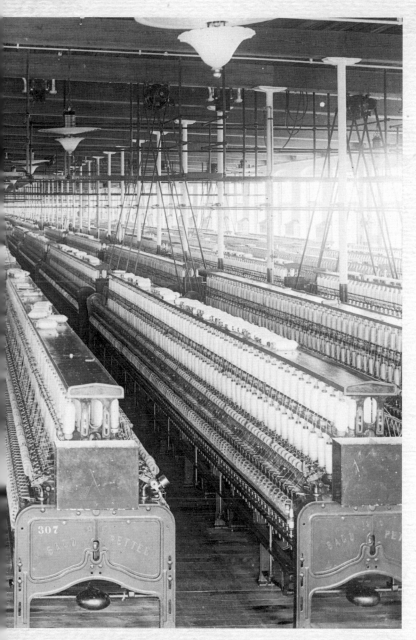

(Above) **There are many thousands of spindles in the immense main spinning room of the Coolidge Mills in Manchester, New Hampshire, c. 1920.**

(Top, right) **The original Slater spinning frame is depicted in** *Harper's Weekly,* **in. 1890.**

technology was forbidden to leave the country under severe criminal penalties. Slater himself had to pretend to the authorities that he was just a farmer, because men with textile industry experience were also forbidden to emigrate.

Soon Slater and his American collaborators had numerous imitators and competitors, and by the 1830s, there were hundreds of water-powered mills, large and small, across the face of New England. They were America's first workplaces devoted to mechanized mass production, where, according to one-time Lowell mill girl, Lucy Larcom, "the buzzing and hissing and whizzing of pulleys, and rollers and spindles" displaced the traditional, quieter music of spinning wheels and hand looms.

The years between the 1830s and the 1930s would see many refinements, large and small, in textile technology, but the basic principles of the spinning frame that Slater introduced remained unchanged. The frames in the main spinning room of the Coolidge Mills in Manchester, New Hampshire, were made of cast iron and steel, not wood, and were no longer water-powered. But in their shape and principles of operation, they were very similar to Slater's original model.

The vision of Lowell as a mill girls' Utopia, of a factory city without permanent factory workers, faded away, yielding to the harsh realities of the market economy. "As the wages became more and more reduced," remembered former mill girl Harriet Hanson Robinson, country girls abandoned Lowell, "until there were very few of the old guard left." For a couple of decades, factory work on the Lowell model had been a respectable option for farmers' daughters, but by 1850, this was no longer the case. Some stayed home rather than labor for dwindling wages, while many went to what Robinson called "the other employments that were fast opening to women." The most important of these was teaching. Traditionally dominated by young men, it was becoming a primarily female profession. Teaching offered modest salaries but greater respectability than manual labor. Yankee working families in the smaller factory villages had never expected Utopia, but they too began to leave the mills as wages fell. Native-born Yankees would remain as owners, managers, and foremen, but they soon became a rare sight on the factory floor.

Their places were first taken by Irish immigrants, whose arrival, triggered by the devastating potato famine of 1845, greatly increased New England's pool of unskilled labor. Low wages did not deter the Irish, most of whom

(Left) **Polish and French Canadian mill girls, all in their teens, stand on the street in front of the Pacific Mills in Lawrence, Massachusetts, c. 1910.**

(Below) **Textile factory with two women at machines, c. 1910.**

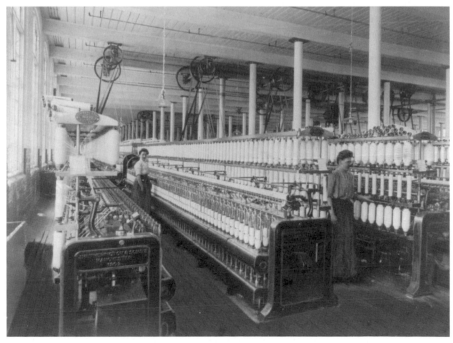

had come to the United States nearly penniless and were desperate for work. In successive waves, other immigrant groups would follow the Irish into the mills. By 1880, the *Atlantic Monthly* noted, the Irish were leaving the textile factories in their turn, as their American-born sons and daughters moved on to better-paid work.

Replacing them were French Canadians, moving south by the tens of thousands from the overpopulated farms of Quebec. In the following decades French Canadians would be joined in the mills by Italians, Poles, and Portuguese—all agricultural peoples fleeing overcrowding on the land and poor harvests. "These successive influxes," the *Atlantic Monthly* noted, "seem like peaceful invasions, in each case the new arrivals gradually supplanting their predecessors."

(Above) Operatives tend the spinning frames in a Lawrence, Massachusetts, factory, c. 1916.

(Right) Portuguese mill workers in Lowell pose in their best clothes, c. 1910–15.

(Inset) Textile printing operations like the one shown here in 1916 primarily employed men, who were better paid than the operatives in spinning and weaving rooms, but still felt the same downward pressure on wages.

Struggles:

WORKER PRODUCTIVITY

Nearly sixty years after Dickens's visit to Lowell, Charles Hubert stood gazing at "the noble buildings" of the Boott Mills, "the largest in New England and perhaps in the world." It was "bell time," when the great steam engines and waterwheels came to a stop and the workers headed home. He watched "an army of five thousand operatives" leave the mills "in a dense stream of humanity, male and female, big and little, until the broad iron bridge was packed and shook under the strain." Hubert was struck even more powerfully by the mills' physical immensity, with their 60 acres of flooring, "three hundred thousand spindles . . . eight thousand looms . . . and thousands of

other ponderous machines, ingenious and effective almost past belief." Dickens had looked at the fleeting possibility of a different kind of factory, a workplace without permanent industrial workers. Hubert was celebrating the mills as a miracle of American productivity.

Hubert was right in many ways. The mills had become larger and their machines faster; the spinning and weaving rooms of late-nineteenth-century factories dwarfed those of the 1840s, and steam had supplemented water power so that there were few limits on their expansion. But as for "the army of operatives," they remained machine tenders, and the nature of their work did not

change much even as the machines became more complex. Hours of work gradually shortened, from a thirteen-hour day at midcentury to ten to eleven hours by 1900. At the same time, little had been done to improve the health and safety of workers, who still risked injuries from unguarded, fast-moving machinery and faced respiratory problems caused by the inhalation of cotton dust—byssinosis, or "brown lung." Wages moved up and down, reflecting the industry's volatile cycles of demand and production. Supporters of the mill owners argued that over the long run, conditions in the mills were improving. Others believed that the trend was downward. Due to "close competition," the *Atlantic Monthly* maintained

in 1888, "the work of the individual operative has been increased and his pay reduced." Improving technology simply accelerated "this doubling-up process," because "in many places where a workman was required, an automatic attachment now does the work."

Most employers pressed their workers ruthlessly for productivity. In 1912, a new law in Massachusetts reduced working hours for women and children from fifty-six hours a week to fifty-four; almost immediately, the mill owners in the city of Lawrence lowered their pay to match the reduction in hours. Worker outrage led to what was called the "Bread and Roses" strike, in which thousands of workers confronted not only management but also the city police and state militia. The strikebreaking tactics of the authorities, extensively covered in the press, were so violent and repugnant to public opinion that the owners were forced to give in to the strikers' wage demands. Yet as the spotlight of public attention moved away and economic conditions worsened, the workers lost most of these gains within a couple of years.

(Left) **Boott Mill workers in Lowell walked across this bridge every morning and evening.** *Historic American Building Survey.*

(Above) **Massachusetts state troopers, protecting strikebreakers, confront strikers in Lawrence during the Bread and Roses strike, c. 1913.**

HEADING SOUTH

The mills that Charles Hubert described were immense and impressive in their scale and productivity, but their prosperity would not endure. Those "noble buildings" in Lowell and elsewhere rested on shaky economic foundations, because the pressure to increase profits and cut labor costs did not relent. Now that factories could be driven completely by steam, they could be located anywhere. Textile manufacturers began to look outside New England for a cheaper workforce.

By the 1890s mills were springing up in rural communities across the upland South. Here manufacturers found what they wanted: large numbers of poor white farming families looking for work, a tradition of low wages and hostility to unions, and state governments uninterested in enforcing child labor laws. The Southern mills swiftly became the nation's low-cost producers, rocking the New England industry to its foundations. In 1905, North Carolina, South Carolina, and Georgia together were producing more cotton cloth than Massachusetts, and New England's specialized makers of textile machinery were finding new customers down south.

One by one, manufacturers in Massachusetts, New Hampshire, and Rhode Island cut back, folded up, or moved south themselves; hundreds of thousands of textile jobs left the region. This huge migration of industry

A "help wanted" advertisement for the Inverness Mills, in Winston-Salem, sits on the side of the railroad tracks in North Carolina, c. 1912.

These two-family mill workers' houses sit just behind the Floyd Cotton Mill in Rome, Georgia, c. 1913.

from one region to another, taking place over three decades, made the South the center of American cotton manufacturing in the twentieth century, as New England had been in the nineteenth.

The great Boott Mills in Lowell suffered a deeply ironic fate. Not long after 1900 their managers and owners decided to abandon all major upkeep and capital investment in that enormous factory complex, judging that it would no longer be profitable. For many years they ran their production operations into the ground, squeezing the maximum profit out of the buildings—and the workers.

The new Southern mill villages resembled not Lowell but the small manufacturing communities of New England nearly a hundred years before, although they centered on a factory chimney rather than a millpond. Most of them were set deep in the countryside, relied on family labor, and often paid their workers in tenement rental and trade at the company store.

The South's cotton-mill workers were new to factory life, but they were hardly recent immigrants. Their families had been working the land for generations, with American ancestries that went back at least to the eighteenth century. But they had stayed poor. Like the New England mill village families of nearly a century before, they were farmers without land—laborers, tenants, and sharecroppers.

The story of the Haithcocks family of North Carolina illustrates the path that many of these families took into the mills. In 1938, an interviewer for the WPA spoke to three surviving Haithcocks sisters, Clara, Frieda, and Effie, who were living together with their surviving husbands, children, and in-laws in a cramped and dirty house in the mill village of West Durham. Their father, Perry Haithcocks, had begun as a struggling tenant farmer; the 1910 census shows the family still on the land in Orange County, and records him as illiterate. The interviewer summarized what the sisters told her, noting, "Their life on the farm was dull and hard and empty of promise . . . Perry felt that the cotton mill offered his family a slightly better chance than the farm had ever given."

By 1920 the Haithcocks had moved a few miles away, to the village around the hosiery mill in Chapel Hill township, and the census reveals that Perry was

The entire workforce of the Elk Cotton Mills in Fayetteville, Tennessee—one of thousands of small factories throughout the South—stands together outside the factory in November 1910.

working there along with his four oldest daughters. "He took his . . . children to the mill, and as soon as it would have them he put them to work."

Going into the mills sometimes brought people like the Haithcocks a bit more than they had previously had, but not much. They had been marginal farm people, and they became property-less industrial workers. In dealing with their employers they had no more power than sharecroppers had, and in the terrible years of the Depression, they suffered only a bit less than black farm workers. By 1938 Perry and his wife Annie were dead, and none of their children had managed to accumulate anything. The mills had slowed down, although they had not closed completely, and of the seven adults in the household, only two were working. One of the Haithcocks women, Frieda, had become an occupational casualty after twenty years as a spinner in the mills. Her years of breathing cotton dust had given her the symptoms of "brown lung" disease. Forced to give up her job at age thirty-six due to multiple bouts of pneumonia, she sat at home "like an old woman, stooped and sallow and wrinkled."

Mary Branch, who worked in the Royal Cotton Mill in Wake Forest, North Carolina, from the 1890s to the 1930s, summed things up another way: "The life of a textile worker," she wrote, "is trouble and worry and fears. We can never get through what we're expected to do, if we work at it ninety-nine years."

A cotton-mill family stands for their portrait in front of their rented house in May 1911. According to Lewis Hine, this was the "[f]amily of L. W. Money. Father, daughter and two boys work in spinning room of Washington Cotton Mills, Fries, Virginia. Smallest worker said he was thirteen, but it is doubtful."

Small Hands:

THE COTTON MILL: "THAT IS HOW WE MANAGE IT"

Children had always worked in American textile factories. Most mill jobs required dexterity rather than strength, and many tasks were suited to workers with small, nimble fingers who could reach under and around machines more easily than adults. They could also be paid a great deal less. For several decades they were a large and crucial part of the workforce. Over time, as New England's cotton and woolen mills yielded to changing public sentiment and emerging state regulations, their numbers declined. By 1900, most states in the Northeast barred children under the age of fourteen from factory work.

But as textile factories and textile jobs moved south, child labor in the mills became an increasingly serious issue. The South's levels of child employment compared with those of New England nearly a century earlier. "The number of children employed in all southern mills has greatly increased in the past few years," reported A. J. McKelway, the assistant secretary of the National Child Labor Committee in 1904. The Committee's best estimate was that there were at least thirty-two thousand cotton-mill workers in the South under fourteen, and no fewer than ten thousand under twelve. Most of the

Southern states barred children under age twelve from factory work, but the laws were very loosely enforced; parents needing additional income, and employers wanting cheap labor, often colluded to get around them.

Lewis Hine, the Committee's photographer and researcher, documented child labor in the mills, taking over a thousand pictures of child mill workers across the South between 1907 and 1916. In 1908, Mr. Smith, an overseer in the Wylie Mill in Chester, South Carolina, explained the system to Hine. There were "plenty of children below 12 in his mill," he told Hine. But their names were not on the payroll books. The younger ones came to work with their older brothers and sisters, who were credited for their siblings' work as well as their own. This was, he said, the common practice all through the South. "That is the way we manage it." Smith posed for Hine on the front steps of his house in Chester, with his own four young children. He drew the line on child labor with them. "He will not let his children work in the mill," added Hine. "Says it is no place for them."

Huldah Foster, "unlettered but not unintelligent," had been one of those children working off the books. Born in Gaston County, North Carolina, she remembered that at ten years old her parents had sent her to work as a spinner in the Belmont Mills. From that time, around 1905, mill work was the only life she knew. "She tells you," reported her WPA interviewer in 1938, "how glad she was as a little girl to hear the six o'clock mill whistle in the afternoons because it meant that as soon as she had eaten supper her playtime would begin." She was able to claim the two hours after supper, until eight thirty, for herself, "to join the other children of the neighborhood in their games." But as she grew up and gave up

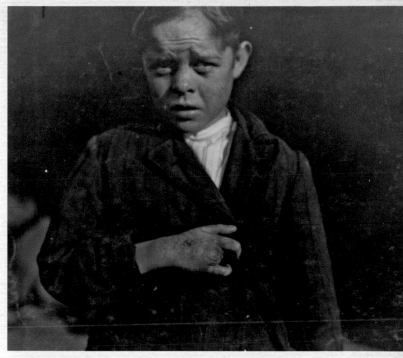

Lewis Hine persuaded a "young cotton mill worker" in Bessemer City, North Carolina, to pose for him, c. 1912, showing his maimed hand. "A piece of the machine fell on his foot, mashing his toe. This caused him to fall onto a spinning machine and his hand went into the unprotected gearing, crushing and tearing out two fingers."

the games of childhood, she found nothing else to take their place, and mourned these brief hours of play as the best memories of her life. Everything else was the daily routine of the textile factory. After the mill closed in 1937, she missed the sound of the machinery as much as her weekly wages. It had been "the one rhythm to which her life was attuned."

The child mill workers of the South figured prominently in the National Committee's campaign to legislate national regulation of child labor, which began in 1904. The Committee won much of the American public to its side, but attempts at federal legislation were ruled unconstitutional in 1918 and 1922 by a conservative Supreme Court. Nationwide standards had to wait until the passage of the Fair Labor Standards Act in 1938, which established the age of fourteen as the minimum age for after-school employment, and sixteen as the minimum age for work affected by interstate commerce.

All of these children were employed at the Loudon Hosiery Mills in Loudon, Tennessee, in 1910. Lewis Hine noted that "all are regular workers."

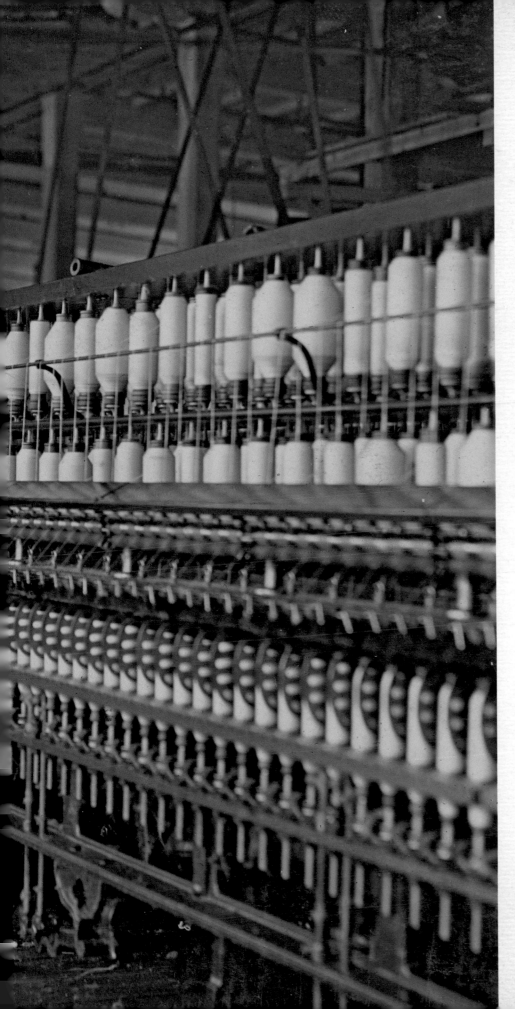

The superintendent of the Catawba Cotton Mills in Newton, North Carolina, looks over the work of one of his very young spinners, c. 1908. "Others smaller still," wrote Lewis Hine. "Ten boys and girls this size and smaller out of a force of 40 employees."

(Above) Mr. Smith, an overseer in the Wylie Mill in Chester, South Carolina, poses on his front steps with his children, c. 1908.

(Right) "This little girl (like many others in this state) is so small she has to stand on a box to reach her machine," Lewis Hine wrote. "She is regularly employed as a knitter in Loudon Hosiery Mills. Said she did not know how long she has worked there." (Loudon, Tennessee, 1910).

Working on the Railroad

"The force that operates a railway," wrote Marshall Kirkman in his multivolume management manual of 1894, *The Science of Railways*, "is like an army. It is methodically organized and drilled. It has its commanders, its rank and file, its officers, sub-officers and privates." At first glance, this is puzzling to anyone familiar with the disorderly expansion of American railroads in the nineteenth century. As financial enterprises, America's railroads were far from disciplined. Their rapid growth was often marked by stock manipulation, the bribery of congressmen and state legislators, and outright fraud. Even the building of the transcontinental railroad was marked by dubious financing and, in some places, shoddy construction.

But as large-scale transportation systems, railroads became, almost despite themselves, the nation's first modern business organizations. Within a few years after they began in the 1830s, the railroads were crossing state lines, and operating day and night, seven days a week. Moving goods and passengers safely and predictably across the country required the constant coordination of schedules for hundreds, and eventually thousands of trains. The railroads created the nation's most complicated structure of work, involving hundreds of thousands of employees performing a wide variety of specialized jobs.

THE EXPRESS TRAIN.

In 1870, this Currier & Ives image of the express train was the epitome of speed and mechanical power.

This elaborate lithograph of 1882 advertises the Illinois Central Railroad and shows the railroad system spanning North America and superseding earlier forms of transportation like the stagecoach and canal boat, shown in the insets. Well-dressed passengers wait to board the train. The poles and wires of the telegraph—critical for coordinating and managing the system—are visible to the left. Behind this scene is a globe showing the major railroad routes across the country and outlining the Illinois Central system in red.

Superintendents, stationmasters, dispatchers, and telegraphers managed the flow of orders and information. Engineers, firemen, and brakemen drove the trains. Conductors managed passenger trains and porters served passenger needs. Switchmen, signalmen, and laborers maintained the signal systems and the track infrastructure. Freight checkers and freight handlers took care of the goods. Roundhouse crews repaired equipment and cleaned the cars. Rate clerks and bookkeepers, purchasing agents and sales agents looked after money, materials, and traffic. Station clocks, engineers' watches, and published timetables had to be synchronized. It was hardly surprising that the railroads led the successful campaign to create standard national time zones—often against bitter opposition—to replace local "sun time."

Marshall Kirkman's own career was testimony to the size and complexity of the "railway service" to which he devoted his professional life. Over the course of nearly forty years he published a torrent of books and articles that tried to systematize railroad accounting, freight handling, personnel management, safety, construction, locomotive technology, and the work responsibilities of every possible kind of employee. *The Science of Railways*, in twelve volumes, was not quite a best-seller, but it was an industry bible, in print for many years and constantly updated.

Kirkman had vast technical knowledge, but he took a rigid and idealistic view of how work in his industry should be organized. His thinking echoed that of others in the late nineteenth century who tried to apply Darwin's biological theory of natural selection to the organization of society (something Darwin had never suggested). There was a "natural law of selection," he wrote, "that assigns every person to his appropriate sphere of duty." This would demand that each worker "must fit perfectly the place he fills, must be familiar with his duties, and able and willing to perform them effectively." Subordination of workers to management had to be absolute, and their labor "must be continuous, systematic and orderly." He was confident that this "discipline of corporate life" worked out for the best, rewarding talent and hard work. After all, everyone knew "that promotion will follow intelligence, faithfulness, and industry."

But actual work on the railroads, throughout the great nationwide system that Kirkman had helped to create, was very different. Railroad workers were thoroughly aware of their responsibility to keep the trains moving, and of the necessarily organized and interdependent nature of their work. But they often experienced the "discipline of corporate life" as dehumanizing and demeaning. Workers rarely thought that the company's interests were identical to their own, and never thought of themselves as soldiers in a railroad army. The railroads responded to cyclical economic downturns with massive wage cuts and sought ever-tighter control over what workers did, reacting to worker

A summary timetable of the Baltimore and Potomac Railroad describes its service from Washington, D.C., to Philadelphia, New York, New Haven, and Boston, 1876.

(Right) **Maurice Livingston, a baggage handler, pulls a wagon loaded with suitcases and trunks at the Mountain Grove, Missouri, railroad station, 1916.**

(Below) **Perched on top of a freight car, a brakeman on the Atchison, Topeka and Santa Fe Railroad, c. 1943, sets its brakes for a long, gradual descent between Summit, California, and San Bernardino—one long downgrade of more than 2,700 feet.**

militancy with every possible form of coercion. Pushed to desperate extremity, railroad workers in the 1870s and 1890s engaged in some of the bloodiest strikes in American history. The meaning of railroad work is to be found not in Kirkman's talk of unchanging principles, natural selection, and military organization, but in their own stories.

ACROSS THE CONTINENT

The completion of the first transcontinental railroad in 1869 was a feat that stirred the imagination of the American people after the trauma of the Civil War. The joining up of the Central Pacific and Union Pacific Railroads at Promontory Summit in Utah was widely celebrated as a great unifying event for the nation. But most of the actual work of grading the route, laying the tracks, and blasting the tunnels had been done by men who—so many Americans thought—hardly belonged in the country at all. Over the course of three years, twenty thousand Union Pacific laborers, largely Irish immigrants but also Mexicans and African Americans, built the road west from Omaha. Another twelve thousand Central Pacific workers, nine-tenths of them Chinese, advanced it east from Sacramento.

A popular lithograph sold in San Francisco at the time illuminates widely held American attitudes. It shows American identity under threat; Uncle Sam is being swallowed at one end by a brutal-looking Irishman and at the other by a pigtailed "Chinaman." After Uncle Sam is disposed of, the Irishman is then swallowed up in turn by the Chinaman. The Irish were partially and grudgingly accepted, although under great suspicion because of their Roman Catholicism. Seen as an alien people with incomprehensible customs, the Chinese, who had been arriving in California since the 1850s, were monumentally unwelcome—

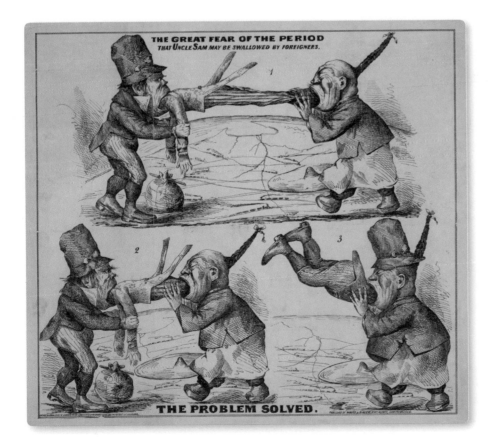

This anti-foreigner lithograph was published in San Francisco in 1869. Its caption reads: "The great fear of the period—that Uncle Sam may be swallowed by foreigners. The problem solved."

except for their labor. "One can hardly help laughing at the strange race," wrote Lucy St. John in the children's magazine *Merry's Museum* in 1870, "they seem such a queer sort of patch in the mottled quilt of California life. They do everything in such a comical way!" Yet, she continued, "queer as they are, they have built for us the great Pacific Railway."

The work that these men—"Patrick" and "John Chinaman"—accomplished, using picks and shovels, steel drills and sledgehammers, had been an enormous struggle. The arithmetic for laying track was simple—three strokes to drive one spike, ten spikes to fasten one rail, and four hundred rails to lay for each mile. Managers and foremen, most of "native" American stock, drove them relentlessly to multiply the miles. The speed record for a single day went to an extraordinary Chinese crew who laid 10 miles of track in a twelve-hour shift.

The hardest-won miles were those that had to be blasted through the mountains. When tunneling through solid granite, work crews might measure

Heading for their next work site, Central Pacific workers ride across a newly built wooden trestle on flatcars pushed by a locomotive, c. 1868.

their daily progress in inches. Robert L. Harris was a civil engineer who in 1867 had helped survey the route of the Central Pacific railroad through the Sierra Nevada Mountains in California. In early 1869 he returned to visit the work site at the Summit Tunnel, where crews were drilling through "1,659 feet of solid granite . . . cut in the face of a precipice." The work had been going on "night and day" in three eight-hour shifts—unusually short because of the exhausting nature of the labor of drilling. He saw the white foremen pressing the men onward, "goaded to exertion" by the promise of bonus pay, and the seemingly impassive Chinese workers, members "of the army of labor."

Moving toward the rock face, he found himself "elbowing my way between crowded workmen, dodging my head from their striking hammers, and my feet from their picks." He arrived to find "two hundred and fifty men . . . working, crowded together in a space of two hundred and fifty feet." One member of a team held a heavy steel drill, while two others, alternating blows, drove it into the rock with hammers. When the hole was judged deep

A. R. Waud's sketch, made in early May of 1869, shows Chinese and European workers meeting up as they complete the last mile of track.

As a professional engineer and a white "native American," Robert Harris strongly felt his superiority to the laborers. He probably dressed in formal business attire while out in the field, like these surveying engineers of a South Dakota railroad, the Deadwood Central, who are shown working with their measuring sticks and transits, 1888.

enough, it was filled with black powder, or the newly developed nitroglycerin, and detonated. There was a "constant succession of blasts," Harris wrote, and each time there was "a rush of three-score Asiatics" to take cover from the flying fragments of rock.

The workers lived in camps, temporary cities that were taken down and put up as the tracks progressed. "Changed every thirty or forty days," wrote the Massachusetts editor Samuel Bowles, "these settlements were of the most perishable materials—canvas tents, plain board shanties, and turf-hovels." The westward-moving camps of the Union Pacific were disorderly and violent places, very much like mining towns. Hangers-on, saloonkeepers, and prostitutes traveled along with the railroad workers. Visiting one settlement at the end of the tracks in the summer of 1868, Bowles found it full of "gambling and drinking, hurdy-gurdy dancing and the vilest of sexual commerce."

The Central Pacific's camps were far less debauched. "The Chinamen were as steady, hardworking a set of men as could be found," reflected John Gillis, one of the tunnel engineers. Chinese workers did not drink, fight, or look for prostitutes, although they smoked opium to relax on their Sunday off. However, reflecting the racial attitudes of his time, Harris was openly contemptuous of "Asiatics," hardworking or not, and did not like the look of their settlements. "Here is a 'camp,'" he wrote of the one near Summit, "but alas none of the old style of snow-white canvas" of the surveyors' encampments. "No it is a Chinese camp, resembling a collection of dog-kennels, which in fact it is—each hut hastily made of 'shakes' about four feet high by six feet broad, and eight feet long."

These graders' cabins in Echo Canyon, Utah, photographed c. 1868–1870, are similar to the huts in the Chinese railroad camps, described by Robert Harris.

No exact records were kept, but it is clear that at least a few hundred workers died in accidents, whether from mishandled nitroglycerin or infections from a crushed hand or foot. As Samuel Bowles noted, at least a few Union Pacific laborers died in brawls and knife fights. Far more—perhaps two thousand—perished from diseases contracted in the crowded and unsanitary camps, just as soldiers had in the Civil War. "Almost everybody [is] dirty, many filthy," Bowles wrote of the ones he saw. A smallpox outbreak in a Nevada camp carried off many Chinese workers, who had never been vaccinated.

Although the Chinese outworked their European counterparts, they were paid somewhat less. In June 1867, Chinese workers on the eastern slope of the Sierras went on strike for higher wages and shorter hours. By American standards it was a remarkably peaceful strike, without protest demonstrations or violence, but the Central Pacific met it with unrelenting force; the railroad's executives cut off the workers' rations, and then sent a group of well-armed white enforcers into the camp. The strike ended after nine days.

At the "Golden Spike" ceremony in Utah on May 10, 1869, when the railroad lines were finally joined, a Chinese crew laid the final section of track from the Central Pacific side. But unlike the Irish workers who joined up with them, they were quickly pushed aside from the ceremonies. They are nowhere to be seen in the "official" photographs and engravings that commemorated the day. During the 1870s, anti-Chinese sentiment grew rapidly in the American West, with riots, increasing segregation, and restrictive laws.

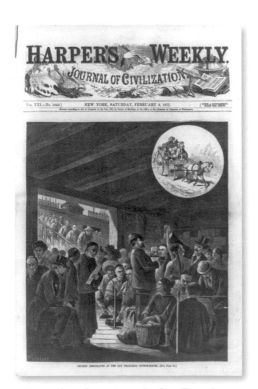

Chinese immigrants at the San Francisco Custom House, 1877.

Chinese workers were not shown in pictorial accounts of the Golden Spike ceremony in May 1869.

In 1882, Congress passed the Chinese Exclusion Act, ending Chinese immigration and uniquely stigmatizing the people who had "built for us the great Pacific Railway."

ENGINEERS

Charles Allen must have been a fast learner. After two years "in his boyhood days" as a railroad fireman—shoveling coal into the steam engine's voracious boiler—he was given full responsibility for a locomotive on the New York and Erie line in 1857, a few days after he turned eighteen. Except for his three years of service in the Civil War, he spent the rest of his working life—fifty years—as an engineer for the Erie.

By the time Allen retired, he was a byword in the company for competence, professionalism, and reliability. His "steady and faithful performance," the Erie's company magazine noted in 1909, set an example "that young employees will do well to follow." In the course of five decades, he had a reputation for exceptionally good care of his locomotives, "seldom having his name appear on the engine failure sheet."

He also met, unfailingly, the railroad's demands for speed and punctuality. In 1865, not long back from military service, he was chosen to be at the throttle of a special express train that was to carry a party of British and American railway executives from Salamanca, New York, near Buffalo, to New York City. All other trains were taken off the main track during Allen's high-speed run; he made record time and delivered his party safely. The railroad's other engineers were watching him, literally, "from the sidelines."

Allen and his family lived quietly in Warren, New York, not far from the Erie's main track across upstate New York. But in 1887 he made the newspapers. On December 22, he and Fireman Perry were taking Passenger 29 westbound toward Buffalo. They had just rounded a deeply cut bank with a blind curve when they saw an eastbound freight approaching. Allen just had time "to reverse his engine and set the brakes before the crash," reported the Hornellsville, New York, *Weekly Tribune*. Knowing that they could not avoid a collision, Allen and Perry jumped from the locomotive's cab. Engine 29 was "made a total wreck and struck with such force that it was turned completely over on its side," the article continued. Thanks to Allen's quick action in setting the brakes, no passengers were injured.

This 1884 Currier & Ives print shows a crash about to happen. As another train approaches on a collision course, the engineer and fireman are blowing the steam whistle, throwing the engine into reverse, and applying the brakes.

Allen and Perry were badly bruised but otherwise unhurt. Engineer Smith of the freight train was another veteran railroad man with a good record; he had simply confused Passenger 29 with an earlier train and thought it had already gone past. "We called upon Engineer Allen this morning," wrote the *Weekly Tribune*'s editor, "and found him at the breakfast table heartily enjoying his morning repast." In a few days he was back on the line. "Mistakes and accidents must happen," the editor concluded.

Charles Allen's railroad career had been not only exemplary, but dangerous. The American railroad network spanned vast distances and had been built up rapidly; American railroads, like packinghouses, steel mills, and coal mines, paid far more attention to productivity than safety. "Accidents," wrote Brit-

Although there is no picture of Allen and Perry's accident, similar wrecks were frequently photographed. Here, in Farmer City, Illinois, c. 1909, what's left of a wrecked locomotive is being hauled away amid the widely scattered debris from the accident.

(Above) One passenger was killed and twenty-five were injured at the Farmer City wreck, a head-on collision. Spectators have gathered to watch the aftermath.

ish railway traveler Charles Richard Weld in 1855, "are thought so little of in America" that it was useless even to talk about them. Railroading in the United States remained a hazardous business throughout the nineteenth century and into the twentieth. "In spite of all the improvements and precautions, the number of deaths and injuries is appalling," observed Englishman S. Reynolds Hole, fifty years after Weld's visit. Collisions due to errors by engineers or dispatchers, derailments due to excessive speed or faulty tracks, and injuries to crew members working outside on moving trains continued to claim lives.

In 1893 the new Interstate Commerce Commission reported that 7,346 people had been killed on American railroads in the previous year, and 40,393 injured. Passengers were at risk, but workers were far more endangered. Between 1889 and 1901—the first years for which statistics are available—American trainmen were more than twice as likely to die on the job as British workers.

Although Allen was a paragon of steadiness and safety, the official *Erie Railroad Magazine* reported that over the decades, he had "experienced several narrow escapes from death" and had more than once been badly injured. In one accident even more dramatic than the one in 1887, his engine had been derailed, and toppled "down the bank, turning over twice on the way." Fortunately, the magazine went on, "his splendid physique" had allowed him to recover quickly each time, and he had never been judged at fault. His proudest achievement was that no passengers had ever lost their lives on one of his trains.

The Erie Railroad was glad to heap praises on Charles Allen at his retirement, but that did not mean that engineers were happy with their working conditions. Railroads rarely compensated employees for job-related injuries or assisted the families of workers who had been killed. The engineers organized in 1863, primarily to protect themselves and their families from the risks of injury or early death in a dangerous trade. The first purpose of the Brotherhood of Locomotive Engineers, the oldest continuous labor

(Facing page) This is a blank certificate of membership in the Brotherhood of Locomotive Engineers, c. 1877, the oldest continuously active labor union in the United States, founded in 1863. Four other skilled railroad brotherhoods were organized in the following decades.

An engineer sits in the cab of a locomotive about to pull out of a Chicago and Northwestern Railroad yard, c. 1942.

organization in the United States, was to provide its members with accident benefits and mutual life insurance. Men in the other operating railroad trades took the same path, creating brotherhoods for firemen, signalmen, brakemen, and conductors.

Once organized, the engineers also began to struggle with the railroads over pay, scheduling, work rules, and seniority; in 1877, a time of severe wage cuts and economic desperation across the nation, thousands of engineers joined other railroad workers in what came to be called the Great Railroad Strike, a sequence of often-violent conflicts stretching from Philadelphia west to Chicago. As fears of a workers' insurrection mounted, state governors called out the militia and President Hayes sent in federal troops. The strike was broken at the cost of numerous lives and an enormous amount of wrecked railroad property. The engineers struck again in 1888, this time against the arbitrary personnel policies of the Chicago, Burlington and Quincy Railroad, but suffered another crushing defeat. Badly bruised, the Brotherhood became far less militant; the engineers refused to participate in the Pullman boycott and strike of 1894, and adopted an official policy of extreme reluctance to strike.

CONDUCTORS

Foreigners traveling across America during the nation's railroad age spent a good deal of time in the company of conductors—the men who took tickets, announced stops, helped the crew with emergencies, and had charge of the train's schedule and non-mechanical operations, including the comfort and safety of passengers. Their travel accounts tell us most of what we know about conductors' work.

In Britain, these employees were called "railway servants"—and were expected to be deferential to passengers and unfailingly polite. But from the 1830s into the twentieth century, American conductors did not think of themselves this way. Like stagecoach drivers and tavern keepers in earlier times, they were proudly independent, and determined to stay on an equal footing with their passengers.

In 1840, English novelist Charles Dickens encountered one of these men for the first time on the railroad between Boston and Lowell, Massachusetts. "The conductor or check-taker, or guard, or whatever he may be," Dickens wrote, was not overly concerned about his duties. Instead, he "walks up and down the car, and in and out of it, as his fancy dictates; leans against the door with his hands in his pockets and stares at you, if you chance to be a stranger; or enters into conversation with the passengers about him."

However, by the mid-1850s, the conductor's work had become standardized in a routine that is still familiar to those who ride American trains today. William Chambers described it after touring the eastern United States by rail in 1854:

This 1893 sketch shows a conductor besieged with passenger questions while the train is stopped in a storm.

> *Walking down the middle, with a row of seats on each side, and each seat holding two persons, he holds out his hand right and left as he proceeds, allowing no one to escape his vigilance. All he says is "Ticket!" . . . If you have already bought a ticket, you render it up to this abrupt demand, and a check-ticket is given in exchange. Should you . . . have no ticket to produce, the conductor selects the ticket you require from a small tin box he carries under his arm, and you pay him the cost of it, increased in price to the extent of five cents, as a penalty for having had to buy it in the cars.*

Dickens's conductors wore no uniform at all; in 1854 Chambers noticed that they still wore civilian clothes, but had badges on their hats with their office "blazoned in metal." But whenever a conductor got off the train, Chambers realized, he removed the badge and became "an ordinary human being." This anonymity would not last. After the Civil War, as railroads became more disciplined and efficient organizations, conductors increasingly were required to wear uniforms that identified them both on and off the train.

Routines were broken—and the conductor's responsibilities became much more important—when there was trouble on the line. In 1884 Joseph Hatton, who was traveling between New York and Baltimore in the midst

A conductor swings aboard his departing train, c. 1918–20.

of a fierce snowstorm, observed his train's conductor at work. As the snow piled up on the tracks, their heavily laden train slowed to a few miles per hour, and then stopped completely. A train just ahead of them had broken down and was blocking their way. The conductor ceased to be a ticket-taker and became the train's emergency manager. He spent several hours outside in the storm, clearing away snowdrifts, placing warning lamps, and working to clear the way, even "kicking at the rails with his boots." Coming in once for a warming gulp of Hatton's brandy, he was in charge of the work party that was "digging the [switching] points out of the snow" so that the disabled train could be moved to a siding—"to push these cars on to another track," he told Hatton, "and get round ahead of the train that's broke down." Finally he helped arrange for extra locomotives to be brought on to pull—and push—the train to Baltimore through the snow. The conductor described his special responsibility to Hatton: "[I]f anything went wrong they'd blame me." He was a very experienced employee who had been given this bad-weather assignment as "a special job."

A conductor was responsible for the management of his train, sharing overall responsibility with the engineer. Given the speed and power of trains, and the number of passengers or value of freight involved, this could be a heavy burden, as Hatton noted. A photograph taken around 1930 portrays this partnership, already nearly a hundred years old. Dressed in their work uniforms, the two men check their watches before setting out on their run. The engineer's overalls and cap are stained with engine grease and coal dust—impossible to avoid in the cab of a coal-burning steam locomotive. The conductor's uniform reflects his "inside job" and his position as the company's representative and a figure of authority for the passengers.

Engineer and conductor consult their watches, c. 1930.

Eyewitness:

The Life of a Perfect Checker

Mr. Lord, the freight checker who lived only for his job, was a legendary figure around the yards of the Northern Pacific Railroad in Seattle in the 1930s. J. J. Stauter of the Federal Writers' Project took down this account of his life in November 1938, from a railroad worker who knew Lord but wished to stay anonymous.

A checker working at his portable table. These tables are moved about from car to car as each is loaded in the freight house at a Chicago and Northwestern Railroad yard, c. 1942.

Did you see old Mr. Lord, that was an N. P. freight checker for so many years? I guess that was before your time. Old Lord was the perfect checker. He was a tall man, over six feet, slim but with broad shoulders. He got his first job as a freight checker with the N. P. somewhere back in the early eighties, and he just sort of settled down that first day to make it his life work. He seemed to figure that the best way to enjoy life was to be the best checker on the road, nothing more and nothing less. The others could go after promotions for all they were worth. They could beef about the thousands of regulations that they had to follow. They could slip away while a car was being loaded for a cup of coffee or a glass of beer. They could blow about the jobs they once held, or was going to get pretty soon. They could buy automobiles on the installment plan. But not Lord.

Lord was just a checker. Company regulations never bothered him in the least; as a matter of fact, he had thousands of private regulations of his own that he followed along with the printed ones. It would take the company fifty years to even think up all the rules he set for himself, let alone get them approved by the proper authorities and posted up. That was one way to get perfect peace of mind in spite of the Company—to beat them at their own game.

He never got married, or even, as far as anybody knows, stepped out with a woman. That would take attention off his work—get him to thinking about other things besides tallying freight into cars—and he was a checker. He lived in a plain little three-room house which he had bought with his first year's savings. They say that one of his three rooms was completely filled with copies of his tally sheets—he kept every one since the first day he worked.

His clothes were plain and neat and seemed to date back to the year he started work, like everything else about him; and yet they never looked old or threadbare. He always wore a flowing black tie done in a perfect bow, with the ends hanging down about a foot, like girls used to wear with a "middy blouse." His face never wrinkled, even when he was over seventy; I guess it was because he had nothing to worry about.

When it came retirement age, he faced it without any emotion; didn't seem to be either sorry or glad, nor to have any plans as to what to do with his new leisure. Like so many other railroad men, he only lasted a few months after his retirement. The regulations said he couldn't be a checker any more, and—well, he couldn't be anything else, so that was that.

Section Hands and Gandy Dancers

Building the railroad across the continent was enormously dramatic if often deadly, and engineers and conductors were the most visible to the public. But for the railroads to run, thousands of miles of track had to be kept constantly in repair. Track laborers, or "section hands," had to rebuild the "ballast" or gravel roadbed after washouts, replace rotted wooden ties, straighten steel rails, and keep the tracks properly aligned around curves. They were the most poorly paid railroad workers; most of them were transient unmarried men, who worked in a section gang for a few months or a year, and then moved on.

Although he had farmed for over fifty years, John Grosvenor's years as a railroad laborer were still vivid in his memory. Twenty-one and newly married in Logan, Kansas, in 1880, he needed work. The Central Missouri Pacific Railroad had just been completed, and he was hired on a Wednesday for the track gang, "as long as I wanted it . . . for $1 a day and pay my own board . . ." They worked to prepare their section of track for the arrival of "the first regular train to go through" three days later on Saturday. They put in "ten hours a day, and they had to be ten big ones."

He spent most of 1880 working on the tracks, and came back in 1882, which he remembered as "a very wet year." The newly built roadbed proved vulnerable to washouts. During every big rain, trains passing through the

(Above) Three railroad workers posed standing on their handcar, c. 1850–60. Track workers used these small hand-cranked vehicles from the mid-1850s well into the twentieth century, when they were replaced by electric-powered vehicles.

(Left) A crew of section men at Salina, Kansas, is heading off to their work site on a handcar in 1867.

vicinity of Logan slowed down to a crawl for their own safety. The track crew traveled just ahead, moving slowly on their handcars. "We had a flag to wave," Grosvenor recalled, "if we run into a real soft spot or a washout." The hardest work of that year came when they had to re-lay 3 miles of track that had been completely washed away. Working day and night in the rain with picks, shovels, and pry bars, they replaced ties and jacked up the tracks with "timbers, lumber, poles, iron, anything and everything," so that the trains could creep through. "We had no raincoats, only boots," he recalled. "We were soaked through. Food was short. We finally got home. Many of the men were just dead on their feet and it was some job to wake them up." He had worked hard for five decades on his Kansas farm, but nothing had quite equaled that week in the rain, working on the railroad.

In Southern railroad yards, most track laborers were African American. Mary Louis started working for the Missouri Pacific—"the Mop," as she called it—around 1900. For two decades she was a housekeeper in the Mop's Pine Bluff, Arkansas, yards She took care of the railroad shanties —the rough wooden buildings where workers took shelter from rain and snow, waited until they were needed for a job, ate, and napped when they had a break in their often-unpredictable schedules. She also cooked for the more than thirty African American men who worked on the tracks, giving them a hot noonday meal. "The railroad gang all like my cookin' and I nevah had no complaints." When section hands had to travel out from the yards for several days, they traded the shanties for a traveling bunkhouse, sometimes just a boxcar. In 1938, John Marshall remembered one of the calls used to rouse the men for work in the morning:

I know you're tired
You're sleepy too,
I hate to disturb you,
But I've got it to do,
I don't mean one,
I don't mean two,
I mean the whole
damn crew.

African American and white railroad laborers work to repair and clear the tracks after a derailment on the Baltimore and Ohio in 1922. The locomotive has been partially overturned, and a completely overturned freight car is visible at the left.

A section gang lays track for a switch that will move traffic to a siding, c. 1900–1910.

In the window of a railroad employment office near Union Station in Chicago (c. 1943), a sign advertises for track laborers at $5.00 PER DAY.

John Grosvenor never had a special name for the work he had done as a young man, but by the early twentieth century, there was one widely in use. Mary Louis spoke of cooking for the "gandy dancers—that what they call the fellahs that take care of the railroad tracks." It's a wonderfully evocative name but a mysterious one. Was there a specialized tool for tamping down the ballast around the track called a "gandy"? Did workers carrying heavy railroad ties walk in a way that resembled a gander's waddle? Every attempt to track down its origins has so far met a blank wall. No one now alive knows for sure. The origin of this piece of railroad slang seems lost to history.

Porters

Before the Civil War, some African Americans had worked as engineers and firemen, but after 1865, due to the antagonism of most white railway workers and their emerging labor organizations, they were systematically pushed out of the skilled and better-paid positions. They were left with work as track laborers, particularly in the South, and as porters—the men who handled travelers' baggage at the station, or took care of their needs on the sleeping and dining cars. Increasingly visible as railroad passenger travel expanded, porters' jobs were almost exclusively reserved for African Americans.

Within the segregated confines of the African American community, porters had high status: They wore uniforms, were regularly employed, and had some opportunity for advancement. But their work was in many ways like that of a trusted servant in a wealthy household. To keep employed—and even more, to be successful—they had to provide swift, efficient service while maintaining a constant facade of deference and good cheer.

An African American waiter is shown serving two travelers in a Pullman dining car on the Cincinnati, Hamilton & Dayton Railroad, 1894.

A young woman sits on her berth in a Pullman sleeping car while a porter hands her a glass of water, c. 1905.

Nat Love was one of the few Americans who wrote extensively about his career as a Pullman porter. Love was an unusual man. Born a slave in Tennessee, he went to Kansas as a teenager after Emancipation and worked there and in Arizona for twenty years as a cowboy, winning fame as a range rider, roper, and crack shot. His nickname was "Deadwood Dick," given to him after he won a target-shooting competition in Deadwood, South Dakota.

But after Love married at thirty-five, he needed a different kind of work that would allow him to support his wife and family. The free-riding cowboy became a different kind of rider, a sleeping-car porter who in his years with the Pullman Company "traveled from the Atlantic to the Pacific and from the Gulf of Mexico to the borders of Canada, over nearly all the many different lines of railroad."

Love's choice reflected not only his lifelong need to keep moving, but also the restrictions he faced as a man of color. On Love's first trip, he discovered "that the difference between a Pullman car and the back of a Texas mustang is very great." Unaccustomed to providing personal services, he began disastrously, "getting the shoes of passengers which had been given to me to polish, badly mixed up." He received no tips, and tips made up half or more of a porter's income. He quit in disgust, but then returned to the work a year later.

Gradually, Love learned the "secret" of success in the job—unrelenting attention to "pleasing a whole car full of passengers." He began to be curious about the district superintendent's detailed knowledge of what went on in the trains. "It was a mystery," he wrote, "how the superintendent managed to find out things that happened on my car when he was not present. Sometimes when I went to report or met him he would question me about things that happened on my run, such as pleasing the passengers and other things, which I did not suppose he knew a thing about, and inquiries among the other trainmen only deepened the mystery."

No one would officially explain it, and Love began to feel that the superintendent was clairvoyant. Finally he discovered the truth: The company employed special agents who traveled the rails as ordinary passengers and reported back to headquarters. As Love recalled, he decided to assume that his work was constantly under surveillance, "and governed myself accordingly." He worked harder to keep his passengers happy, "to make all the friends I could on my runs"; the undercover passengers' reports became more and more favorable, and his income from tips increased steadily. As his experience grew, he was frequently made "porter in charge" of his Pullman car, meaning that on many runs, he did not have to report to a white conductor.

Love prided himself not only on his efficiency but his ability to get even the sourest travelers into a good humor and "laughing with the other passengers." He also recalled the many times that he had given compassionate service, watching "by the bedside of a sick passenger, feeding him, giving him medicine, bathing him, and in fact becoming for the time being a hospital nurse." Still, he measured his success primarily by his tips. Very few did not tip at all; the smallest he recalled was two cents from a man who told him that, as black men, "some of us porters needed . . . knocking down." At the other extreme was "one of the Rothschilds," a member of the great French banking family, who gave him $25 for his services on the four-day trip from Chicago to San Francisco.

Nat Love ended his autobiography with a chapter of extended praise for the Pullman Company, the railroad system as a whole, and the scenery and civilization of the United States. He exhorted his readers to "See America and let your chest swell with pride that you are an American." A black man in a white man's world, he was still pleasing his passengers and making friends.

Wearing his winter uniform, a Pullman porter poses for his portrait at Chicago's Union Station, 1943.

Steelworkers: "The Splendor of American Civilization"

Twelve hours. I go off at six and on at six . . . Twelve hours work without stop.

—Steelworker, Homestead, Pennsylvania, 1894

All prices. From a dollar and forty cents up to the tonnage men, who get five and ten dollars a day when the mills run smooth.

—Steelworkers' wages, Homestead, Pennsylvania, 1894

As most observers saw it, the American steel industry near the turn of the nineteenth century was a marvel of high technology and immense, efficient production. R. R. Bowker, editor, business executive, and political reformer, greatly admired the great integrated steel mills of Pennsylvania, Ohio, and Illinois. "Such establishments," he wrote in 1894, as "the Carnegie Steel

Joseph Pennel made this surprisingly beautiful watercolor sketch of the Bethlehem, Pennsylvania, Steel Works in May 1881.

Schoolboys walk home up the hill with the myriad chimneys of the Homestead Works in the background, c. 1907.

Works at Pittsburgh and Homestead . . . represent the highest triumphs of engineering and technical skill." They were amazing places, whose "ingenious mechanical contrivances" made American steelworks—and workers—more productive than those anywhere else. The United States had just overtaken Great Britain as the world's leading producer of steel, and steel was building railroads, bridges, skyscrapers, and steam engines.

At the same time, Hamlin Garland was taking a very different look at steelmaking. As a journalist and novelist, he had written eloquently about farm work and the lives of men and women in America's Midwest. In 1894 he ventured east to Homestead, Pennsylvania, the center of American steel-making and the site of the nation's largest steel mill.

Garland agreed that Homestead was an amazing place, but it was also a terrible one. Taking a ferry across the Monongahela River in the rain, he saw "great sheds" with grim chimneys spewing smoke. Poorly built tenement houses ascended the hill behind the mills "in dingy rows," and the town's streets were dangerous to walk in, full of sticky yellow mud with sidewalks "sunken, swaying and full of holes." It was an extraordinary contrast—the poverty of the town against the wealth it generated.

Grimy communities like Homestead, he thought, with their "gangs of foreign laborers" and jagged industrial landscapes, were "American only in the sense that they represent the American idea of business." Garland was a fine observer, but here he was wrong. Homestead was as American as a cattle drive or a Nebraska farm.

Garland walked through the mills with a native guide—a young man who had grown up in Homestead, had previously been a steelworker, and "thoroughly understood" what they would see there. Both for eye and ear, the steel mill was the most dramatic of American workplaces. Textile manufacturing copied the human-scale processes of spinning and weaving, but multiplied and at high speed. Steelmaking was on a different scale completely. It dealt with high temperatures, huge machines, enormous forces, and crushing weights of material.

As Garland entered the mill yard, he was struck at once by the noise— "the crashing thunder of falling iron plates, the hoarse coughing of great engines, and the hissing of steam." Then he was nearly stunned by unexpected beauty. "Suddenly through the gloom," he wrote, he saw a "mighty up-soaring of saffron and sapphire flame." It was the flash of one of the mill's great Bessemer converters, which turned pig iron into strong, flexible steel. The flame made "a magnificent contrast to the dusky purple of the great smoky roofs below."

Garland entered "an immense shed, open at the sides, with a mixed and intricate mass of huge machinery"; it was a mill for making steel beams, "one of the finest in the world," he was told. He admired "the beautiful glow of a red-hot bloom of metal" as a newly made steel beam was swung in the air

(Below, left) Steelworkers at Homestead are drawing off molten slag at the lowest level of a blast furnace, c. 1907.

(Below, right) Steel mill laborers are making sand molds to receive molten iron, c. 1905. The resulting ingots of pig iron will be used in the steelmaking process in a blast furnace or Bessemer converter.

by a crane, and then watched an enormous saw cutting the steel beam into lengths, "a saw that melted its way through a beam of solid iron with deafening outcry . . . a glowing wheel of spattering sparks of golden fire." The mill was no less dangerous than its flames were beautiful. Its workspaces were designed for steel, not for men. Even with his experienced guide, "every inch of ground" seemed to have its dangers.

Garland tried to puzzle out the workers, who labored in such an extraordinary place, so far from the fields and barns of Nebraska. In the rolling mill, where white-hot ingots were passed through enormous rollers to make steel plate, he watched men tending the soaking pits or belowground furnaces with huge shovels and bars; "it takes grit to stand there," his guide said. "The men work over them when it's hot enough to burn your boot soles." Controlling the entire process from above was a single man, more highly skilled and better paid. He was the "chief roller," who guided the machinery "like a mahout on his elephant."

The steelworkers were for the most part "lean men, pale and grimy." Unlike farm workers, they were rarely touched by the sun. At rest, they often "wore a look of stoical indifference." But in action, they were athletes, swift and skilled, working with "silence and certainty" and an "almost desperate attention and alertness." Garland watched the transformation of an ordinary-looking, "pale, stoop-shouldered" man as he climbed to his work station on the steam-powered traveling crane that moved the steel beams. Suddenly he became "alert, watchful and deft."

"The work is hard?" Garland asked one of the men. "Hard. I guess it's hard," he replied. "I lost forty pounds the first three months I came into this business. It sweats the life out of a man. I often drink two buckets of water during twelve hours." He had no more time to talk, and went back to his station. "It's all the work I want, and I'm no chicken," said a muscular young man, who estimated that the tools he handled weighed 150 pounds. "Feel that arm." The journalist complied. "It was like a billet of steel. His abdomen was like a sheet of boiler iron." Garland's companion added, "It's a dog's life . . . [T]hose men work twelve hours, and sleep and eat ten more. You can see a man don't have time for anything else." Even the best-paid men were "heavily marked by labor."

Garland finally made his way to the Bessemer converter, "the most gorgeous and dangerous of all" the mill's workplaces. There, in "two immense pear-shaped pots," each with "a ferocious geyser of saffron and sapphire

Steelworkers line up to receive their pay at the Homestead works in 1907.

Two Bessemer converters are shown running at full blast in 1886. *(Harper's Weekly)*.

flame," iron was transformed into steel. When the molten steel was ready, one of the great vessels was upended and its contents were poured into an enormous ladle, which "exploded like a cannon," shooting flames and splashing liquid metal. The workmen crowded under the ladle to prepare the converter and its heating furnace for the next pour. At times, Garland was told, the process would have to stop while men jumped into the unlit furnace or the converter pot to rebuild its heat-resistant lining.

"They call this the death-trap," his companion shouted over the roaring. "[T]hey wipe a man out here every little while." He explained: "Sometimes a chain breaks, and a ladle tips over . . . sometimes the slag falls on a workman from the roadway up there. If a man watches out, why, all right! But you take it after they've been on duty twelve hours without sleep, and running like hell, everybody tired and loggy, and it's a different story."

There were no old men to be seen in the steel mills. "The long hours, the strain, and the sudden changes of temperature use a man up," said the former steelworker. Almost all the workers left the mills before they turned fifty. "I can see lots of fellows here who are failing. They'll all lay down in a few years." His own decision to leave the mills had come much earlier. "I used to come home so exhausted," he remembered, staggering with fatigue like a drunken man. "I finally came to the conclusion that I'd peddle groceries rather than kill myself at this business."

The mill's common laborers made $1.40 a day; more-skilled men could earn $2 or $3; the few men at the top of the occupational ladder, paid according to the tonnage they produced, might make $5 or as much as $10 a day, "when the mills run smooth."

Working conditions at Homestead and elsewhere in the steel industry had improved over the decades, Garland learned. The introduction of heavy machinery for handling and cutting steel had come, he wrote, "to lessen the horrors of the ironworker's life, to diminish the number of deaths by exploding metal . . . or breaking beams." Still, the casualties were high.

Garland wondered what kept them at this work. The skilled men he spoke to kept on for the hope of high earnings at their dangerous trade. As for the others, the predominantly foreign-born men who shoveled slag and hauled pig iron, they had little choice. "A man'll do almost anything to live," said another onlooker.

Eight hours a day, or six, would make the work less destructive, the men agreed. "A man could stand work like this six hours a day. That's all a man ought to do at such work." The steel companies "wouldn't make so much, but the hand would live longer." Of course, "mill owners don't run their mills for the benefit of the men."

Not all of Homestead's workers may have agreed, but this was Garland's final assessment of work in the mills. It was "a place into which men went like men going into war for the sake of wives and children, urged on by necessity, blinded and dulled by custom and habit; an inhuman place to spend four-fifths of one's waking hours." Yet Homestead and the other great mills like it were among the nation's greatest technological glories. "Upon such toil," he wrote, "rests the splendor of American civilization."

Eyewitness:

"You Ain't an Ironworker Unless You Get Killed"

Even riskier than making steel was the work of the men who assembled the beams and girders into buildings. With the steel-framed skyscrapers that transformed the American city came a new trade—that of the high ironworker.

Chris Thorsten told his story in a New York City union hall, as he sat playing cards with other high ironworkers. In February 1939, they were passing the time, waiting to hear about the possibility of work. "All we got is hard luck," one of them said. "If they'd give the damn work back to the contractors, we'd all be workin'." All the men, Federal Writers' Project interviewer Arnold Manoff wrote, shared a taut calmness that probably came of their dangerous work. They were quiet and poised, with faces that were "solid, hard and set in straight deep lines."

Thorsten had come a long way to work high above the streets of Manhattan. Born on board a fishing boat moored to a dock in New Orleans, he had grown up rough. His whole family were fishermen—"herring catchers," he called them. His mother had died young, and after his father perished at sea, he wound up living unhappily with two stepparents. Given a little money and a packet of clothing, he "ran away from New Orleans when I was a kid" and went north.

Thorsten became an ironworker at the age of nineteen, in 1907, when tall, steel-framed buildings were transforming the skyline. "I been in this racket thirty-two years," he said in 1939, and he was still a powerful man at 6-foot-2 and 200 pounds, hard-muscled, with hands twice the size of an ordinary man's. "You wouldn't believe I was fifty-one years old," he told his young interviewer. "Take a good look."

Doing work that would terrify most of their fellow citizens, ironworkers prided themselves on toughness, and gave way to nobody. Thorsten repeated a common saying about ironworkers: "Ya see, dem guys—on Friday, they walk a narrow little plank

"Building the great steel-framed skyscrapers—working high above the street," New York City, c. 1906.

away up in the air, and on Saturday, the sidewalk ain't wide enough for them."

Most of Chris Thorsten's memories were of his three decades working on narrow platforms hundreds of feet above the city's streets. He "drove rivets all the way" when the Hotel New Yorker was built in 1928–30, and worked "with the hoisting gang" on the Parcel Post Building in 1920, hauling "32-ton girders" up from the street. That work, he recalled, paid well: "We made money." But the price was a punishing schedule. He "worked straight through five days and four nights," with "two hours for breakfast, one hour for lunch, one hour for supper, and one hour at night." On the fifth night, he fell so deeply asleep in a nearby saloon that his friends couldn't wake him up to go back to work. True to his ironworker's code of invincibility, he "felt kinda ashamed of myself that I couldn't take it."

Thorsten knew the risks of his work very well, and carried the scars. Men were hurt on every job, he said, and often enough, they were killed. Two had been killed while he was working on the Hotel New Yorker; they had died on the Triborough Bridge, the George Washington Bridge, and the Empire State Building. "You ain't an ironworker unless you get killed" was a grim running joke in the business.

Thorsten finished the interview with one last story. Once he had seen a friend die up close, knocked from the scaffold right next to him. George Morgan was tying a safety railing onto the platform when a swinging steel beam struck him, sending him down to the street. The next day, everyone went back to work at the site, and Thorsten, still thinking about his friend, lost his concentration. Pinioned between a beam and a moving crane, he recalled, "[I broke] my collarbone, all the ribs in my body, and three vertebrae. I was laid up for four years." Then he turned back to his card game.

"Erecting the 23-story steel skeleton for the new Times Bldg," Broadway, New York, 1904.

Steel Mills:

Two Stories from the Steel Mills

I. "I Don't Know How True This Story Is"

Nelson Walton had worked for many years at the great South Side Works in Chicago; when interviewed in 1939, he was living in the neighborhood where both my parents had grown up. He told a story that Chicago steelworkers had passed along for decades.

> *I don't know how true this story is; I have been hearing it for years. Every time I try to pin the guy who tells the story—down about what year the accident took place, where, and who the poor son of a bitch was—I am evaded. But the boys say it is true. The story goes that a guy fell off, or was pushed off, one of the bridges into a ladle. You know what happens then. He goes pouff into nothing. Then the company buried the guy with the steel until the family got over the accident, or until they moved away. After that the company dug up the metal and used it in the process of making steel.*

II. Who Was Joe Magarac?

In the 1930s, stories began to circulate in steelworker communities and American magazines about a fabled Slavic steelworker named Joe Magarac, a seven-foot-tall giant who could outwork the strongest man in any steel mill. Joe, so the stories went, wanted to do nothing but make steel; he even turned down marriage to a beautiful girl to have more time to work. Joe, it turned out, was actually made of steel himself—a tireless, cheerful living machine.

The tale of Joe Magarac became a popular one—repeated in steel towns, and also favored by the public relations department of U.S. Steel. What did this story mean and where did it really come from? The first writer to put it in print, Owen Francis, thought that it had been created by Croatian workers in Pennsylvania at the end of the nineteenth century, and that it expressed pride in their strength and capacity for hard work.

But it is very likely that the legend of Joe Magarac began as a joke. *Magarac* means "jackass" in Serbo-Croatian, and it was rarely a term of affection or pride. The Croatian steelworkers who told the story to Owen Francis could well have been pulling his leg—he did not speak their language, and took a condescending view of the "Hunkies," as he called them. The story, as stories do, took on a life of its own over the years, both in conversation and in print. Memorable images of Joe were created, including a dramatic oil painting by William Gropper. Many readers and listeners surely enjoyed the story just because they took pride in Joe as a Slav, a steelworker, and an incomparably strong man. But it seems that Joe was widely publicized in the 1940s for another reason: His story symbolized productivity and patriotism—just what the steel companies, and the war effort, needed. Joe Magarac, after all, was no union man defying the bosses; he was the perfect worker, who could make steel with his bare hands and labor twenty-four hours a day.

Ore docks, blast furnaces, and steel mills, South Chicago, Illinois, c. 1907.

A Wonder and a Horror: The Stockyards

For visitors to Chicago, all across the long century that followed the Civil War, there was one sensation that they would never forget. It was the stench of the world's largest stockyards, an olfactory wall that you encountered for the first time like a blow on the head. "It hit me squarely between the eyes," wrote Englishman Nicholas Everitt in 1915. "It penetrated through handkerchiefs, gloves, or deodoriser . . . there was no escaping it." The stockyards were an immense concentration of cattle, hog, and sheep pens, holding an average of thirty thousand animals a day, surrounded by dozens of enormous slaughterhouses and processing factories. The smell they created, said Everitt, was "strong, pungent, rancid, unforgettable." It was the smell of manure, blood, meat, and money.

In early America, the great bulk of butchering had been done on a small scale by individual farmers. As cities grew in the early nineteenth century, urban livestock markets and slaughterhouses expanded to feed a growing

This 1873 lithograph depicts pork packing in Cincinnati, once the nation's most important meatpacking center. It shows an early, smaller-scale version of the animal disassembly line—first developed here but greatly expanded in Chicago.

KILLING.

CUTTING.

RENDERING.   SALTING.

PORK PACKING IN CINCINNATI.

population of families who did not slaughter and preserve their own meat. By 1840, there were large markets outside major cities, like Boston's Brighton Market, where farmers brought their animals to sell to dealers and butchers. Cincinnati, the largest city in the West at that time, became known as "Porkopolis," the central point of the pork trade; Midwestern hogs were slaughtered; packed as salt pork, smoked ham, and bacon; and shipped in barrels by river and wagon to cities and plantations south and east. By 1870, continued urban growth and the expansion of the railroad network meant that urban livestock markets had grown enormously, along with some kinds of meatpacking. Only salted and smoked meat could be transported long distances, and slaughtering had to be confined to the winter months to avoid spoilage.

But the 1870s and '80s saw far greater change, with the advent of safe canning for meat as well as vegetables and fruit, workable large-scale refrigeration, refrigerated freight cars, and increasingly rapid rail transportation. These innovations created a continent-wide market for meat and meat products, a flow of production and consumption that began with Western cattle and Midwestern hogs and ended on the dining tables of millions of city and small-town families. At the midpoint of the flow, and in control of it, were the

This panoramic view of the Union Stock Yards, c. 1897, shows livestock pens, packing plants, and the elevated, covered chutes along which animals were driven to be slaughtered.

great meatpackers of Chicago and the Union Stock Yards. There were other meatpacking centers—Omaha, Kansas City—but Chicago, where most of the nation's major rail lines intersected, was dominant. By 1900, it was producing four-fifths of the processed meat consumed in the United States.

"A City of Animals"

The stockyards and the packinghouses were both a wonder and a horror. Some observers were completely undisturbed, like Willard Glazier in 1886, who simply noted the many miles of road and railroad track within the yards' expanse, the elegant exchange office, the banks and hotels for the cattlemen. Most had more complicated reactions. The stockyards were "one of the most interesting sights in the United States," Frank G. Carpenter's *Geographical Reader* told its young readers in 1898. "The cattle which we see this morning," it continued, "will a few days later be on the breakfast tables of the people of New York, Washington, and other cities and towns." The yards were "a city of animals within a city of men," and their story was one of vast scale and amazing technological progress. But the *Reader* offered only uneasy praise. The men who ruled the yards, it added, were "the most bloodthirsty rulers any city ever knew. They fill the yards with new animals day after day, only to kill them."

Novelist and reformer Upton Sinclair was the meatpacking industry's most devastating critic, recounting and publicizing its abuses. Yet he too was awed by the scale of the yards. He wrote in *The Jungle* (1906) of the vast extent of the cattle pens. "North and south as far as the eye can reach," he marveled, "there stretches a sea of pens. And they were all filled—so many cattle no one had ever dreamed existed in the world. The sound of them here was as of all the barnyards of the universe; and as for counting them—it would have taken all day simply to count the pens."

There was something about the enormous scale of the yards and the plants, their impressive efficiency, and their unrelenting, mechanized violence, that both attracted and repelled. By the 1890s, despite the stench, the stockyards had actually become a tourist attraction. Both the Swift and Armour companies, the two largest packinghouses, established reception centers for visitors and offered guided tours. At the time of Chicago's great World's Columbian Exposition of 1893, the stockyards proved more popular than most of the Exposition's more-elegant exhibits. In the early 1900s, Armour was counting one hundred thousand visitors a year.

Surrounding the stockyards and the packing plants was Packingtown, or "Back of the Yards," a sprawling community of workers and their families that had grown as rapidly as the industry itself. Irish and German workers had settled there first, followed by waves of Eastern European immigrants—

Visitors are assembling for a tour in the reception room of the Armour Packing Plant in Chicago, c. 1909.

Czechs, Slovaks, Poles, Croats, Lithuanians, and Ukrainians. The neighborhood was intricately divided by language and ethnicity, with separate churches and social organizations—divisions frequently exploited by the employers to break strikes and prevent successful labor organization. Divided in most ways, packinghouse families had only their difficult, poorly paid work in common.

When taken together, the plants clustered around the stockyards at the turn of the century constituted the single largest industrial center in the United States—perhaps in the world. Within a single square mile worked thirty-five thousand men and women, toiling for five major packing companies, including the giant firms of Swift and Armour, and several smaller ones. Brought in along 250 miles of railroad track, between eight and ten million cattle, hogs, and sheep moved through the stockyards every year.

Unlike steelmaking, butchering is not a highly complex process. Animals are killed, drained of blood, and cut apart; then the parts, as the *Geography* said, "are turned into food and other things for the use of man." In earlier

Several drovers, brokers, and cattle buyers for Armour's packinghouse stand to be photographed on one of the cattle-pen fences, c. 1909. Others are down in the pens inspecting the livestock. Along with hundreds of others, these men graded, bought, and sold eight thousand to ten thousand head of cattle every day.

Sticking hogs at Armour Packing Plant, Union Stock Yards, Chicago, c. 1893.

times butchering had been a wasteful process as well, discarding over half the weight of animal carcasses as unusable. But the great Chicago meatpackers searched for ways to eliminate this waste, turning their slaughterhouses into ruthlessly efficient factories. The production cycle, from the arrival of animals at the stockyard through slaughter, processing, packaging, and shipment, took no more than forty-eight hours.

The key to this efficiency was the *disassembly* line, the mirror image of, and inspiration for, Henry Ford's later innovation in automobile production. As animals arrived at the packinghouse, they were hoisted onto overhead rail lines, which took them through dozens of specialized work stations. They were stunned, killed, drained of blood, skinned, emptied of their entrails, split, and turned into cuts of meat or processed for sausage and mincemeat. The plants were designed to waste nothing of the animal—to use "everything but the squeal," as the oft-repeated phrase went. Not only lard and tallow, but hides, hooves, hair, tendons, ligaments, bones, and blood, were collected and transformed into salable commodities, usually in nearby factories. Products included leather, soap, fertilizer, glue, ivory, gelatin, shoe polish, buttons, perfume, and violin strings.

From the 1860s through the 1930s, the packinghouses were extraordinarily difficult workplaces, marked by a detailed division of labor, relentless pressure for speed and productivity, and little concern for health and safety. The human cost of this work was great.

THE DISASSEMBLY LINE

Although Sinclair crusaded against the packinghouses, he was a careful observer of their work. In one chapter of *The Jungle,* he described the multitude of tasks performed on just one section of the hog production line. Swiftly killed and then "strung up by machinery," the dead hogs passed between two lines of men, "each doing a certain single thing to the carcass as it came to him." Different men scraped hair off the legs, sides, and back; others severed the head, opened the body, cut expertly through the breastbone, pulled out the intestines, cleaned out the body cavity, and washed it. At every step they made sure that usable parts of the hog would slide down "through a hole in

(Below, left) Hog scrapers at work on the rapidly moving disassembly line, propelled by the overhead rails, at the Armour Packing Plant in Chicago, c. 1909.

(Below, right) After the hog carcasses had been processed (c. 1897), they were, as Upton Sinclair wrote, "rolled into the chilling room . . . where a stranger might lose himself in a forest of freezing hogs."

the floor" for further processing. "Looking down this room," Sinclair wrote, "one saw, creeping slowly, a line of dangling hogs a hundred yards in length; and for every yard there was a man, working as if a demon were after him."

Since animal bodies were far more variable than cotton thread, a packinghouse could not be mechanized as fully as a textile factory. Human hands were needed at most steps in the process. A few packinghouse jobs required unusual dexterity, experience, and strength, and were performed by men with the butcher's traditional craft skills. The "splitters," Sinclair reported, were "the most expert workmen in the plant" and the best paid; they made the difficult, precise cuts that split the animal down the middle so that it could be processed further. Next in skill and pay came the cleaver men, "great giants with muscles of iron" who used two-foot blades to cut the split carcasses into sections. As the meat moved rapidly across the cutting table, the cleaver man's assistants would "slide the half carcass in front of him on the table, and hold it while he chopped it, and then turn each piece so that he might chop it once more"—work in which they could easily lose their fingers. Such skill impressed Sinclair, who noticed that good cleaver men "never made but one cut."

At the corporate level, Swift and Armour were creating highly efficient business organizations, with "progressive" training and promotion policies for their white-collar and engineering employees. But work in the packing plant itself was a different matter. Most of its minutely subdivided tasks, repeated hundreds or even thousands of times a day, required little skill. The production system had been designed so that it could employ unskilled workers who could learn their jobs in a few days. Drawing on a large pool of unskilled immigrants who were eager, often desperate, for work, the meatpacking firms were able to keep wages low.

The slaughtering floor (or "killing bed") was a terrible place, although the men who worked there quickly hardened themselves to its conditions. Amid the screams of terrified and dying animals, men labored on a floor drenched in blood that sometimes came up to the tops of their shoes. On the cattle line, "knockers" stunned steers with sledgehammers, while other workers shackled them to the overhead trolley line, and still others cut their throats with "a swift

In this 1905 view of the Swift and Co. plant, cleaver men, among the most-skilled and best-paid meatpacking workers, are cutting up the hogs after the carcasses have been split.

stroke, so swift that you could not see it—only the flash of the knife." Several men on the killing floor did nothing but shovel blood into disposal holes on the floor; others used brooms to sweep entrails into chutes where they could be saved and washed out for sausage making. Due to the pace of the production line, the men "worked with furious intensity, literally upon the run."

The packing plants were fiercely hot in the Chicago summers—except in the refrigerated chilling rooms where the meat was stored—and cold in the city's winters, except for the cooking and canning rooms. The slaughtering floors had no heat at all, Sinclair wrote, and when the temperature dropped below zero, the workers would find themselves covered in frozen blood. Injuries were frequent in the plants; human blood, and the occasional severed finger, sometimes joined the animal parts in their finished product.

Women—just as they had done while butchering on the farm—did the fine processing. They made sausages and mincemeat, packed lard from hogs and tallow from cattle, filled cans with smoked beef and deviled ham, and packaged bacon. Boys ran messages and helped out in the packaging departments.

(Below, left) **A knocker prepares to stun this steer with his sledgehammer before it goes down to the killing beds at Swift & Co.'s packinghouse, c. 1906.**

(Below, right) **These workers on the cattle slaughtering floor are scraping, cleaning, and rolling up the hides after the animals have been skinned. Note that the floor is covered in a half-inch or more of blood, 1906.**

Emblems:

"THE DEAD CHILD OF A STOCKYARDS HUNKY"

The Right to Grief by Carl Sandburg (1905)

Take your fill of intimate remorse, perfumed sorrow,
Over the dead child of a millionaire,
And the pity of Death refusing any check on the bank
Which the millionaire might order his secretary to scratch off
And get cashed.

Very well,
You for your grief and I for mine.
Let me have a sorrow my own if I want to.

I shall cry over the dead child of a stockyards hunky.
His job is sweeping blood off the floor.
He gets a dollar seventy cents a day when he works
And it's many tubs of blood he shoves out with a broom
day by day.

Now his three year old daughter
Is in a white coffin that cost him a week's wages.
Every Saturday night he will pay the undertaker fifty
cents till the debt is wiped out.

The hunky and his wife and the kids
Cry over the pinched face almost at peace in the white box.

They remember it was scrawny and ran up high doctor bills.
They are glad it is gone for the rest of the family now
will have more to eat and wear.

Yet before the majesty of Death they cry around the coffin
And wipe their eyes with red bandanas and sob when
the priest says, "God have mercy on us all."

I have a right to feel my throat choke about this.
You take your grief and I mine—see?
To-morrow there is no funeral and the hunky goes back
to his job sweeping blood off the floor at a dollar
seventy cents a day.
All he does all day long is keep on shoving hog blood
ahead of him with a broom.

Struggles:

"Antanas Kazlauskas" and the Stockyards Strike

In 1904, young journalist Ernest Poole wrote the story of Antanas Kazlauskas, a Lithuanian immigrant who came to Chicago in the late 1890s to work in the stockyards. He published it in the *Independent*, a New York magazine sympathetic to social reform.

Who exactly was Antanas? Very few packinghouse workers have left their stories, and at more than a century's distance, it is not easy to be sure. It seems most likely that Poole combined the voices of several Lithuanian workers to create his account. He interviewed many of them during his stay in Chicago in 1904.

Antanas, as Poole told his story, left Lithuania, poverty-stricken and under the domination of the Russian czar, to find both work and freedom in America. The new country's size and speed dazed him at first, as he got off the ship in New York and within a few hours boarded the train to Chicago.

I felt everything get bigger and go quicker every day. . . . We were driven in a thick crowd to the railroad station . . . I was mixed up and could not think long at one time. Everything got quicker—worse and worse—till then at last I was in a boarding house by the stockyards in Chicago, with three Lithuanians, who knew my father's sisters at home . . .

Chicago was not exactly the golden city of his expectations.

We were tired out when we reached the stockyards, so we stopped on the bridge and looked into the river out there. It was so full of grease and dirt and sticks and boxes that it looked like a big, wide, dirty street, except in some places, where it boiled up. It made me sick to look at it. When I looked away I could see on one side some big fields full of holes, and these were the city dumps. On the other side were the stockyards, with twenty tall slaughterhouse chimneys. The wind blew a big smell from them to us.

He came to realize that life in America would be a bitter economic struggle.

Then we walked on between the yards and the dumps and all the houses looked bad and poor. In our house my room was in the basement. I lay down on the floor with three other men and the air was rotten. I did not go to sleep for a long time. I knew then that money was everything I needed. My money was almost gone and I thought that I would soon die unless I got a job, for this was not like home. Here money was everything and a man without money must die.

He defended the men who did the punishing work of the packing plants.

My job was in the cattle killing room. I pushed the blood along the gutter. Some people think these jobs make men

Eastern European workers are preparing meat to be preserved and barreled in the City beef department of Armour & Co., Chicago, c. 1893.

bad. I do not think so. The men who do the killing are not as bad as the ladies with fine clothes who come every day to look at it, because they have to do it.

I soon saw that every job in the room was done . . . to save everything and make money. One Lithuanian, who worked with me, said, "They get all the blood out of those cattle and all the work out of us men." This was true, for we worked that first day from six in the morning till seven at night. The next day we worked from six in the morning till eight at night. The next day we had no work. So we had no good, regular hours . . . The foreman in that room wanted quick men to make the work rush, because he was paid more if the work was done cheaper and quicker.

Poole had come to the city to write about the bitter strike, led by the Amalgamated Meat Cutters and Butcher Workmen's union, that was convulsing the stockyards and the packing plants. Far from an impartial spectator, he was a passionate advocate for the workers' cause. After organizing in 1897, the union had made some gains in the plants for workers, securing some protection for seniority rights and more uniform wage scales.

Antanas praised the union for what it had done for him.

I had been working hard in the cattle killing room and I had a better job. I was called a cattle butcher now and I joined the Cattle Butchers' Union. This union is honest and it has done me a great deal of good. It has raised my wages . . . It has given me more time to learn to read and speak and enjoy life like an American. I never work now from 6 a.m. to 9 p.m. and then be idle the next day. I work now from 7 a.m. to 5:30 p.m., and there are not so many idle days. The work is evened up . . . The best thing the union does is to make me feel more independent. I do not have to pay to get a job and I cannot be discharged unless I am no good. You must get money to live well, and to get money you must combine. I cannot bargain alone with the Meat Trust. I tried it and it does not work.

In 1904, union leaders looked for more. They took the men out on strike for higher wages and an end to the relentless speeding up of the production line. But the

Young women are packing mincemeat into jars at the Armour plant in 1893—easier work than on the killing floors, but more poorly paid.

companies struck back, hiring strikebreakers from Chicago's huge pool of underemployed, unskilled workers, and blacklisting the most active union members so that no stockyards employer would hire them. In their most incendiary move, Swift, Armour, and the other large packers brought in African Americans as replacement workers, a move that stirred up considerable violence.

Distracted by racial animosity and divided by language and ethnicity, the packinghouse workers were unable to sustain the strike. Workers returned to their jobs under the previous conditions, and even lost some of their earlier gains. Antanas's hopefulness was short-lived. The union made significant gains for workers during World War I, a time of great prosperity for the stockyards, but wages were cut again when bad times returned in the early 1920s and another strike failed. Labor relations in the stockyards improved by the late 1930s, when the great packing companies finally signed contracts with the unions.

MAKING CARS

In 1913, it seemed to English writer Stephen Graham that American roads were rapidly becoming crowded with automobiles. Graham was taking a pedestrian's-eye view of American life, walking the roads of Illinois on his way to Chicago. "The farmer," he wrote, "commonly tells you that hundreds of automobiles whirl past his door every day." About 70 miles from the city he counted the traffic and observed that cars vastly outnumbered carriages and bicycles. Farmers still cursed them for frightening livestock and endangering hay wagons, but they were becoming inescapable.

Although Graham suspected that many new American drivers had mortgaged their property to buy their automobiles, they were "far more of a general utility in the United States" than anywhere else in the world. Of course, there were drawbacks to this emerging form of rapid personal transportation. "Inexpert driving is no crime," Graham noted, "accidents are nothing to weep over; badly constructed cars are driven along loose springy roads with blood-curdling speed and recklessness." Still, it was clear that in a country of great distances, most of whose people had "a readiness to adopt and utilise any new thing right off," automobiles would shape the future.

Automobile traffic is heavy on Fifth Avenue in New York, c. 1913. A horse-drawn delivery wagon can be seen at the right.

American drivers confront a traffic jam on a rural road in 1919.

As with any new technology, early automobiles had frequent problems with reliability. In 1914, there was still a good deal of popular amusement at the sight of a broken-down motorcar overtaken by a horse and buggy.

This c. 1860–80 engraving shows the interior of a traditional carriage shop, where two men are building a vehicle by hand. The older man is holding the vehicle's shaft before attaching it. The younger worker, perhaps an apprentice, is making an adjustment to the carriage's interior. The earliest automobiles were built in this traditional way, which was displaced by the assembly line.

The automobile created a revolution in American life in the space of a single generation. In 1900 it had been an expensive rarity, with no more that 8,000 automobiles on the road—about one for every 10,000 Americans. By the time Graham wrote, there were nearly 1.8 million. By 1920 there were more than 10 million, and in 1929, almost 27 million—one automobile for every 4.5 Americans. The automobile would reshape American patterns of travel and leisure, as well as the structure of cities and suburbs. Its enormous success required changes that would transform the American landscape—the building of a national network of paved roads, and the creation of a far-flung system of refineries, distribution channels, and service stations for gasoline to fuel internal combustion engines.

But all of this would have been impossible without a revolution in the workplace. Early automobiles were very expensive because they were built like elaborate, custom-made carriages. They were constructed individually and slowly by groups of skilled workmen, each with a different specialty. Automobiles could not become affordable and widespread until they were mass-produced. Parts and manufacturing processes had to be standardized, and machinery had to replace crafts skills. Finally came the development of the mechanized assembly line, with its stunning decrease in the cost of production. This triumph of engineering and organization would create an American culture of unfettered travel, individual freedom, and the virtual idolatry of the automobile. As one of the mainsprings of twentieth-century economy, it would have complex consequences, both good and bad, for American workers.

THE ASSEMBLY LINE

Frank Dilnot, another English journalist, wrote in 1919 of "the miracle known as Ford's factory," which he called "one of the sights of the world." Henry Ford did not invent the American auto industry all by himself, although he was its most important architect. Automobile manufacturers before Ford had been striving to standardize and mechanize the way in which they built cars, and had steadily increased their output. In addition, the assembly line itself was not new—versions of it were already in use in the meatpacking industry and in the manufacture of guns, clocks, and bicycles. But Ford—in the service of his vision of "a car which anyone could afford to buy, which anyone could drive anywhere, and which almost anyone could keep in repair"—pulled together a team of engineers and production managers who organized, improved, and combined existing technologies to create a radically new form of production.

Workers in the machine shop at Dodge Main in Hamtramck, Michigan, turn out thousands of identical parts, c. 1915.

Dilnot, like thousands of other visitors, marveled at the assembly line for Model Ts at Ford's factory in Highland Park, Michigan. He saw it "winding its way through hundreds of yards of the factory," with workmen standing "at intervals of a yard on either side." Conveyor belts brought a steady flow of parts to the workers at each station, as the gradually assembled cars, traveling on a larger conveyor belt of their own, passed on a "continuous journey between the two lines." As each car moved by, "each man does something . . . or adds something as it passes, and by the time it has traversed over the winding line it has been built up by the hundreds of workmen into practically a complete car. And these cars follow each other at intervals of seconds only."

The first Model Ts took Ford workers 12.5 hours to assemble. After the fully powered assembly line was completed at Highland Park in 1913, it took less than 6 hours, and after a year of tinkering with the process, improving it step by step, assembly time was down to 93 minutes. "What was worked out at Ford," recalled manufacturing executive Charles Sorensen, "was the practice of moving the work from one worker to another until it became a complete unit, then arranging the flow of these units at the right time and the right place to a moving final assembly line from which came a finished product."

Ford's innovations were so clearly superior that they were swiftly taken up by his competitors, and assembly-line production became the industry standard. Only a few very expensive automobiles would continue to be built in the traditional pattern of carriage making, by teams of skilled artisans.

Transforming Work

Compared to previous methods, mass production and the assembly line produced cars at great speed and low cost. But it radically changed the work of vehicle building by systematically reducing the level of skills required. The assembly line worked most efficiently when the work of attaching or adjusting parts was broken into the smallest possible steps. Recognizing this, the designers of the production process steadily reduced the skill and judgment needed to perform each task. "The Ford Company," wrote the authors of a detailed study of its industrial methods in 1919, "has no use for experience in the working ranks, anyway." Its managers preferred workers "who have nothing to unlearn . . . and will simply do what they are told to do, over and over again." A few years later, Ford estimated that 80 percent of the jobs in his plants could be learned in a week or less.

As these new methods were adopted, the traditional carriage makers, machinists, and upholsterers who had built the first generation of cars saw their status and independence disappear, along with the need for their specialized skills. For them it was a bitter degradation. Mort Furay remembered

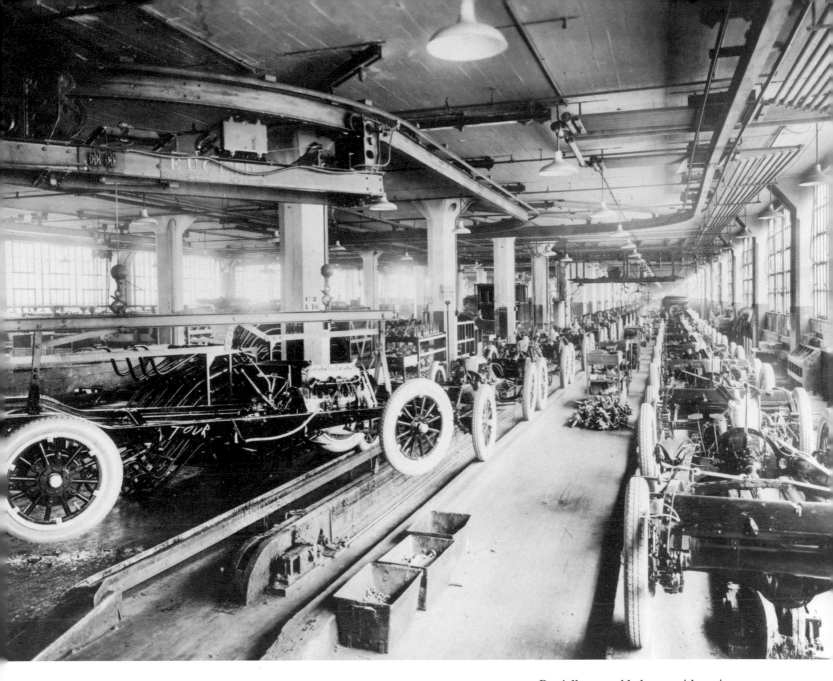

Partially assembled cars, with engine, axles, and wheels attached to the frame, move down the assembly line at the Dodge Main plant in Hamtramck, Michigan, in 1915. *Historic American Building Survey.*

of his father, an upholsterer for the Cadillac Motor Company, that "gradually he lost all the components of his trade" to new machinery and the division of labor. As his father's craft was "taken away . . . piece by piece," he was "reduced to the status of other men in the neighborhood who were just plain ditch-diggers."

But such workers were a dwindling minority. Most autoworkers did not experience a painful transition from skilled craftsman to factory operative because they had not been craftsmen to begin with. In the course of its rapid growth, the industry recruited its workforce from those without industrial skills—newly arrived immigrants from Eastern Europe, laborers in heavy industries like steel, and farm workers. They had a different, but also difficult, adjustment to make as they grew accustomed to the realities of the assembly line and the tight industrial discipline that it required.

Assembly-line workers had to focus on the constant, accurate, and rapid repetition of a single task—inserting a bolt, tightening a nut, lubricating a joint. The work was not physically exhausting, but workers risked the twin extremes of anxiety and boredom. Many of them adjusted to these conditions, and Ford himself declared, "I have not been able to discover that repetitive work injures a man in any way." However, a Ford executive in 1918 took a different view of the tension involved, noting confidentially that "a good many men" could not tolerate the work; he quoted one exhausted worker who explained how he felt: "If you have to drive eight tacks into every Ford cushion that goes by your station, within a certain time," he wrote, "and know that if you fail to do it you are going to tie up the entire platform, and you continue to do this for four years, you are going to break under the strain."

Management in every auto plant controlled the speed of the line, and relied on the "speed-up" to increase the pace of production. "You wouldn't tell them to go faster," remembered W. C. Klann, an assembly plant supervisor in the 1920s.

As vehicles move down this Ford assembly line in 1923, one worker connects the gas tank while another adjusts the steering wheel.

Workers at the Dodge Main plant in Hamtramck, Michigan, pose at the end of the assembly line with the first models of the new 1919 Dodge four-door sedan.
Historic American Building Survey.

"You would just turn up the speed of the conveyor to go faster, that's all, until they kicked that it was going too fast and they couldn't do it. Then we would drop it back a notch." If many workers experienced unrelenting tension on the line, even more found their work boring. It became a common saying among auto-workers that you had to "check your brains at the door" before starting work.

On the other hand, the industry's rapid expansion and high productivity meant that automobile workers were quite well paid, considering their skills. In 1914, the Ford Motor Company famously raised the wages for most of its workers to five dollars a day, nearly doubling them. Henry Ford was widely praised as a visionary but excoriated in industrial and financial circles; the *Wall Street Journal* called him foolishly irresponsible, and "a traitor to his class." This in part reflected Ford's vision of a widely affordable car—a belief that with higher wages he could create customers for his cars from among his own workforce, generating a reinforcing cycle of prosperity. But he also saw it as a way to reduce high rates of employee turnover; given the stress and tedium of the assembly line, autoworkers were exercising what freedom they had by moving from one company to another.

The five dollars per day proved a great success; turnover and absenteeism at Ford were greatly reduced, and productivity and profits shot up. The rest of the industry was forced to follow, offering higher wages and bonuses. For some years, a number of manufacturers, including Ford and the Dodge brothers, sustained reputations as benevolent employers who cared about their workers, sometimes providing charitable help and intervening in family problems. But this did not last: Ford lost interest in paternalism and turned to harsher measures to control productivity; the Dodge brothers died young in 1920; and automakers turned their full attention toward increasing production and cutting costs.

In the 1920s, autoworkers remained just about the best-paid industrial workers in the nation, considerably better off than coal miners, railroad section hands, steel mill laborers, meatpackers, and cotton mill operatives. Still, their relative prosperity was precarious. Hours of work could be unpredictable, week by week. If needed parts failed to arrive, workers could be sent home only minutes after coming to the factory. Fluctuations in sales over the year, and retooling for new models, meant seasonal layoffs in early winter and late spring for some workers. Even in a prosperous decade, they also experienced sharp (albeit, relatively brief) peaks of unemployment when demand for automobiles dipped.

A COMPANY TOWN

In the 1920s, the automobile industry accounted for 350,000 to over 400,000 jobs. The great majority of them were in the upper Midwest, and over half were concentrated in the single state of Michigan—where, by historical happenstance, most the industry's early innovators had lived and worked. Many communities in Michigan became one-industry towns—places where life was completely intertwined with automobile production. Hamtramck, a suburb of Detroit, was one of them. Settled in 1798, it had been a small farming community for over a hundred years until the Dodge brothers—at first, Ford's close collaborators and suppliers, and then his formidable competitors—began to build the Dodge Motor Company's main plant there in 1910. As the huge plant, one of the largest in the United States, took shape, the town grew rapidly around it.

Hamtramck had just under 3,600 inhabitants in 1910; by 1920, it had almost 49,000, in an area of only 2 square miles. Eighty percent of them were Polish immigrants and their children who had settled there to find family security, familiar community life, and employment at Dodge Main, which at full capacity employed around 35,000 workers. Hamtramck grew along the axis of the Joseph Campeau Avenue streetcar line, which brought workers

(Facing page, background) **The Dodge Main plant is shown here in 1930, in the midst of Hamtramck, Michigan, the small city it dominated. Stretching south of the plant are some of the city's thousands of autoworkers' homes.** *Historic American Building Survey.*

to the plant's main gates. For many years, Polish was more commonly heard than English in the town's streets and workplaces. The fabric of the city's life—its thousands of small houses; its Roman Catholic parishes, schools, and benevolent organizations; its doctors, dentists, and grocery stores—all depended on Dodge Main wages.

(Left) When this bird's-eye view of the Dodge Main plant in Hamtramck was made, c. 1929–30, the plant employed about thirty-five thousand workers. *Historic American Building Survey.*

Struggles:

The End of Prosperity and the Strikes of 1937

In 1929, automakers celebrated a record year for production and employment. Ford, General Motors, Chrysler (which had absorbed Dodge), Studebaker, Packard, Nash, and smaller firms together built 5,358,420 cars and employed 447,448 people. But the American economy had already started to collapse by the end of the year, and the industry would not see such prosperity again for many years.

Along with other Americans, autoworkers slid into the abyss of the Depression. The production of vehicles fell to levels not seen since 1916. Between 1929 and 1933, the average yearly earnings in the industry fell by nearly 40 percent, as hours and wages were cut. But that was for the fortunate workers who had managed to hold on to their jobs. Nearly half of the workers counted in 1929 were unemployed in 1933.

Manufacturers responded to falling demand and declining profits by demanding greater output from those employees who remained. Production lines felt the speed-up even more intensely than they had in the 1920s. "Workers were being fired," remembered Everett Francis, "if they slowed down and were unable to make production." Joseph Ferris recalled that "you either had to put out or get out . . . you thought you were lucky to hold on to your job."

Until the 1930s, autoworkers had had what amounted to an unspoken agreement with the companies: They would perform tension-filled, tedious, and repetitive work, under strict managerial control, in exchange for high wages. Because of those wages and the diversity of its workforce, the industry had seen relatively little union activity and few strikes in its first three decades. The Depression shattered that implicit agreement by destroying the precarious economic security of the workers and their families. As the companies offered only a harsher work regime for lower rewards, an increasing number of workers became more receptive to union organizing, and to confronting management directly over work rules

and wage cuts. This led to the organization of the United Auto Workers (UAW) in 1935, and to the "Sit-Down Strikes" of late 1936 and 1937. In order to prevent the employment of strikebreakers, General Motors workers in Atlanta and then in Flint, Michigan, occupied the plants to force the company to negotiate.

Led by union organizers, the workers at GM's Fisher Body Plant No. 1 occupied the building on December 30, 1936. The strikers were sustained with food supplied by the union's Women's Auxiliary. When the Flint police stormed the plant with tear gas in early January, the strikers fought back with the plant's own fire hoses; outside, other union members and sympathizers broke windows to dissipate the gas. After several hours of struggle, the police withdrew, leaving the strikers still in possession. Early in February, organizers were able to spread the sit-down strike to one of Flint's Chevrolet plants, forcing General Motors to recognize the union.

In March, workers secured union recognition from Chrysler after staging another sit-down strike at the Dodge Main plant in Hamtramck. Ford Motor Company held out until 1941, as an increasingly isolated and erratic Henry Ford remained determined to keep the union out at any cost, including violence and intimidation against his workers. Ultimately, a sit-down strike at Ford's River Rouge plant forced the issue, and Ford joined the other two large automakers in recognizing the UAW. For the next several decades, work in the automobile industry would be structured by union contracts; workers would not be exempt from tension, tedium, and the risks of unemployment, but they would have a greater share of protection and power.

Steering linkages move down the assembly line in the Dodge Main plant in 1934. During the difficult Depression years, workers who still had jobs pushed especially hard to keep them. *Historic American Building Survey.*

(Right) Sit-down strikers are using car seats as improvised couches in the Fisher Body plant, Flint, Michigan, early 1937.

Chapter 5
Ordinary Jobs

This broadside advertises the sale at auction of the complete inventory of a failed dry goods merchant in Boston, 1858.

Away from farms, factories, and mines, or the traditional routines of households and workshops, millions of Americans worked at undramatic jobs selling goods, keeping accounts, managing files and correspondence, and ensuring the flow of messages and information. They labored as small merchants and storekeepers, as peddlers on country roads and city streets, as clerks and copyists. Beginning in the late nineteenth century, young women entered the world of the office and store in increasing numbers as typists, "sales ladies," cashiers, and telephone operators.

Barely noticed most of the time, except for an occasional spasm of publicity and reform, was an army of ragged children, some as young as six or seven, working on the streets of American cities: running errands, shining shoes, and selling the newspapers that kept the adult population informed.

Some women took up work even farther in the shadows, in the world of sexual commerce. Prostitution was socially shameful, generally illegal, and risky, but it was a significant form of work in America, shaping the lives of hundreds of thousands of women and affecting many millions of men. It would be hard to create an honest portrait of work in America while ignoring these women.

MINDING THE STORE

Starting in the early nineteenth century, American men turned to "keeping store" by the hundreds of thousands, working as small retail merchants in country towns and city neighborhoods. Laboring at the far end of the supply chain for consumer goods, their work was distinctly undramatic. Unlike peddlers, they stayed in place, owning or renting the building that Americans always called a "store."

In some ways storekeepers' work remained very much the same over time. They bought from wholesalers, received and unpacked goods, assembled their stock for display on the store's shelves, and waited for customers. Storekeepers set prices and recorded sales, often bargaining with their customers for both price and terms of payment. They struggled with the questions of how much credit to extend to their customers, and how much credit to request from their suppliers. For several decades they went directly to wholesale merchants to pick out their stock in person; then, they increasingly dealt with jobbers and traveling salesmen who brought samples of the goods to them. The prospect of owning an independent business that promised hard work, but not physical exhaustion and danger, drew American men into storekeeping every year.

Stores often opened at dawn or not long after, to catch early rising customers, and rarely closed early, so that merchants spent long hours within the store's confines.

Country storekeeper D. M. Moody posed for his portrait, c. 1830, with his ledger books behind him. Recording sales, payments, credit arrangements, and inventories of goods, a merchant's books were the indispensable tools of his trade. *Old Sturbridge Village.*

J. M. D. Burrows, a country merchant in Davenport, Iowa, remembered in 1881 that "we hardly ever closed . . . until midnight" on the busiest trading days in spring and fall, so that the store could accommodate farm customers who came from a distance but wanted "to do their trading so as to start home early next morning." With next day's early opening and other store work to attend to, these days "made our business very laborious." Of course, in contrast to times inundated with trade, weeks could pass in the slower seasons of winter and midsummer with only a trickle of customers. Still, merchants generally kept long hours, even in slow times, as a matter of business practice; it was important not to miss any opportunity for a sale.

City storekeepers normally dealt in cash, but in the countryside, where money was in short supply for much of the nineteenth century, storekeepers played a vital role as marketers of agricultural produce. Taking cheese, butter, pork, corn, or wheat in exchange for goods, they then organized shipment to city markets, where they would be paid in credits to city wholesalers.

"Ninety per cent of American merchants fail," Thomas Nichols estimated in 1864. It was due, he said, to "boundless credit . . . active competition, and the frequent occurrence of financial crises." Nichols exaggerated, but he caught sight of an important reality. From great international trading firms to major urban retailers to small country stores, periodic business failure was a common feature of American commercial life. Most storekeepers lived on credit from their wholesale suppliers; country merchants in particular were expected to pay for them when the harvest came in and their customers could pay off their own accounts. Retail merchants often found themselves overwhelmed by accumulated debts to suppliers and lenders, overextended credit to their customers, or unwise expansion of store premises. They sold off their inventories and buildings, paid what they could, and moved on.

Americans, Nichols continued, saw business failure as a temporary condition that could, and often would, be reversed in the future. "Where a man can fail a dozen times," he wrote, "and still go ahead and get credit again, ruin does not amount to much." This too was an exaggeration, but most American merchants survived one or more brushes with the collapse of credit and the dissolution of a partnership.

THE RISE AND FALL OF A COUNTRY MERCHANT

Seth Tinsley was a country merchant whose life bore ample witness to the American cycle of ambition, expansion, prosperity, and ruin. In the early 1830s, he came to Springfield, Illinois, from Kentucky as the town became both the state's capital and a major center for the marketing and transportation of farm produce. In the early 1830s he set up as a "Dealer in Dry Goods, Groceries, etc." Tinsley advertised his goods weekly in the town's newspapers, letting customers know when he had received new shipments of cloth, footwear, foodstuffs, tobacco, and hardware, offering to take country produce in pay but promising good discounts for cash. He worked with a number of different partners, but always remained the central figure in his enterprise. Like most Western merchants, he or one of his partners made buying trips twice a year to Philadelphia, New York, or Boston to examine the new lines of spring and fall goods.

His trade prospered, enough so that in 1841 he was able to build a substantial four-story brick store on the public square in Springfield, across from the State Capitol building. Tinsley's new building would also house the town's post office, the federal court for the district of Illinois, and the law offices of an up-and-coming young attorney named Abraham Lincoln. Throughout the 1840s Tinsley seemed to have a golden touch. His store remained successful, and he used the profits, as well as a good deal of credit, to move into ventures well beyond storekeeping.

Tinsley's partnership bought a sizable cooper shop that made tubs and pails, and then invested heavily in ways of bringing Illinois agricultural goods to Eastern markets. In December 1843, Seth M. Tinsley and Company in-

This engraving of Seth M. Tinsley's store building in Springfield, Illinois, was made sometime between 1849 and 1851; the signs on the building show that he had sold part of his original mercantile business to Hurst and Taylor, although he continued a store under his own name. *Author photo.*

Wearing an apron, a store clerk waits on customers in a dry goods and grocery store, c. 1840. *Author photo.*

formed their customers that they were buying pork for shipping to "St. Louis, New Orleans, Baltimore, Philadelphia, New York or Boston." Ventures in flour milling and whiskey distilling followed, and then a plan to make illuminating oil for household lamps from Illinois lard. In 1844 Tinsley was looking for twenty thousand bushels of wheat to be milled to sell in Eastern markets, and in 1845 posted an advertisement for one hundred thousand bushels of corn. Starting as a modestly prosperous storekeeper, Tinsley now owned what R. G. Dun, the then-new business reporting service, called "the heaviest concession in this part of the country."

But in the early 1850s Tinsley's empire unraveled. His huge investments in barreled pork and Illinois flour went sour when the bottom fell out of the markets. Having guessed wrong about the changing prices of pork and wheat, he lost heavily and went deeply in debt. He sold his store to one of his junior partners and tried to save his other businesses, but ultimately failed. He went back into the store business for a while, competing with his former partner, and then gave it up and sold off all his goods. The rest of his life saw a string of modest business enterprises and frequent failures, and he began to drink heavily. By 1868 he had lost his house and was reduced to a "sleeping room" in a lumber mill that he had once owned; it burned down, sparing his life but destroying what was left of his furniture. Five months later he was dead at the age of sixty-two. His obituary remembered him as "a dashing, industrious, adventurous keen trader." But he had long outlived his successes.

In a Country Store

Thomas Waterman Wood's 1873 painting, *The Village Post Office* (shown below), gives us a carefully realized view of the interior of a country store, probably in Vermont, just after the Civil War. Goods of many kinds—ceramics, hardware, hatboxes, patent medicines, rugs, ox yokes, even a bugle—are visible on the shelves. At the left, a clerk watches while a female customer examines a bolt of cloth. At the right, several people wait in line to pick up their mail; in small communities, storekeepers very often doubled as postmasters. At the center, a number of men have settled down next to the stove to argue and read the newspaper. A basket of eggs is on the floor near the counter, one of the items of farm produce that storekeepers took in exchange for goods.

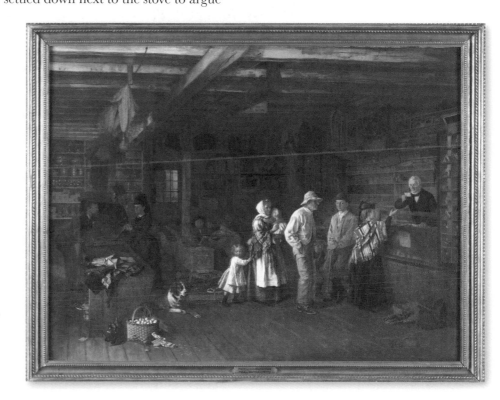

"This morning I let down the heavy, old-fashioned shutters . . . and kindle a fire," wrote Joseph O. Goodwin in 1870, recalling his daily routine in another New England country store. He went on: "I sweep the dirt from the floor . . . I sell a codfish to a little Irishwoman . . . an axe-helve, two quarts of beans, a *Farmer's Almanac*, a box of cinnamon, to others. Away from the cities," Goodwin continued, "the whole range of lesser everyday wants turns for fulfillment to the country store."

Thomas Waterman Wood painted *The Village Post Office* in 1873, probably based on a store in the Vermont countryside that he knew well. *New York State Historical Association.*

Goodwin had spent most of his early life looking at these everyday wants; he had grown up around his father's store in East Hartford, Connecticut, and had worked there until he was twenty. If a customer "wants anything, from a wash-tub to an ounce of paregoric, she knows where to find it."

Goodwin recalled the multiplicity of goods on the shelves, from the cloth and dress trimmings, coffee, tea, and hardware that were consistently in demand, to secondhand spectacles and ancient boxes of polishing powder and curative elixirs.

The storekeeper within his community was not only a source of goods but almost always a significant public figure, "used in a variety of ways—as banker, oracle, reference, newspaper, directory, intelligence man." Storekeepers listened with seeming interest to all their customers, presided affably over

(Above, left) **A storekeeper weighs out items for a customer in this c. 1840 engraving.**
Author photo.

(Above, right) **Customers examine dry goods displayed by a merchant, c. 1845.**
Author photo.

sessions of local gossip, and tried not to take sides in political discussions. They also dealt with many thousands of individual purchases and payments each year.

Storekeepers could not be "in the least exclusive," as Goodwin noted, because they needed to welcome all sorts of customers. But there were always some who seriously taxed both their equanimity and their profits. On the one hand were the "deadbeats" or credit risks. In his father's store, every year brought a new group of transient families to town, replacing "a dozen vanished predecessors." Unfortunately, every year at least one or two of them left town owing the store substantial amounts; predicting the deadbeats in advance always seemed an insoluble problem. Just as difficult were those whose payments were always "a little short of the exact amount of the bill." Less costly, but more wearing, were the ultra-suspicious, who the storekeeper found were "always questioning his weights, his prices, his figures and his books."

Goodwin had left the store to become a printer, then a writer. He was glad to leave the endless small details of retail trade to his father; the older Goodwin, a man at the center of his community, kept the store open for many more years. It remained a place for customers "with trading to do," but also continued to serve those "who came only to hear and tell what may have transpired during the day."

Country stores diminished in number with the coming of the automobile, the depopulation of rural districts, and the expansion of suburbs and chain stores, but into the 1930s there were still many thousands of them. Owning one was still an ambition for many men. John Briscoe, whose work in the Texas oil fields in the 1920s was recounted in Chapter 3, had always wanted to be a country merchant. With the savings from his difficult and dangerous job, he bought a store in the small town of Graford, Texas, in 1928, and kept his business going for another twenty-five years.

A VERY SMALL MERCHANT

Coley P. White of Wilson, North Carolina, "was busy dusting the shelves in his store" when Stanley Combs, an interviewer for the Federal Writers' Project, arrived in early July 1939. White was a storekeeper, but one on a very small scale. "His stock," wrote Combs, "consists of a line of candies, cigars, cigarettes, cold drinks, a few pies, cakes, and canned goods." White's store served the convenience needs of a down-at-the-heels neighborhood at the edge of Wilson's downtown. In order to attract additional customers, Coley White had added a slot machine and a billiard table to the small space. He was twenty-eight years old, and had learned the retail trade as a young helper at another small grocery, and then as a clerk at the town's A&P store.

The porch of a country store in Gordonton, North Carolina, is a gathering place for these African American men, c. 1939. Like many rural stores in the 1930s, it features a gasoline pump for automobiles and, on the right, a kerosene pump for lamps and lanterns. The white store owner is working inside, while his brother stands in the doorway talking.

Dorothea Lange's 1939 photograph shows the shop window of the "Golden Rule" store in the small town of Mebane, North Carolina, with its display of bags of flour.

What surprised Combs was that White, a young, single man, was living on his own right in the store. Adjacent to the main room was an office that he had outfitted with a bed and other furniture, and "in this he has worked and lived for the past several years." White had had a difficult childhood and a fractured family, and seemed to prefer living in this self-contained way.

White had to work long hours to make his store at least a little profitable, and found it helpful to be "right here on the job all the time." This also ensured that no one could break in and steal from him. Despite his meager surroundings, Coley White said, "It's all paid for, and I run things my way." About his storekeeping life, he said, "I am working here and doing well enough. Seems like I ought to make some money, but I manage to spend it all."

Tools:

ONE PRICE AND A PERFECT FIT

In American cities, with their much denser populations, retail stores had become far more specialized by the middle of the nineteenth century. In country stores, selling shoes merely involved inviting the customer to pick out a pair from the shelves—or in some stores, out of a shipping barrel.

But store owners and sales clerks in urban shoe stores had begun to develop the art of attractive displays, and of selling directly to the customer. A Currier & Ives engraving of 1871 (shown at right) shows a female customer and a shoe salesman, both fashionably dressed, in a dance of mutual appreciation over the "perfect fit."

A slightly later lithograph (shown below), from 1878, shows the exterior of what may well be the same store. A crowd of men, women, and boys are gathered outside and at the entrance, looking over its elaborate displays of styles and sizes. Here too the concern is with a "neat fit,"

The clerk in this "one-price" shoe store assures his customer that she has found the "perfect fit," c. 1871.

with a gouty man in slippers, a surveyor with new knee-high boots, and a messenger boy on his way to deliver packages of shoes. The poster is marred by a racist image of an African American man changing his shoes on the sidewalk. Here the shoes do the talking—the shopkeeper and clerks are inside.

These images display something else, another of the new tools of commerce. They are "one-price cash" stores. The store owner and clerks take only cash in payment, and will not bargain for the price. With thousands of potential customers passing by every day, and the increasing anonymity of city life, they do not need to maintain the long-term debit and credit relationships that were essential to the country store.

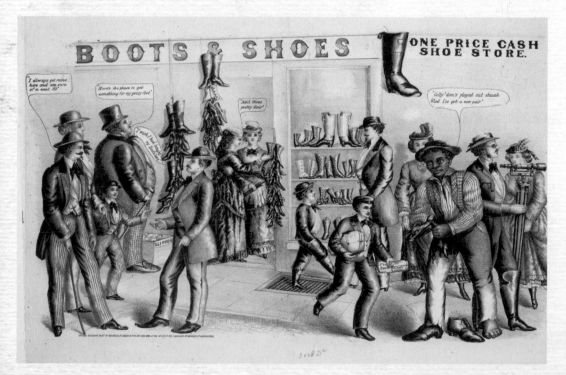

"One Price Cash Shoe Store" lithograph, c. 1878.

THE PEDDLERS WITH THEIR PACKS

Beginning early in the nineteenth century, peddlers were the advance men of the American commercial economy, carrying consumer goods out to the scattered farms of the countryside. James Guild of Tunbridge, Vermont, was one. Years later he recalled that in 1821, he had been a "farmer boy . . . confined to the hoe or the axe," who hated working in the fields. He bought a load of goods on credit, hoisted the heavy pack onto his shoulders, and "put on a peddler's face." Then, over rudimentary roads, he walked west to Rochester, New York—a distance of 340 miles. Over the course of that two-month journey, he stopped at every house he could see from the road, and asked the invariable question: "Do you wish to buy some hair combs, needles, buttons, button molds, sewing silk, beads?"

By the 1840s, peddlers were visiting "every inhabited part of the United States"; on foot or driving small wagons, they were a familiar sight on the back roads. They were mostly young men, and for decades came primarily from New England, with its strong tradition of aggressive entrepreneurship. The great majority of peddlers were reasonably honest, but the more devious among them generated a vast rural folklore. Stories abounded about Yankee tricksters and gullible consumers. They were accused of selling wooden

This young peddler stands with his fully loaded walking pack, braced and harnessed to his shoulders, c. 1840–60.

A peddler displays his wares, c. 1850–60: scissors and other fine hardware, mirrors, and sewing notions.

nutmegs—carved to resemble the expensive spice—or peddling clocks that stopped running as soon as they left. Scotsman James Alexander met a couple of the less-scrupulous peddlers and was "much amused with . . . the tricks they had played in the South, selling barrels of rotten apples with a few sound ones at the top, and barrels of damaged flour." Still, on the whole, peddlers were expected and generally welcomed, if not always loved; they brought goods that families wanted and could not easily obtain.

Later in the nineteenth century, even with the revolution in transportation and communications brought by the railroad and the telegraph, and a vast expansion in the number of country stores, peddlers maintained a place in the American economy. There were still great stretches of countryside where farms were widely separated and villages were difficult to reach; families looked forward to seeing a peddler coming down the road.

"A Newspaper and a Department Store"

Hyman Bernstein understood this well. He spent fifty years as a peddler on the back roads of Illinois and Iowa, from 1871 to 1921. A Russian Jew, he came to Chicago at the age of eighteen. "I had learned no trade in Russia," he recalled, and for him, "the easiest thing to do" was to buy "some dry goods" and start to sell them door to door. Initially, he thought that he would earn his living in the neighborhoods of the fast-growing city. But the great Chicago Fire of 1871 intervened, devastating the city and bringing most economic activity to a standstill. "Many of the hopes were burned," Bernstein remembered, and thousands left the city, looking for a way to live. "A great many men became country peddlers," and he was one of them, "walking from farm to farm" carrying a heavy pack. It would become his life's work.

Bernstein told his story in 1938, when he was eighty-five. "There was no rural mail delivery in those days," he said, and "the farmers very seldom saw a newspaper." He found that his customers were just as hungry for news from the city as for the goods he brought: "You see, I was a newspaper and a department store."

The first two years of peddling were the hardest, before Bernstein had saved enough to buy a horse and small wagon. In some of the districts he traveled, the houses were miles apart, and it would "take a day sometimes to walk from one farm to the next one."

For fifty years he spent most of his life on the road, in summer and winter, good weather and bad. The farm families he visited fed him well, and there was always a place to sleep—a hayloft in warm weather, and a spare bed or the floor near the stove when it was cold. His wintertime visits were especially welcomed: "The farmers were very lonely during the long winters, and they were glad to have anybody come to their homes."

This 1868 engraving depicts a peddler showing his wares to a rural family—cloth, brooms, brushes, tin wares, pails, and buckets.

Bernstein always returned to Chicago at the end of every journey. He married, bought a house, and had six children. He remembered that he always came home for Jewish holidays, and returned for a week each time one of his children was born. But then he "was off again in my wagon." He made "pretty good money, but never got rich." His earnings went to bring his and his wife's families over from Russia and to put their children through college. "I feel that we made a good investment," he said. He did not regret it.

Bernstein was proud of what he had done: "The peddlers with their packs," he said, "did their share to make life more comfortable for the farmers, while they were ploughing the ground and raising food for America."

"IT DOES MIRACLES"

Still traveling in 1938 was Clement Flynn, another Federal Writers' Project interviewee, but a very different sort of peddler. He sold not dry goods but a universal cure for human ills. Born in Michigan, Flynn had come to Yuma, Colorado, to homestead a farm and cut timber, work he did until 1893, when he made the discovery that would define his life. He "got a receipt [recipe] for a medicine," he said, "which I have made and sold 45 years . . . I call it the

A country peddler—a short man with a white beard and a round "slouch" hat—poses in front of his wagon, surrounded by customers, c. 1889. A peddler's chant remembered in rural New York State goes: "Sam Wilson, pots and pans / Calico, candy, toys and cans / Medicine, dishes, brooms and wares / Sam is here, forget your cares."

Itinerant photographers could also be counted among the nation's peddlers. City people could easily find a photographer's studio, but in the late nineteenth and early twentieth centuries, hundreds of men traveled the back roads of rural America, taking and selling family portraits. In 1906, a photographer poses a country family in front of their house.

Emblems:

The Cries of New York

In 1938, it was estimated that New York City had about three thousand licensed pushcart peddlers, and almost as many unlicensed ones. Most of them worked in the eighty or so places in the city that over the previous three decades had been set aside as permanent pushcart markets. But there were still some peddlers who sold their goods on the streets by calling out to their customers with distinctive cries—a tradition that went back to the eighteenth century.

Terry Roth of the Federal Writers' Project described how the criers carried out their street commerce: "The peddler winds in and out of the streets of the city, bellowing, yodelling, whining, purposefully indistinct cries that will attract the curiosity of the housewife and bring her to the window to discover the cause of the commotion; a philosophy similiar to that of the extra news hawks. She is met by the tempting display of the wares and the attractive prices. The crier has made his contact."

The criers could still be heard in 1938, but it was clear that they were gradually vanishing from the city's streets. Roth and his coworkers collected the "Cries of New York" for what they hoped would be an enduring piece of American folklore.

When I cry it will be so loud that the people come to the windows, look out. They come down with bedroom shoes on, with bathrobes, and some have pans or newspapers to put the fish in.

When I first come in a block nobody pays any attention. Then I start singing, get them to laughing and looking, and soon they start buying. A lot of them just hang around to hear the song. I always try to give the best I can for the money, the best fish for the money, and that makes repeated customers. A lot of people wait for my individual cry.

—Clyde "Kingfish" Smith, a fish vendor in Manhattan

A customer samples a clam from a pushcart vendor on Mulberry Street, c. 1900.

(Top) A hair tonic pitchman peddles his wares, Seventh Avenue at 38th Street, c. 1936.

(Bottom) A banana peddler displays his wares to a New York City housewife, c. 1900.

This watch I hold in my hand is genuiiiine!
Step up closer!
Listen to it—examine it—what a beauty!
Only one fourth of a dollar. Twenty-five cents!

—CHEAP WATCH PITCHMAN,
LOWER EAST SIDE

Wahooooo!
Fresh Fish!
Wahooooo!
Fresh Cod!
Wahooooo!
Fresh Mackerel!

—THE FISH MAN, THE BRONX

Ahps! (apples)
Peeeeeches!
Flowxrwrwhers!

—THE FRUIT AND FLOWERS MAN,
THE BRONX

Pickled,
Pickled,
Piiiiickled watermilyons!
Mops,
Brooms
Everything tin!

—PICKLE AND HARDWARE SELLERS, EAST
HOUSTON AND ORCHARD STREETS

Great Remedy." A tall, bearded bachelor never seen outdoors without an umbrella in his hand, Flynn had spent decades selling his remedy to the far-flung farm and ranch families of eastern Colorado and western Nebraska.

He had complete faith in the herbal ingredients he concocted and bottled every year. "It cures anything. Pains, Colds, Coughs, Pneumonia, Rheumatism, Arthritis, Burns," he said. "When you don't feel well, just take a teaspoonful twice a day and it will do the work." Patent medicines have always had a powerful appeal to American consumers, and "The Great Remedy" clearly found many repeat customers out on the Great Plains. But although he believed that his elixir was "a miracle," Flynn was never ambitious to make a fortune. Without a family to support, he would "work a while, then lay around during the winter or until I needed money again." Then he would fill and label his bottles, hitch up his wagon, and go back on the road.

CLERKS

As the American economy grew in the early nineteenth century, its institutions, and the transactions in which they engaged, became ever more complex. Keeping the books, carrying on correspondence, taking inventories, copying documents, preparing goods for shipment, calculating profit and loss, all made up an immense and constantly expanding burden—the work of clerks. They worked in wholesale warehouses and retail stores, law offices and auction firms, insurance brokerages and import firms. By the 1840s many thousands of young men were leaving farm and country villages every year to work in the offices of New York and Philadelphia, Boston and Baltimore, and many smaller places. Hunched over writing desks or checking off bills of lading, their work was visually undramatic, but vitally important. Even though they were not directly producing the goods, they were managing the new American marketplace.

"The young men engaged in the commercial houses of this metropolis are innumerable," wrote Reverend James W. Alexander about New York in 1857, and every few years their "numbers rise by tens of thousands." What he called "an increasing centripetal force" was attracting "the youth of rural districts towards the great emporium." In its own way, this flood of young men into city offices was one of the important migrations of American history. Young men came to work as clerks, to keep accounts and copy letters, because it was the path to success—to becoming a merchant, a banker, a partner in the firm. Some would succeed fully, while others would achieve part of their ambition or fall into disappointment. But this ambition was the engine that propelled them into counting houses and offices.

In this c. 1840 engraving of an importing merchant's countinghouse, the merchant himself is seated, reading a letter. One clerk is supervising the off-loading of goods from a ship, while others are writing at the high desk, scrutinizing accounts, and pulling a heavy ledger book down from the shelf. *Author photo.*

Three young men in New York City are photographed discussing business papers, c. 1860.

August Kollner's view of Wall Street, New York City, in 1847 includes places where men of business and their clerks worked: the Stock Exchange, banks, and the offices of brokerages, insurance companies, and major mercantile firms.

In 1834, Theodore Dwight described the tide of clerks and men of business that poured into lower Manhattan every working day. "Then come the clerks of all degrees," he wrote, "the youngest generally first: and these, in an hour or thereabouts, give place to their masters, who flow down with more dignity, but scarcely less speed, to the counting-rooms of the commercial streets."

It was a commonplace view among clergymen, as well as among anxious parents in the countryside, that this unstoppable flood of young clerks into the cities put them and the nation in great moral peril. "The newly arrived boy or young man plunges into trouble and danger the hour he sets foot in the city," Alexander wrote. In the eighteenth century, clerks as well as apprentices would have lived with their employers. But that was long in the past.

Now they lived anonymously in boardinghouses or rented rooms, outside the reach of family or their superiors at work. The loss of religious faith threatened, and then might come "drink, gambling and unholy love." Moral reform associations were formed to rescue these young men, churches reached out to them, and lecturers arrived to tell them about the dangers of alcohol and sexual excess.

From the 1830s to the 1850s, the five Dolbear brothers were teachers of penmanship who wrote handbooks on business handwriting, traveled across the country to teach aspiring clerks in many American cities, and were "principals of the New-York and New-Orleans writing academies."

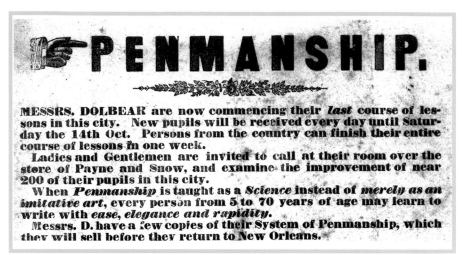

PENMANSHIP.

MESSRS. DOLBEAR are now commencing their *last* course of lessons in this city. New pupils will be received every day until Saturday the 14th Oct. Persons from the country can finish their entire course of lessons in one week.

Ladies and Gentlemen are invited to call at their room over the store of Payne and Snow, and examine the improvement of near 200 of their pupils in this city.

When *Penmanship* is taught as a *Science* instead of *merely as an imitative art*, every person from 5 to 70 years of age may learn to write with *ease, elegance and rapidity*.

Messrs. D. have a few copies of their System of Penmanship, which they will sell before they return to New Orleans.

Despite these moral risks, the American economy grew, and the number of clerks steadily multiplied. A number of young men did become "rakehells," but many others joined churches and temperance societies. Most would marry and become commercial men of one kind or another in the city. Still, all that really mattered to their employers was their work. They sold hardware and bolts of cloth, kept the ledgers and filed the promissory notes, and spent the tedious hours "packing, invoicing and replacing goods" that made the commercial economy function.

They were the young men "who get their living in one way or another by penmanship," as educator and writer Horace Mann described them in 1850. They were also young men in a hurry, working later hours, frequently moving their lodgings and changing their jobs. They were looking for their own success. Ultimately, they all wanted the moment when they could give up penmanship, counter sales, and recordkeeping and make decisions—striking bargains, ordering goods, directing the enterprise themselves.

Interestingly, the most famous clerk in nineteenth-century American literature was not one of these hopeful, ambitious young men. Herman Melville's "Bartleby the Scrivener" of 1853 was, instead, a passive and hopeless figure. He stood for the losers in the race for success, for those who would remain subordinate clerks all their working lives.

Melville describes how Bartleby began by doing "an extraordinary quantity of writing" for his employer, working "silently, palely, mechanically"

As this 1845 view of the New York post office, the nation's largest, makes clear, city postal clerks were already facing an enormous volume of routine work. Melville's Bartleby had been one of them.

at his desk. Then, he gradually, yet inexorably, abandoned his tasks. Saying only "I would prefer not to," he refused to copy documents, proofread, or run errands—that is, to do a clerk's work at all. After abandoning his work, he gave up eating, sleeping, and then speaking, finally disappearing from life altogether. Bartleby reflects the anguish of those who had lost the race for wealth and position and found themselves trapped permanently in the world of routine and small rewards.

Bartleby's despair—Melville tells us that he had previously been a clerk in that least-optimistic of workplaces, the Dead Letter Office—was, of course, extreme. Melville was portraying the plight of a lost soul in the business offices of his own time. But his powerful image of a clerk frozen in place at his desk foreshadowed what would soon be happening to the nature of office work.

In the years after the Civil War, business organizations became much larger. "Railways, telegraphs, canals, steamships," wrote George W. Beard in 1881, "have made it possible to transact a hundred-fold more business" than in the past, and with a vast "increase in business transactions." As partnerships gave way to corporations, the flow of documents and information became a flood, and jobs within them became increasingly hierarchical and specialized. The actual work of recordkeeping—and in retail establishments, the task of dealing with customers—became disconnected from management.

**Panoramic picture view of Armour &
Co.'s General Office, Union Stock Yards,
Chicago, c. 1900.**

Penmanship and bookkeeping were no longer a young man's path to power
and promotion. Men "on their way up" increasingly began in technical or supervisory work. Clerical work became more and more routine, a "dead end"
that ambitious men avoided.

A panoramic view of the offices of Armour & Company in Chicago
(shown above), around 1900, tells the story of the increasing scale and complexity of office work. Only a few hundred feet from the organized butchery
of the stockyards, hundreds of formally dressed workers are gathered into a
large, open but highly organized space. Everyone is reading, writing, or moving paper. Partitions divide workers into numerous specialized groups, organized around the flow of paper. Then there are three critical signs of ongoing
change: the telephone, the typewriter, and a half-dozen or so young women.

Cash Girls and Sales Ladies

Shortly after my wife and I moved into our c. 1876 Victorian house in the
small town of Warren, Massachusetts, we made an unexpected discovery.
Left behind in the dusty and partially finished attic was a small diary, kept
in pencil, for the year 1875. The diarist was a teenage girl named Nellie
Northrop, who had moved into the house the year it was built. She was then
sixteen, living with her grandmother and uncle and attending high school.
We read her little volume with growing fascination. Picking up clues from her
diary, we turned to the federal census, local town records, and city directories
to find out as much as we could about her later life.

Nellie's diary describes her days in high school—crushes on boys, and the
difficulties of Latin grammar—as well as the social life and gossip of a New
England village. Her mother had died a few years earlier, and her father had
become an alcoholic and abandoned her. But Nellie's story was also part of

Panoramic picture of Armour Co's General office, Union Stock Yards Chicago

a larger narrative about how women's lives were changing in the later part of the nineteenth century.

Articulate—and, with her high school diploma, well educated for her time—Nellie would never marry. She became a "spinster"—the word traditionally used to describe a single woman. But unlike her counterparts in early America, she would not live as a household dependent earning her keep at the spinning wheel. Instead, she became part of a major transformation of work that in the late nineteenth and early twentieth centuries would send hundreds of thousands of women like her into retail shops and offices.

One of the most vivid sections of Nellie's diary describes a trip to Boston to visit Henrietta Nichols, her youngest aunt. Henrietta, who was then thirty, was an occupational pioneer: She was living on her own in the city, working as a saleswoman in one of the early department stores that were beginning to dominate the retail landscape of American cities.

In the 1870s, as Francis King Carey wrote, women had begun "to be employed as attendants in shop as never before." By 1880, journalist William Rideing noted that "thousands of young women are occupied in the retail stores of Sixth Avenue and Grand Street" in New York City. The census of 1880 noted about 30,000 of them nationwide, ten times more than had been counted in 1860, and their numbers were increasing every year. By 1900 they numbered over 150,000, and in 1920, there were half a million.

Many of these young women began as teenage "cash girls." Paid meager wages on which they could not support themselves, they were expected to live at home. Rideing thought that if their families were comfortably off, the women often used their earnings

In this 1090 engraving for *Harper's Magazine,* W. A. Rogers depicts a group of young New York "shop girls" or "sales ladies,"—three of the thousands who by then were working in the city's department stores—looking at the Easter bonnets on display in a millinery shop.

Dorothy Leonard, a saleswoman in a large retail tobacco shop (c. 1910), finds an item for a customer.

to dress well. If they pleased their employers, he wrote, they could look forward in a few years to "be promoted to the positions of saleswomen," where they could earn considerably more—particularly if they had the skill "that brings a hesitating customer to conclude a purchase." Saleswomen could earn just about enough to support themselves and live independently.

In 1883, Emily Faithfull, a well-known English writer and advocate for women's work, took a careful look at these working women, whose numbers had grown so rapidly since her last visit in 1872. "American shop girls," she noted, often wanted to be called "sales ladies," which she saw as a mark of their typically American need for respect from employers and customers. It followed that by English standards, they were not particularly obliging or deferential. "By way of proving their independence and equality," she observed,

At eight thirty on a February morning in 1910, two young salesclerks walk into the employee entrance of Wanamaker's Department Store.

many of them "continually carry on conversations with each other while attending to their customers, and act as if they were conferring a great favor in supplying the goods needed."

On the other hand, Faithfull acknowledged that American shoppers were not easy to deal with; they often spent a great deal of time "visiting the stores . . . to inspect the goods, without the remotest intention of buying anything at all." Department store salesclerks had to take their customers as they came; after spending two days with her aunt behind a sales counter in Boston, Nellie Northrop noted in her diary that "some of them are awful disagreeable." Still, sales work involved little or no manual labor, and could be seen as a ladylike option for middle-class young women. Physically, it was far less taxing than seamstress work or tending power looms. Its primary drawback was the need to stand perpetually behind the counter. Faithfull

Nine young women, cashiers or "cash girls" in the Holmes Department Store in New Orleans, pose for Lewis Hine's camera in 1917.

noted as one of the occupation's drawbacks "the absence of seats for proper rest during the long hours the girls are obliged to work."

In 1914, English journalist Stephen Graham found poetry in their procession home from work:

> *First, the flood of the homeward tide at six-thirty in the evening, the thousands and tens of thousands of smartly dressed shop-girls hurrying and flocking from the lighted West to the shadowy East—their bright, hopeful, almost expectant features, their vivacity and energy even at the end of the long day.*

Neither Henrietta nor Nellie would marry, and the pattern of their lives would be similar to those of many thousands of working women. They would live as boarders in furnished rooms in respectable urban neighborhoods and work in a succession of sales and clerical jobs. Henrietta stayed in Boston and remained a "sales lady." Census and town records tell us that between 1880 and 1900 Nellie worked successively as a retail clerk for a druggist in Springfield, Massachusetts; as a postal clerk for her uncle, the postmaster of her home town of Warren; and as a bookkeeper for a store in the Boston suburb of Saugus. In 1910 she, too, was in Boston, working as a department store "sales lady."

Female workers leave the offices of T. B. Reardon's Heating and Plumbing, c. 1903.

INTO THE OFFICE

Although women had moved in large numbers into retail work by 1880, the labor force of the American office was still almost entirely male. The census for that year reported only a minuscule number of women doing clerical work—just over four thousand, or less than 1 percent of the total. But the next twenty years saw the feminization of routine office work in thousands of American companies, large and small.

Coming to America in 1883 at the beginning of this transformation, Emily Faithfull was enthusiastic about the introduction of that "marvellous machine," the typewriter. It would greatly expand opportunities for women, she predicted. "Girls quickly learn to use the type-writer," she wrote, and "seem quite to enjoy manipulating the keys." With "a few months' practice," they were soon able to write "three times as fast as with a pen, and with perfect neatness and accuracy." Women who could use the typewriter—particularly if they had also learned the Gregg or Pittman shorthand system for rapidly taking dictation, and could also become stenographers—were looking at the prospect of "a good living."

As corporations increased in size, and the complexity of commercial and financial transactions grew, the burden of record-keeping, data collection, and correspondence expanded immensely. The demand for office workers grew more rapidly than for any other occupation. By 1900 the number of women in the office had grown thirty-fold, to 125,000, and by 1920, there were over 1 million women at work typing, filing, keeping records, and taking dictation. Employers maintained that women were better at detail work, were faster and neater at their tasks, were more likely to do what they were told—and, of course, could be paid substantially less.

My father's older sisters, Florence and Isabel Larkin, became part of this new female workforce just before 1920. Their parents encouraged them to take the girls' commercial course in high school, and they both became adept at typing and shorthand. They spent their long working lives as stenographers and secretaries, taking the train every day from their family's home on Chicago's South Side to the great office buildings downtown.

CHAMPION TYPIST

A very few stenographers moved out of obscurity to become well-known. One of them was Rose L. Fritz of New York City, the daughter of a Jewish real estate broker, who for several years was famous as the world's fastest typist.

As the United States moved rapidly to a war footing in 1917, the federal government needed not only soldiers for the fight overseas, but also clerks and typists to staff the new offices for armaments, control of industry, and food production. As this recruiting poster suggests, stenographers' skills were in great demand.

(Above) This 1920 advertisement for a Chicago office supply company clearly testifies to the feminization of office work.

"I attended a business school for about three months," she told a newspaper interviewer, "during which I put in two or three hours daily on the typewriter." She discovered that she was exceptionally fast, and worked to get faster. Her aptitude was a gift, she acknowledged, but her continued improvement was just the result of her daily work as a stenographer on her first job, which kept her so busy that she "did not have time to practice outside working hours." She quickly impressed her employer with her speed and accuracy.

Soon she would impress everyone else. With her talented fingers, Rose had entered the working world just as formal speed-typing competitions—echoing earlier ones for typesetters—were beginning. Rose entered one of the first, in Chicago, at the International Business Show of 1907. She won that competition when she was nineteen, and held the title for six years. In that

(Right) Rose Fritz, six-time speed-typing champion, poses with her machine in 1911.

Surrounded by onlookers, three women compete in a typing contest in 1923 in one of the bureaus of the Navy Department in Washington, D.C.

early age of automobiles and airplanes, speed of any kind was admired, and she quickly found herself a minor celebrity.

When asked to give advice to other young women going into office work, she was happy to oblige. The first requirement, Rose said, was "absolute accuracy"; speed would come later. Typists should cover the keys on their machines lest they be tempted to look, and strike each key with "a sharp staccato blow." Just as important, they needed to take meticulous care of their machines: "[I am] astonished when I go into a business office to see the condition in which the average operator keeps her machine." A dirty, sticky machine would win no prizes for speed, and "a blurred letter is a disgrace to the operator and to the firm for which it is written."

Rose's unusual skills allowed her to move beyond regular office work. After winning her first title, she was hired by the Remington Company, a major typewriter manufacturer, to serve as both stenographer and symbol. She was given abundant time to practice and to enter competitions. Posed attractively with her typewriter and steno pad, she was photographed as "Miss Remington" in the company's advertisements. By 1920 Rose Fritz had become a teacher in one of New York City's private business schools, teaching the next generation of typists about speed, accuracy, and neatness.

TELEPHONE GIRLS

Emily Faithfull was also alert to the significant role women would play within another realm of technology. The telephone, already on its way to being "an indispensable adjunct to all places of business" in America, would soon, she predicted, "afford a suitable employment for women." Women's voices, in addition to their clerical skills, would give them the advantage. "A telephonist requires a clear voice and a good ear," she wrote, "and owing to the timbre of the ordinary female voice, girls are more adapted for the work."

Again, Faithfull saw the future. There were only a hundred or so female operators in 1880, but women workers swiftly became crucial to the rapidly expanding telephone system. Driven by the same economic forces, 20,000 of them were at work in 1900, 80,000 in 1910, and 170,000 by 1920. They became the voices at the other end of the line that Americans heard daily. Working at their switchboard consoles amid a forest of wires, they literally plugged the nation's callers in to their destinations.

Telephone operators work their switchboard at a central exchange office, c. 1915.

My great-aunt, Agnes Long, was one of them. She grew up poor in an Irish laborer's family on the South Side of Chicago, and at age fifteen was tending a machine in one of the city's many small factories. The telephone company offered her a way to better herself, and around 1905, she went to work for Illinois Bell at one of the "telephone exchanges" that the company was building throughout the city. She made her way from file clerk to operator and finally to "chief operator," or supervisor—retiring just as automated switching equipment was eliminating the sound of the human voice for most calls.

Telephone work "was awfully complicated at first," remembered Palmira Fernandes, an operator at the exchange in Barre, Vermont, who was interviewed for the Federal Writers' Project in 1939. She recalled that it had been "hard to get used to the switchboard."

People would occasionally call with the oddest requests, she continued. Heavy sleepers would sometimes request wake-up calls, and visitors to Barre would ask about the movie schedule or "a good but cheap beauty parlor." Strangest of all, though, was a call that had come in to her on the night shift the year before. A local man had been listening to the now-legendary Orson Welles broadcast of "The War of the Worlds" on Halloween eve, and was frantic with fear. He wanted her to "call New York and get the truth"—which of course, according to phone company policy, she couldn't do. Palmira hadn't heard the broadcast since she'd been working, and "didn't know whether to be scared or to set him down as a lunatic." She had to wait until the morning to find out.

Like many operators, Palmira also found the need for constant repetition, good cheer, and politeness more than a little wearing. "You get darn sick of saying 'Number, please,' and 'Yes, thank you' all the time," she explained. "You get so used to those words they're apt to roll out of your mouth anytime. I was shopping in the dime store the other day, and when the clerk handed me the change I said, 'Yes, thank you.' " When Palmira started with the phone company, she thought that she would only stay for the summer, but "it seemed so good earning my own money that I decided to stay the year. Then I stuck." On the whole, she thought, it was "not a bad job."

WORK AND THE SINGLE WOMAN

Most of the young women who took up these occupations left them after a few years to marry. Perhaps one out of ten—like Nellie, Henrietta, my great-aunt Agnes, and my aunts Florence and Isabel—would remain single and stay in the workforce until retirement.

It is important to realize that all of these hundreds of thousands—and, eventually, millions—of jobs were for single women only. Up through the 1920s, married women made up a very small percentage of the workforce

A telephone operator for the New England Telephone and Telegraph Company poses for an idealized portrait with headphones and speaker in 1911.

Oliver Herford's drawing of 1919, "Telephone Girl Becomes Stenographer," shows a young working woman being courted by two competing instruments—the typewriter and the telephone receiver.

Struggles:

THE OFFICE ROMANCE

The entry of millions of women into business offices changed the emotional temperature of the work environment. Men, both married and unmarried, worked alongside women who were mostly young and almost always in subordinate positions. Office romances became a commonplace reality, as well as a staple of popular fiction. The workplace became a theater for flirtation and courtship, one of the primary places where couples could match up. Many young managers, engineers, and accountants met their wives while they were working as stenographers and file clerks.

But there was a much darker side to the office romance; men could and sometimes did abuse their positions of power to exact sexual favors from their female employees, turning the office into a place where they could exploit young women and be unfaithful to their wives. Popular culture tended to take this lightheartedly, portraying outraged wives storming into the office to find their philandering husbands embracing the "young hussies" who were supposed to be taking dictation. Just as with the depiction of young servant girls as seductresses, it was easier to blame the victim. The reality was rarely so amusing.

(Below) **This William Jacob drawing from 1902 illustrates one of the popular themes about life in the new office setting. Here a business executive says to his young and attractive stenographer, "I regret having to let you go, Miss Keys, but my wife doesn't seem to like you, and, er . . . you see, I . . . er, can't discharge my wife."**

(Above) **Part of a humorous series from 1907 about life in the new American office, this stereograph view shows an executive's wife breaking in on him as he embraces his secretary.**

outside of the household, farm, or family-owned small store. Work outside the home was virtually unthinkable for most married women, a violation of the norms of family life and the proper role of men as the principal family breadwinners. Few employers would knowingly hire them.

This was underlined in a terrible and dramatic way in my wife's family. Her grandmother, Harriet Knapp, went to work for Macy's Department Store in New York around 1920 in order to supplement her family's income—but of course, to get the job she had to remain silent about her married status. Over a few years she rose to become an assistant buyer in the housewares department. It seems that she kept her secret well. No one in authority knew that she was married, let alone that she had children, until in 1927, one of her sons was killed in a horrific automobile accident that was splashed over the front pages of the New York newspapers. She never returned to Macy's.

Newsboys: An American Institution

Darting in and out of street traffic and "hawking" newspapers to pedestrians at the top of their lungs, newsboys became an American institution with the beginning of the "penny press" in the early 1830s. Previously, daily newspapers had been considerably more expensive, costing more than most passersby were willing to pay on the street. With the advent of one-cent papers the first successful one was the *New York Daily Sun*, beginning in 1833—a young and ragged sales force emerged to put these cheap dailies into the hands of clerks, merchants, and workmen.

In 1845, caricaturist D. C. Johnston pictured a Boston newsboy, shoeless and ragged, being apprehended by one of the city's new police officers while a hypocritical bystander laments the boy's immorality. *Author photo.*

H. R. Robinson's 1850 cartoon portrays the competing parties in New York City politics—the Whigs and the "Loco-Foco" Democrats—as tussling newsboys. The Democrats are shown as ragged and barefoot. The Whigs, as the party of business, are depicted as better-dressed than any newsboy was likely to be.

By 1864, Thomas Nichols acknowledged that "the institution of newsboys," although "a very noisy one," was indispensable for the dissemination of information in the cities of the United States. Americans were unable to "wait for news with the stolid patience of Englishmen," and eagerly snapped up "extras"—new editions that came out to report breaking news and could appear "at any hour of the day, and at any time before midnight." By the time Nichols was writing, every major American city had competing daily papers and hundreds of vociferous boys on the street, who "cry murders or battles, fires or shipwrecks over the city."

But newsboys were not just the noisy heralds of shipwrecks and elections, or picturesque figures on the urban scene. They were children, always from poor families, and sometimes orphaned and homeless. Their work, especially at night, exposed them to the dangers of the city streets.

John Morrow's *A Voice from the Newsboys*, published in 1860, is the earliest description of an American newsboy's life. Born in 1844, he was one of seven children of a New York City family wracked by drink and violence. His working life began at seven when his father and stepmother sent him down to the city's docks to steal firewood and coal; later, he and his siblings sold matches on the street. After many drunken beatings, he ran away from home and began a perilous life selling newspapers and living on Manhattan's streets. At various times he was beaten, robbed, and attacked by wild dogs.

His good fortune was to find refuge at one of the few places that cared for children of the street, the Newsboys' Lodging House. There he learned to read, struggled to find ways to take care of his younger siblings, and began his religious education. Encouraged by advocates for the city's poor, and clearly helped by one of them as a ghostwriter, he produced an account of his life at the age of sixteen.

Most of the newsboys he knew, he wrote, had lives like his; they had been "dropped homeless . . . upon the world" by the "drunken barbarity or delirious death" of their parents. Those that still lived at home were forced into the work by constant "stinging abuse." Morrow recalled how he and his companions would wake up in a "bedless den" and rush to the newspaper office at four thirty in the morning to wait for their bundles of papers. They would then spread out over the city with their raucous songs—"Here's the *Herald! Times! Tribune!*" Finishing at around nine o'clock in the morning, they would count their coins, buy a cheap breakfast, and go in search of errands to run, like delivering messages and carrying packages or travelers' luggage. After another cheap meal they would return to the office for the evening papers, and spend another three or four hours on the darkening streets, ending the day just as they began it, "by supplying people with the latest news."

Passersby, intent on their own business, rarely gave the newsboys a second look, Johnny Morrow wrote. If they had, they would have seen small boys "splashing wearily through the mud" of the city's streets and in winter, "chilling their bare feet against the icy flag stones, and drawing their rags about them."

In 1909, Lewis Hine photographed these newsboys in Hartford, Connecticut, at noontime on a Sunday. "Many of them had been out since 5 and 6 a.m.," he noted. He also observed that many of the newsboys were just seven or eight years old.

DETROIT
NEWSBOY
CIGARS.
MANUFACTURED BY
BROWN BROTHERS
DETROIT.

The book earned Morrow some celebrity and a bit of money. Sadly, young Morrow died in 1861, a few days after a risky surgical operation on a chronically lame leg. His gravestone stands today in the city's Evergreen Cemetery.

Morrow hoped that his book would encourage greater compassion toward street children and more help for them, and perhaps it did. City authorities and child advocates paid at least a little more attention to the newsboys, reducing some of the worst savagery of their lives.

Nonetheless, the number of boys plying this trade in the streets continued to grow enormously. By the early twentieth century there were far more city newsboys than there had been in Johnny Morrow's time. Between 1860 and 1910, with the continued expansion of both city populations and newspapers in circulation, their number had probably grown thirty-fold. Americans were buying millions of copies of newspapers on the streets every day.

Some former newsboys recalled their lives as a kind of picaresque adventure. "When papers was a penny apiece," remembered Chicago sign painter Philip Marcus, "was the days when I was selling them." It was around 1910, and Marcus recalled, "[I] was a little lad then, and I lived on the streets practically all day, days and nights both." Marcus's family was poor, but he wasn't pushed into street life; he chose it as a form of defiance. He had begun to "run wild" at seven years old, and ran away from home many times, despite his mother's attempts to get him "to stay off the streets at night." Working as a newsboy gave him a kind of perilous freedom, with his family as an ultimate backstop.

(Facing page) **This 1894 advertisement for Newsboy Cigars emphasizes the picaresque side of a newsboy's life, showing them as happy mischief-makers, playing cards on a cigar packing crate. The cigars were manufactured in Detroit, and the shoulder bag of the newsboy on the left reads** DETROIT FREE PRESS.

Newsboy Joseph Harris was small for his age at nine years old; he told Lewis Hine that he had started work on the streets of Hartford when he was seven.

He and other newsboys "used to sneak in the burlesque houses or the all-night places on West Madison Street and sleep there." The problem, he explained, was that "the ushers would come around every hour or so and throw the flashlight in your face to see was you awake. Sometimes they threw us out." Then the boys would hunt for another place to sleep.

Marcus and his friends spent most of their time selling penny newspapers, but had "a lot of dodges" for making additional money. They practiced dozens of ways of cheating customers out of their change, and stayed alert to chances for petty theft. Marcus remembered being an important part of the city's street life in another way. "The newsboy was always a good source of information in those days," he recalled. "You could find out from us almost anything you wanted to know—where the saloons were . . . the location of the gambling joints, the whorehouses, almost anything." Such information could sometimes yield a tip. "We was always on the make. We had to be."

Marcus spent some time in one of Chicago's reform schools, but survived his newsboy days to become a respectable, if streetwise citizen, with children

In 1913 Lewis Hine photographed and interviewed the three Sasser brothers who were selling papers in San Antonio.

of his own—whom he never would dream of allowing to "live on the streets . . . day and night" as he had done.

As part of his relentless documentation of child labor, Lewis Hine photographed hundreds of newsboys between 1908 and 1917, in dozens of American cities. Hine's newsboys were not as ragged as those of the mid-nineteenth century; standards of clothing, even for the poor, had improved over the years. Boys in Northern cities were shown with shoes and at least adequate clothes—although in Tampa, Florida, and San Antonio, Texas, they continued to work the street barefoot. But they remained strikingly, painfully young. In virtually every city he visited, Hine found many who were seven or eight years old. In Hartford and New York City, he found something that had been rare or nonexistent in the nineteenth century: a few "newsgirls," no older than the boys, also selling on the streets.

Hine photographed these young people and gathered some information about them, but never had the time to investigate their living situations systematically. Still, it seemed clear that at least a few were essentially homeless, and that others had only a tenuous connection with their poverty-stricken families. In 1913 he documented the three Sasser brothers of San Antonio (shown on page 352), ages five, seven and eleven, who "all start out at 6:00 A.M. and sell until 9:00 and 10:00 P.M. nearly every day except Sunday." The oldest brother struggled to keep the two younger ones earning enough to bring back home. "We don't go to school," he told Hine. "Got to sell papers. Father is sick."

Most, however, seem to have had families to return to at night—families that needed their income badly enough to continue sending them out to work, despite their youth, the long hours, and the risks of the street.

Changes in child labor laws and their more rigorous enforcement, the schools' increasing concern with the prevention of truancy, and the advent of newspaper home delivery ended the era of the newsboys. As well, the emergence of radio news took some of the urgency away from the "extra edition." The "newsie" on the street, young, brash, and ragged, ultimately gave way to the newspaper rack and the vending machine.

THE UNDERGROUND LIFE: PROSTITUTION

In 1836, Helen Jewett was twenty-two years old, a beautiful and fashionably dressed woman living in New York City. Early on the morning of April 10, she was found murdered in her bed with her room ablaze. Her killing and the trial that followed became the most sensational story of the year for the city's then-new daily newspapers. But Helen was not a "respectable" young woman. She was a prostitute, and her room was not in her family's house but

Two lithographic images of Helen Jewett were made in 1836 shortly after her death. One (calling her "Ellen") showed her in her bed, partly clothed, immediately after her murder. The other portrayed her as a pretty, fashionably dressed young woman. Both were by the same artist, Alfred M. Hoffy. *Courtesy American Antiquarian Society.*

in the expensive brothel owned by the well-known madam Rosina Townsend. Her real name was Dorcas Doyen, and she was a country girl from a poor family in Temple, Maine, who had come to the city at eighteen to find a new and more prosperous life. It is virtually certain that she was killed by one of her repeat clients, Richard Robinson, but he was acquitted after the judge ordered the jury to ignore the testimony of her fellow prostitutes, and the defense was able to portray her as a wily, cold-hearted temptress. Helen's terrible fate set her apart, but she had thousands of sisters in her trade in America's greatest city, and many more thousands elsewhere.

Despite oft-repeated civic boasts about the virtue, as well as the freedom, of the American people, visitors to the United States found

In 1873 C. S. Reinhart drew "Underground Life in New York," showing prostitutes and drunken men in a bawdy house, and Board of Health inspectors taking filthy rugs, bedding, and furniture from a cellar "dive" while a partially dressed woman gestures angrily.

SKETCHES FROM OUR ARTIST'S NOTE-BOOK.

Helen's occupation shockingly prevalent. "In no cities of Europe are prostitutes more numerous in proportion to the population," wrote Englishman Andrew Bell in 1836, "than in New York, Philadelphia, and Baltimore." Each of these cities, and others as well—including Boston—had a kind of sexual marketplace, with services elaborately graded by price and location. Services ranged from the most expensive "parlor houses" situated near the best hotels, to the women congregating in the uppermost balconies of theaters, to the cheapest dockside dives.

In a smaller American community, young writer Nathaniel Hawthorne found things much the same in 1836. He confided to his travel notebook that he had been talking with a group of men on the porch of a tavern in Augusta, Maine, when a young man walked up and asked if anyone knew the whereabouts of Mary Ann Russell. "Do you want to use her?" was the crude response from one of the bystanders. Mary Ann was, in fact, the young man's wife, but she had left him and their child to become "one of a knot of whores" that plied their trade near the state capitol.

These patterns, laid down in the early nineteenth century, had changed little over the years for this "oldest of professions." Prostitution grew along with the country. By 1855, it was estimated that there were "full 500 resorts of prostitutes" in New York, and over 200 "dance-houses" where they could be found. Prostitutes moved west with the frontier, arrived in California along with the forty-niners, and were abundant just about everywhere working men congregated in substantial numbers—in mining camps, lumber and railroad towns, oil fields, and the "red light" districts of cities.

Campaigns against prostitution came and went in the nineteenth and twentieth centuries, including massive police raids, powerful movements of

In most American cities in the nineteenth century, the theater served as a place of assignation as well as popular entertainment, including this theater in Boston, c. 1858–59. Prostitutes frequented the uppermost tier of seats, often called "the guilty third tier," and men climbed the stairs to meet them, often leaving the theater together to go back to the women's lodgings.

Built in 1892, the Copper Block housed many of the prostitutes that worked in the copper-mining city of Butte, Montana. *Historic American Building Society.*

religious reform, and public health crusades, but none were permanently effective. The trade remained ineradicable. Sexuality could not be completely tamed, or completely divorced from commerce.

Prostitution took women into the demimonde, a shadow world with some opportunities and many risks. Many prostitutes took up their trade out of poverty and domestic disaster. A young widow, or a country girl, arrived in the city, and dependent on her own resources, often faced desperate economic choices, because most women's work paid too poorly to provide decent food, clothing, and shelter. But others entered the profession because they sought excitement or independence from their families, or because they were attracted to the lure of fashionable clothes and furnishings that their earnings could provide.

Men of all ages, married and unmarried, from city lawyers to visiting country storekeepers to sailors on the docks, turned to brothels for sexual release, but most of the brothels' customers were young men, living away from home and increasingly unlikely to marry until their late twenties.

Prostitution was rarely a long-term career; as women aged and "hardened," they increasingly lost their economic value. Women in bawdy houses were generally in their teens, and twenties; their "housekeepers" or madams were older ex-prostitutes. Some saved enough from their high-earning days to open small businesses or live in some comfort; many spent their later years eking out a living as barmaids, laundresses, and seamstresses. The most unfortunate found their lives destroyed by drink and venereal disease. They went, in the words of *The Manufacturer and Builder's Magazine* in 1890, from the "gilded hells" of the bawdy houses "to the pauper's grave in the Potter's Field or the dissecting table of the surgeon."

"INTO A LIFE OF SHAME"

How many prostitutes have worked in America at any one time? "We have 600,000 prostitutes" in the United States, lamented a clergyman in 1900, "and many more doubtless that are not known." But no one has ever produced an accurate count. For obvious reasons, women "in the life" have usually concealed their occupation from census takers and the compilers of city street directories. In the nineteenth century they sometimes identified themselves as "seamstresses," blending in with hundreds of thousands of other working women. In some cities they called themselves "actresses," creating statistical patterns that suggested an unrealistically large-scale devotion to the stage.

One closer look at the prostitutes' world was published in 1888, when pioneering sociologist Carroll D. Wright worked with the Boston police department to study the paths into prostitution of nearly two hundred of the city's women. The largest number had been domestic servants, followed by girls who had worked in textile mills and shoe factories. Almost as many were women who had simply fled their own families, giving up their roles as daughters or wives. Next came seamstresses, dressmakers, and store clerks. One woman had been a music teacher, another a skilled typesetter. What had caused "their entry into a life of shame?" asked Wright. He reported that "17 entered their present life because of ill treatment at home . . . 26 testify that they were driven into the life by poor pay and hard work, while 46 were brought into the life through seduction." Then there were the ones he found most morally culpable. Just as Helen Jewett had a half-century before, 59 of them said that they wanted luxury and fashion—they had made the choice "through love of easy life and love of dress." Just as with Dorcas Doyen, the question of choice was surely far more complicated, but Wright's judgment—mirroring that of society as a whole—was unsparing.

Twenty-two years later, Lewis Hine was documenting one of the places in America where very young girls were being pulled into that "life of shame." In November 1910 he took a series of grim photographs of "Hell's Half Acre," a strip of ramshackle structures just across a shallow creek from the factory village of Avondale, Alabama. The Half Acre's buildings were bawdy houses, he was told, just far enough away from the mills that the owner could disclaim any responsibility for them. Not only did "the mill people patronize these resorts," he learned, but also, many seduced and abandoned "mill girls end up in these houses." Worse still, there were "on court record, three cases within a year of girls under fourteen years of age ruined in Hell's Half Acre." This seduction and abuse of young girls, whose families were too demoralized or brutalized to stop it, was the worst aspect of the underground life, but to Hine's knowledge, little or nothing was being done about it.

The Brothels of Sedalia

Another glimpse of prostitution in America—this time a rare look at daily life in a brothel—emerges from an unusual architectural study.

Sedalia, Missouri, today is a hardworking small city in the central part of the state, but years ago, it was a tough and wide-open town. Sedalia began in the 1860s as a railroad town, a community that owed its existence to the Missouri Pacific and Missouri-Kansas-Texas railroads that intersected there. Well into the twentieth century, Sedalia was a major center for railroad switching and repair, and a railhead, or receiving point, for cattle drives from Texas.

Prostitutes in Sedalia were comfortable enough that they often defied the conventions of concealment, forthrightly listing their true occupation on the census. Still standing in Sedalia is one of its brothels, built in 1874 at the beginning of the town's railroad boom. The two-story brick building at 217 Main Street is ordinary-looking, with shops below and rooms above. But it may have the distinction of being the only brothel on the National Register of Historic Places.

The brothel at 217 Main served as a house of prostitution for sixty-five years, from the time of its construction until 1940. Legitimate businesses— grocery stores, pharmacies, carriage shops, restaurants—occupied the first floor. Ordinary working people had small apartments at the front, facing the street. At the rear were the prostitutes' quarters; their rooms ran off a hall that went back to a separate entrance concealed from the street. The door at the head of the back stairs still has its peephole today, installed so that the women could scrutinize potential customers before letting them in.

The rooms still bear clear evidence of their use for sexual commerce. Amazingly, their plaster walls have survived, covered with graffiti left by the women's customers. "Bertha Best in the House," wrote one. "Josie the best looker on Main Street" appeared in another hand. Some railroad men who were passing through identified themselves by their trade and hometown: "Richard Sittle, Machinist / Moberly, Mo." Walter Beardsley did not give his occupation but boasted unprintably about his physical endowments. F. M. Roberts signed his name with an elegant flourish; he was an instructor of penmanship in a Sedalia business college. The most dramatic of the customers' graffiti is a full-length prostitute's "portrait"—a drawing of a dark-haired young woman clad only in corset and stockings.

Twenty-two women of Sedalia, including those who worked at 217 Main, openly identified themselves as prostitutes in the 1900 census. They ranged in age from eighteen to thirty, and seem to have been nearly as transient as the railroad workers, coming to Sedalia from Illinois and Iowa, Ohio, Kentucky, and Kansas, as well as from other parts of Missouri.

(Facing page, top) **Lewis Hine photographed "Hell's Half Acre" in Avondale, Alabama, in 1910, a settlement of "disreputable houses" near the Avondale Cotton Mills.**

(Facing page, bottom) **Girls and young women are leaving work for the noon break at the Avondale Mills, walking only a few yards from the bawdy houses of "Hell's Half Acre." Lewis Hine noted that some young mill girls wound up there.**

(Above) **Customers drew graffiti on the plaster walls of the brothel rooms at 217 Main Street in Sedalia, Missouri. This sketch of a largely undressed young woman is the most dramatic of them.**
Missouri State Archives.

Despite opposition from local churches, prostitution went on openly in Sedalia because public opinion favored tolerance. Local authorities valued its economic benefits; the keepers of bawdy houses paid high rents to the prominent men who owned downtown buildings, and as late as 1900, prostitutes were paying sizable quarterly fines into the town treasury in order to keep working. And, just as important, it was well known that the town's brothels drew their customers from all ranks of society, including the powerful. For many years, most of the men in Sedalia willingly allowed the brothels to stay.

Brothel customer E. H. Ruef has signed his name on the brothel room's wall, just above the drawing of a grinning, leering face. *Missouri State Archives.*

Eyewitness:

FRANK BYRD AND "BETTY"

Frank Byrd was a New York writer who found work in the 1930s at the Federal Writers' Project. Byrd wrote a series of twenty-two sketches about the street peddlers, preachers, entertainers, and prostitutes in his city. "Betty" was a woman Byrd had known in the 1920s, when she worked for a few years as a "high-class" prostitute. Byrd wrote her story in 1938:

Luigi's speakeasy did an all-night business, but you had to know what to say before they'd let you in. Whenever the bell rang, Jimmy got up and peeped through a little hole in the door. Well, he did the same thing the night Betty walked in. It was the first time I had seen her; I won't forget it. She was the kind of girl men fight for . . . but on a Harlem police blotter, they had "prostitute" scribbled opposite her name. Not that she looked like one. Her eyes were a pale, lovely blue; her hair, soft and brown.

She was in love. The boy's name was Bill.

When Jimmy opened the door, Betty, eyes sad, pocketbook under arm and looking tired, hesitated in the doorway before walking to the far end of the room. No one looked up apparently, but several pairs of eyes followed every movement of her graceful body.

"How's things, Joe?" Betty greets the bartender. "Hiya, Betty," Joe says without looking up. "Note for you." She lights a cigarette and casually unfolds the piece of paper. Her features light up. Business . . . more money for Bill, who understands her and needs her.

Drawing her coat a little more closely near the waistline, Betty walks briskly toward the door. Sam, the taxi-driver, follows. He has that something closely akin to a sixth sense. It tells him whenever Betty wants him to drive her places and, if necessary, collect for her. Both of them disappear into the dark street.

Girls like Betty, they say, are all alike. Perhaps they are. I don't know. But I do know she was a Wellesley graduate . . . and all girls are not Wellesley graduates.

Betty came to Greenwich Village to write. They brought her to Harlem to get "local color." Well, she got it. Bill was working in a nightclub, one of those dingy, smoky little basement places. Betty

liked him and he saw in her all the things he had missed in other women. He sang for her. Afterwards she went home to the Village with her friends. The next time she came to Harlem, she came alone. The place had "got" her, as they say.

Cigarette smoke, fast living, and basement gin put an end to Bill's love songs. He left for Arizona. Betty hoped he might get over it but she knew that wasted lungs are not cured overnight. It cost her $200 a month to keep him in a sanitarium there.

After that, she didn't have to worry about bills and money. She always had more than enough.

Men loved Betty. When she smiled at them, they did anything she wanted. Many of them wanted to marry her, but she only looked at them with a little amused smile playing about the corners of her mouth.

A hijacker once gave her two truckloads for a kiss. A boy from Park Avenue lost a $1,000 bet on her. He thought she'd say "yes" when he asked her to marry him . . . and she knew his family was one of the oldest in the Social Register.

Betty had to have money . . . for Bill. So she got it. Nothing else mattered to her. Men brought it to her and were happy because it made her smile.

But the reason I tell you this is because she came to Luigi's new place on the Avenue last night, and it was the first time I had seen her since the old days. She certainly was not the same carefree Betty I once knew.

Bill, of course, did not come back. "He was too far gone," the doctors said. The kid is still very good to look at, and while she was perched on the stool at the bar, one of the men who used to know her walked over and said something. She shook her head, meaning "no." Then he pulled a wad of bills out of his pocket and showed them to her.

I could see her reflection in the mirror and what her lips said was: "I don't need it."

The man went away puzzled. He couldn't understand such a complete change. He couldn't, of course. He never knew about Bill.

Suggestions for Further Reading

VISUAL COLLECTIONS

The extraordinary visual collections of the Library of Congress can be accessed at its American Memory Web site (http://memory.loc.gov), and also through the Prints and Photographs Online Catalog (www.loc.gov/pictures).

There are many specialized image collections on the Library of Congress site. What follows is a list of those I made substantial use of in this book.

- America's First Look into the Camera: Daguerreotype Portraits and Views, 1839–1864

- Taking the Long View: Panoramic Photographs, 1851–1991

- Lawrence & Houseworth (San Francisco, California) Photograph Collection, 1862–1867

- History of the American West, 1860–1920: Photographs from the Collection of the Denver Public Library

- Prairie Settlement: Nebraska Photographs and Family Letters, 1862–1912

- Kern County Survey Collection: Photographs of Agriculture and Industry in Kern County, California, 1880s

- The Northern Great Plains, 1880–1920: Photographs from the Fred Hultstrand and F. A. Pazandak Photograph Collections

- Touring Turn-of-the-Century America: Photographs from the Detroit Publishing Company, 1880–1920

- Lewis Wickes Hine Photographs, National Child Labor Committee Collection, 1908–1924

- Prosperity and Thrift: The Coolidge Era and the Consumer Economy, 1921–1929

- Farm Security Administration Collections, 1935–1940

AUTOBIOGRAPHICAL AND LITERARY ACCOUNTS

The documentary sources for *Where We Worked* were extremely various and scattered in many places. Here is a short list of the most interesting and widely available autobiographical and literary accounts:

Adams, Andy. *Log of a Cowboy: A Narrative of the Old Trail Days.* Eastbourne, UK: Gardners Books, 2007. (Originally published in 1903) [A Texas cowboy's life]

American Life Histories: Manuscripts for the Federal Writers' Project, 1936–1940. (http://lcweb2.loc.gov/wpaintro/wpahome.html)

Garland, Hamlin. *A Son of the Middle Border.* New York: Penguin Books, 1995. (Originally published in 1900) [Farming in the Midwest]

Love, Nat. *The Life and Adventures of Nat Love.* Salem, NH: Ayer, 1992. (Originally published in 1907) [Life of an African American cowboy turned railroad porter]

Melville, Herman. "Bartleby the Scrivener," 1853.

Robinson, Harriet Hanson. *Loom and Spindle, or Life Among the Early Mill Girls.* New York: Pacifica Press, 1976. (Originally published in 1898)

Rosengarten, Theodore. *All God's Dangers: The Life of Nate Shaw.* Chicago: University of Chicago Press, 2000. [An African American sharecropper in Alabama]

Sinclair, Upton. *The Jungle.* (Originally published in 1905; many recent editions) [Work in the Chicago stockyards]

Stowe, Estha Briscoe. *Oil Field Child.* Fort Worth: Texas Christian University Press, 1989. [Life and work in the Texas oil fields]

SECONDARY ACCOUNTS

The scholarly sources for this book were likewise extremely various and scattered. Here are a few suggestions for further reading:

Green, Harvey. *The Uncertainty of Everyday Life, 1915–1945.* New York: HarperCollins, 1992.

Larkin, Jack. *The Reshaping of Everyday Life, 1790–1840.* New York: HarperCollins, 1988.

Laurie, Bruce. *Artisans into Workers: Labor in Nineteenth-Century America.* Champaign, IL: University of Illinois Press, reprint edition, 1997.

Schlereth, Thomas. *Victorian America: Transformations in Everyday Life, 1876–1915.* New York: HarperCollins, 1992.

Sutherland, Daniel. *The Expansion of Everyday Life 1860–1876.* Little Rock: University of Arkansas Press, 2000.

Terkel, Studs. *Hard Times: An Oral History of the Great Depression.* New York: Pantheon, 1986.

——. *Working: People Talk About What They Do All Day and How They Feel About What They Do.* New York: The New Press, 1997.

Index

A

B

Irish immigrants
   domestic servants, 120, 121
   and farming, 2–3
   textile workers, 242, 243–44
   and transcontinental railroad, 261, 265
ironworkers, 290–91

J

Jewett, Helen, 354–55
Johnson, David, 98–99, 100
Johnston, David Claypoole, 120
Jungle, The (Sinclair), 293, 296

K

Kazlauskas, Antanas, 300–301
Kelly, Alice, 198
kerosene. *See also* oil field workers, 209, 215, 219, 221
Kingman, Lewis, 239
Kirkman, Marshall, 258, 259
Klann, W. C., 308–9
Knapp, Harriet, 347
Knopf, Adolf, 134

L

Lange, Dorothea, 64, 324
Langerfeld, Arthur, 176, 177
Larcom, Lucy, 125, 126, 241
Larkin, Annie. *See also* Larkin, John, 2
Larkin, Florence, 341
Larkin, Isabel, 341
Larkin, Jack, Sr., 230, 232–34
Larkin, James, Sr., 2
Larkin, John, 2–3
Larkin, Morris, 2, 3, 5
Larkin, William, 2
laundries, commercial, 123
laundry starch, 122–23

lead poisoning. *See* housepainters
Leaves of Grass (Whitman), 206, 207
Lee, Russell, 32, 33
Lemmons, Bob, 52, 53
Leonard, Dorothy, 338
"Life of a Coal Miner, The" (McDowell), 163
linotype machine. *See also* printers, 104–5
Livingston, Maurice, 260
logging, 141, 142–57
   mechanical revolution in, 153
   risks in, 151–52
   sawmills, 156–57
   "shanty boys," 144, 145, 146, 147, 148
Log of a Cowboy (Adams), 49
Long, Alice, 345
Longfellow, Henry Wadsworth, 86, 106, 107
Loring, Harrison, 119
Louis, Mary, 277, 278
Love, Nat, 280–81
Lowell (MA), textile mills in, 235–37
Lowery, Robert, 89
Low's Almanack, 1825, 4, 10
lumbering. *See* logging

M

machines and mechanization. *See also* specific industries
   in coal mining, 159, 176–77
   cotton gin, 30–31
   farming innovations, 10–11, 14–16
   hand-cranked washing machines, 122
   linotype machine, 104–5
   sewing machine, 129–33
   spinning frame, 240–41
   spinning mule, 226, 228
machinists. *See* industrial workers
Magarac, Joe, 290
Maier, Annie, 133–34
Mann, Horace, 334
Manoff, Arnold, 288

W

Walcott, Marion Post, 74, 77
Walton, Nelson, 290
washing machines, hand-cranked, 122
Watson, Elizabeth, 133–34, 136
Weekly Tribune, 267
Weir, Robert, 208
Weld, Charles Richard, 268
Wells, Douglas, 105
whalers, 203–9
White, Coley P., 323–24
Whiting, Lyman, 97
Whitman, Walt, 206, 207
Whitney, Eli, 30, 31
Whittier, John Greenleaf, 6
Wilkinson, Smith, 237
women, work of, 316
    cash girls and sales ladies, 336–40
    domestic servants, 118–21, 124, 125
    housework, 110–16
    meatpacking, 298

    migrant workers, 69, 70
    officer workers, 341–45, 346
    prostitution, 354–63
    role in farming, 6, 21–23
    sewing, 125–37
    shoemaking, 98
    teachers, 243
    textile workers, 235–37, 238, 239, 242, 243–45
    typesetting, 103
    wash day, 122–23
    work and marriage, 345, 347
Wood, Thomas Waterman, 321
Wright, Carroll, 173
Wright, Carroll D., 359–60
Wright, William, 187

Y

Young Mill-Wright and Miller's Guide (Evans), 156